WILDFLOWERS OF
THE FLORIDA KEYS

HELP US KEEP THIS GUIDE UP-TO-DATE

Every effort has been made by the author and editors to make this guide as accurate and useful as possible. However, many things can change after a guide is published.

We would appreciate hearing from you concerning your experiences with this guide and how you feel it could be improved and kept up to date. While we may not be able to respond to all comments and suggestions, we'll take them to heart, and we'll also make certain to share them with the author. Please send your comments and suggestions to the following address:

FalconGuides
Reader Response/Editorial Department
246 Goose Lane
Guilford, CT 06437

Thanks for your input!

Second Edition

WILDFLOWERS OF
THE FLORIDA KEYS

A Field Guide to the Wildflowers, Trees, Shrubs, and Woody Vines of the Region

ROGER L. HAMMER

FALCONGUIDES

GUILFORD, CONNECTICUT
HELENA, MONTANA

FALCONGUIDES®

An imprint of Globe Pequot, the trade division of The Rowman & Littlefield Publishing Group, Inc.
4501 Forbes Blvd., Ste. 200
Lanham, MD 20706
www.rowman.com

Falcon and FalconGuides are registered trademarks and Make Adventure Your Story is a trademark of The Rowman & Littlefield Publishing Group, Inc.

Distributed by NATIONAL BOOK NETWORK

Photos by Roger L. Hammer unless otherwise noted
Maps updated by Melissa Baker, © The Rowman & Littlefield Publishing Group, Inc.

British Library Cataloguing in Publication Information available

Library of Congress Cataloging-in-Publication Data available

ISBN 978-1-4930-6211-9 (paper: alk. paper)
ISBN 978-1-4930-6212-6 (electronic)

∞™ The paper used in this publication meets the minimum requirements of American National Standard for Information Sciences—Permanence of Paper for Printed Library Materials, ANSI/NISO Z39.48-1992.

The author and Globe Pequot Press assume no liability for accidents happening to, or injuries sustained by, readers who engage in the activities described in this book. Neither the author nor the publisher in any way endorses the consumption or other uses of wild plants that are mentioned in this book, and they assume no liability for personal accident, illness, or death related to these activities.

TO MY NOVELIST FRIEND AND ONETIME FLORIDA KEYS RESIDENT CARL HIAASEN, WHOSE INVESTIGATIVE EDITORIALS IN THE *MIAMI HERALD* PLAYED A KEY ROLE IN EXPOSING AN ILL-CONCEIVED DEVELOPMENT CALLED PORT BOUGAINVILLE THAT WOULD HAVE FOREVER DESTROYED THE FORESTS OF NORTH KEY LARGO. THOSE FORESTS ARE NOW PROTECTED WITHIN DAGNY JOHNSON KEY LARGO HAMMOCK BOTANICAL STATE PARK AND CROCODILE LAKE NATIONAL WILDLIFE REFUGE. THANK YOU, CARL.

CONTENTS

ACKNOWLEDGMENTS

To my happy-ever-after wife, Michelle, who was my lovely companion on some of the road trips to the Keys and helped carry my camera gear in the field. Thank you, honey! And much gratitude goes to my many botanist friends who shared the gift of their time and wisdom—most notably, Keith Bradley, Edwin Bridges, Kris DeLaney, Alan Franck, George Gann, Joe O'Brien, Vivian Negrón-Ortiz, Rich Spellenberg, Alan Weakley, Steve Woodmansee, and Richard Wunderlin. They helped with this book more than I can express in words, especially my taxonomist friends Keith Bradley and Alan Franck, who tolerated countless emails about current botanical nomenclature and confirming correct identifications. Because many trees, shrubs, and even endangered herbaceous wildflowers are cultivated at Fairchild Tropical Botanic Garden in Coral Gables, many employees and volunteers sent me alerts whenever they saw flowering plants that I needed to photograph. Those kind souls include Lydia Cuni, Brian Harding, Chad Husby, Jimmy Lange, Jennifer Possley, and Marlon Rumble, plus Fairchild volunteers Daniela Champney and Mary Jackson. Valued assistance was also provided by Florida state park and national park employees and volunteers, especially Becky Collins, Janice Duquesnel, Liz Golden, Helen Keller, Kristie Killam, Susan Kolterman, Miranda Murphy, Jimi Sadle, Caylee Sarff, Curry Hammock State Park manager Ken Troisi, and Mary Rose Zigler. I should also thank my nursery friends Marisol Almaraz, Katie Gonzalez, John Lawson, and Stan Matthews, who grow many trees and shrubs native to the Florida Keys and make them convenient to photograph. And then there were many friends who alerted me to flowering plants in the wild that I needed to photograph; they include Maryanne Biggar, Ruth Brooks, Jim Duquesnel, Ashley Grace, Amy Grimm, Beryn Hardy, Linda Haunert, Craig Huegel, Mark and Trudy Kenderdine, Eric King, Debbie McCoy, Michael Scott, and Leigh Williams. Also, much gratitude goes to David Legere, Mason Gadd, and others at Globe Pequot Press in Guilford, Connecticut, for all they do to make field guides like this a reality for wildflower enthusiasts who live in or visit the Florida Keys. While there is great joy and a profound sense of accomplishment involved in writing wildflower field guides, the most satisfaction comes from being the recipient of cherished friendships from so many people. Please know that I am forever grateful.

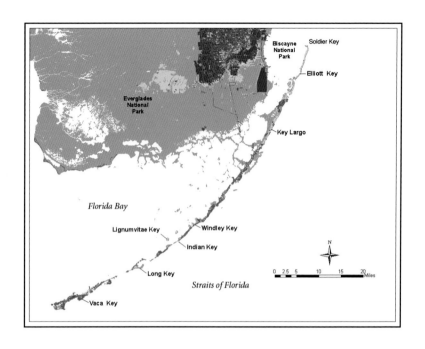

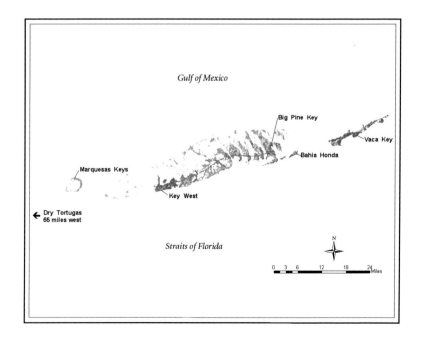

INTRODUCTION

There's an old saying in the Florida Keys that if you're not barefoot, you're overdressed, and that pretty much sums up the laid-back attitude in the part of Florida known locally as the Conch Republic. Despite the Florida Keys being a popular fishing, diving, and partying destination for millions of people each year—and where you can drink a beer naked in a clothing-optional bar in Key West—floristically the Florida Keys are unlike any other region in the United States. This distinction is because the majority of the native plants found in the Florida Keys are tropical species indigenous to the Bahamas, Greater Antilles, and tropical Americas. The Florida Keys even share USDA Zone 11 with the Bahamas, so favorable winter temperatures allow tropical species to flourish in a region that lies wholly within the temperate zone.

Tropical storms and hurricanes have brought tropical plants that rely on natural wind dispersal of their seeds, namely members of the Aster and Dogbane families, ferns, orchids, bromeliads, and even trees such as West Indian mahogany (*Swietenia mahagoni*) and Jamaican dogwood (*Piscidia piscipula*). Favorable ocean currents have brought seeds of countless shoreline plants from the West Indies (which includes the Bahamas) to Florida, but the majority of the trees, shrubs, palms, and vines of tropical origin arrived here in the bellies of birds that migrate to South Florida from the Bahamas, Greater Antilles, and even the Yucatán Peninsula. One consistent characteristic of the vast majority of tropical plants in the flora of South Florida, especially trees, palms, and shrubs, is that they produce small fruits and seeds that birds eat as they migrate from tropical regions each spring. Therefore, it is migratory birds that have had the greatest influence in shaping the flora of southern Florida, and most particularly the Florida Keys.

The Upper and Middle Florida Keys are fossilized coral reefs, referred to as Key Largo Limestone or coralline reef rock, created by receding sea levels that exposed the reefs to the air and sun, and later colonized by terrestrial plant life. Beginning at Big Pine Key and continuing to Key West, you find sedimentary limestone created by small particles of limestone that settled out of the seawater and then fused together to form what is called oolitic limestone (the limestone particles are called "ooids"). This is the same bedrock found at, or near, the surface on the southern Florida mainland and erroneously called "coral rock."

The purpose of this guide is to showcase the interesting array of tropical and temperate plant life that has colonized the Florida Keys over thousands of years. It is like an island vacation without leaving Florida.

PLANT COMMUNITIES

Tropical Hardwood Hammocks

The hammocks in the Florida Keys are quite unlike those on the Florida mainland because they are almost purely Caribbean basin tropical hardwood forests. Tropical hardwood hammocks are found on many islands of the Florida Keys, but the largest stands are on Elliott Key and Key Largo, protected within Biscayne National Park, Crocodile Lake National Wildlife Refuge, Dagny Johnson Key Largo Hammock Botanical State Park, and John Pennekamp Coral Reef State Park. Some tropical trees, such as lignumvitae (*Guaiacum sanctum*), milkbark (*Drypetes diversifolia*), yellowwood (*Zanthoxylum flavum*), soldierwood (*Colubrina elliptica*), and American toadwood (*Cupania glabra*), are restricted to the Florida Keys and do not occur naturally anywhere on the Florida mainland.

Pine Rockland

Pine rockland is a globally imperiled plant community found in southern Florida, Cuba, and the Bahamas. Pine rockland habitat on the Miami-Dade County mainland is characterized by a rich understory dominated by tropical plant species intermixed with clusters of saw palmetto (*Serenoa repens*). The pine rocklands on Big Pine Key, however, are nearly devoid of saw palmetto and more closely resemble pine forests in the Bahamas, where saw palmetto is entirely absent. Conversely, Florida thatch palm (*Thrinax radiata*) and Key thatch palm (*Leucothrinax morrisii*) are common understory palms in pine rockland habitat on Big Pine Key yet are absent in the same habitat on the southern mainland.

Oolitic limestone outcroppings characterize this South Florida plant community, as does the single overstory tree, the South Florida slash pine (*Pinus densa*). Fire is an essential maintenance tool of pine rockland habitat, whether a natural fire caused by lightning or resource managers conducting prescribed burns. In the absence of fire, pine rockland habitat will give way to tropical hardwood hammock formation or be overtaken by invasive species such as Brazilian pepper (*Schinus terebinthifolia*) or Burma reed (*Neyraudia reynaudiana*), so to maintain the character and health of pine rocklands, resource managers purposely set controlled fires every three to five years if there have been no natural fires. Wildflower enthusiasts should pay attention to pine rockland fires—wildflowers will erupt in bloom within weeks after a burn.

Coastal Berms

Coastal berms develop parallel to sandy or muddy shorelines and form lines of trees, shrubs, and other vegetation that colonize storm-deposited sand and shells. Along the shoreline you may find sea lavender (*Heliotropium gnaphalodes*), sea purslane (*Sesuvium portulacastrum*), crested saltbush (*Atriplex pentandra*), and other salt-tolerant species, with a backdrop of coastal trees such as red mangrove (*Rhizophora mangle*), buttonwood (*Conocarpus erectus*), white mangrove (*Laguncularia racemosa*), saffron plum (*Sideroxylon celastrinum*), and sea grape (*Coccoloba uvifera*).

Coastal Rock Barrens

This rocky, harsh, and barren habitat has very little organic soil and is mostly dry but sometimes inundated by brackish water, so it is a very tough and resilient group of plants that call this habitat home. It is a good place to look for such species as false sisal (*Agave decipiens*), joewood (*Jacquinia keyensis*), wild dilly (*Manilkara jaimiqui*), and several species of cactus. This habitat is particularly prevalent in the Middle and Lower Florida Keys, so check Long Key State Park, Curry Hammock State Park, and Bahia Honda State Park.

Mangrove Forests

Mangrove forests are dominated by four tree species. Red mangrove (*Rhizophora mangle*) is the most prevalent and is typically the most seaward, forming extensive forests. Arching prop roots help stabilize red mangroves in muddy shorelines that are affected by tides and storm surges, plus offer an important habitat for juvenile fish, shrimp, crabs, and other marine life. Mangroves are also favored nesting sites for ospreys, bald eagles, herons, night-herons, egrets, cormorants, roseate spoonbills, mangrove cuckoos, and many other birds. Mangrove forests also buffer shorelines from storm surges and help protect what lies behind them, whether upland plant communities or housing developments. The red mangrove may indeed be the most important tree in Florida.

The black mangrove (*Avicennia germinans*) is often intermixed with red mangroves, or it may form extensive forests of its own further inland. It is characterized by upright root projections, called pneumatophores, that help provide oxygen to the roots in anaerobic soils.

The white mangrove (*Laguncularia racemosa*) and buttonwood (*Conocarpus erectus*) are related by plant family and tend to grow farther from the shoreline than the unrelated red and black mangroves. Buttonwood can even be found in pine rocklands and once supported a thriving charcoal industry in South Florida.

HOW TO USE THIS GUIDE

This guide features plants that are native to the Florida Keys, but also includes some of the more prominent invasive exotic species commonly found on roadsides and at other disturbed sites, or adversely altering natural plant communities. Some of these non-native species are listed by the Florida Invasive Species Council (formerly the Florida Exotic Pest Plant Council) as either Category I or Category II invasive species and are targeted for removal by resource managers.

This guide is arranged by the most prominent color of the flower (for convenience, palms are placed in the "Green and Brown Flowers" section, regardless of flower color). Within the six color groups, the plants are first arranged alphabetically by the botanical name of the plant family, followed by the genus, species, and sometimes subspecies or variety. Botanical synonyms are offered when necessary to avoid taxonomic confusion. Plant descriptions are meant to be as brief and nontechnical as possible, and the bloom season is the time of year when the plant is likely to be flowering. The "Habitat/Range" section includes the natural range of each species both in and outside of Florida. The "Comments" section includes botanical name derivation and other interesting trivia about each species.

BLUE AND PURPLE FLOWERS

Whitemouth dayflower (*Commelina erecta*)

PINELAND TWINFLOWER
Dyschoriste angusta (A. Gray) Small
Acanthus family (Acanthaceae)

Description: Herbaceous perennial with erect, 4"–8" stems and opposite, nearly sessile, linear to narrowly lanceolate leaves. The leaves reach ½"–1" long and are covered with small hairs. Funnel-shaped flowers have 5 lobes, with darker purple dots on the lower lobe. The flowers are in the upper leaf axils and measure about ⅜" long.

Bloom Season: All year

Habitat/Range: Pinelands from Central Florida (disjunct in Wakulla County) south into the Florida Keys and the Bahamas

Comments: *Dyschoriste* means "difficult to separate," referring to the valves of the capsule. The name *angusta* means "narrow," in reference to the leaf shape. Some species in this genus are used in the Caribbean to cure "pains in the waistline" and to "relieve women's tiredness." It is a larval host plant of the common buckeye butterfly. Another common name is pineland snakeherb.

GREEN SHRIMP PLANT
Ruellia blechum L.
(Also *Blechum pyramidatum* [Lam.] Urb.; *Blechum brownei* Juss.)
Acanthus family (Acanthaceae)

Description: Square-stemmed herbaceous perennial averaging 4"–8" tall with hairy, ovate, opposite leaves ranging from 1"–1½" long and ½"–¾" wide. Pale violet 5⁄16" flowers appear behind green, overlapping, hairy bracts that line upright spikes to about 3" tall.

Bloom Season: All year

Habitat/Range: Invasive mostly in disturbed sites of Central and South Florida. Native to the neotropics.

Comments: *Ruellia* honors French physician, herbalist, and botanist Jean de la Ruelle (1474–1537), who translated Greek classics into French. The name *blechum* is a Greek name originally applied to a genus. This Category II invasive species can be a pernicious weed in landscapes but is often tolerated by gardeners because it is a larval host plant of the beautiful malachite butterfly in southern Florida. The larvae hide within the floral bracts by day to avoid predators.

MEXICAN BLUEBELL OR MEXICAN PETUNIA
Ruellia simplex C. Wright
(Also *Ruellia brittoniana* Leonard; *Ruellia tweediana* Griseb.)
Acanthus family (Acanthaceae)

Description: Herbaceous perennial 24"–36" tall with narrowly lanceolate, conspicuously veined leaves 6"–12" long and ½"–¾" wide. Trumpet-shaped 5-lobed flowers range from purple, pink, or white, averaging about 2" wide.

Bloom Season: All year

Habitat/Range: Invasive in a variety of natural habitats, including residential landscapes and disturbed sites throughout much of Florida. Native to the neotropics.

Comments: The name *simplex* relates to the simple leaves. This overly popular landscape plant is an aggressive Category I invasive species in Florida and should not be cultivated. It spreads rapidly by explosively dehiscent seeds and underground rhizomes and is difficult to control whenever it invades natural areas. The nursery trade has developed new sterile hybrids, but even those should be replaced with one of the Florida native *Ruellia* species.

THICKLEAF WILD PETUNIA
Ruellia succulenta Small
Acanthus family (Acanthaceae)

Description: Herbaceous perennial averaging 4"–8" tall with green or reddish-purple, opposite, elliptic to lanceolate leaves that are mostly 1"–3" long, ½"–¾" wide, and covered with short hairs. The 5-lobed, trumpet-shaped flowers are 1"–1½" wide, ranging from light purple to pink, rarely white.

Bloom Season: All year

Habitat/Range: Endemic to pinelands and flatwoods from Charlotte County south along the Gulf coast to Miami-Dade County and the Florida Keys

Comments: The name *succulenta* refers to the somewhat succulent leaves. Although common within its range on the Florida mainland, in the Florida Keys it is mostly found on Big Pine Key and is the only native *Ruellia* in the Keys. Butterflies visit the flowers, and it is a larval host plant of the common buckeye butterfly. It was once regarded as a subspecies and variety of the widespread *Ruellia caroliniensis*.

SEASIDE AGERATUM
Ageratum maritimum Kunth
Aster family (Asteraceae)

Description: Rhizomatous perennial to 20" tall but often half that height. The toothed, mostly 1-nerved, opposite, glabrous leaves are somewhat triangular in outline. Flower heads are in terminal clusters measuring about ⅜" wide and range from lavender to pale blue.

Bloom Season: All year

Habitat/Range: Beaches, salt marshes, and other coastal habitats of the Monroe County Keys, Mexico, Cuba, Hispaniola, and Belize

Comments: *Ageratum* is Greek for "old age" and alludes to the long-lasting flowers. The name *maritimum* refers to its coastal, or maritime, habitat. This state-listed endangered species is sometimes cultivated for its butterfly-attracting flowers, and members of the genus are also larval hosts for the tobacco budworm moth. It can be mistaken for the Florida native blue mistflower (*Conoclinium coelestinum*), but there is no vouchered evidence that species naturally occurs anywhere in the Florida Keys.

CAPE SABLE THOROUGHWORT
Chromolaena frustrata (B. L. Rob) R. M. King & H. Rob
Aster family (Asteraceae)

Description: Herbaceous perennial with short, soft, scattered hairs on the stems and with 3-nerved, shallowly toothed, elliptic-lanceolate leaves measuring ½"–1" long. Blue to lavender flower heads are in terminal clusters of 2–6.

Bloom Season: All year

Habitat/Range: Endemic to coastal habitats from mainland Monroe County east to the West Lake region in Everglades National Park and the Monroe County Keys

Comments: *Chromolaena* alludes to the colored involucre bracts of the type species. The name *frustrata* relates to American botanist Benjamin Lincoln Robinson (1864–1935) becoming frustrated while trying to describe this Florida endemic when other botanists were insisting it was a related Jamaican species. The largest populations of this state-listed endangered species are around the Flamingo area of Everglades National Park. In the Florida Keys it is known from Long Key and Lignumvitae Key.

JACK-IN-THE-BUSH
Chromolaena odorata (L.) R. M. King & H. Rob.
Aster family (Asteraceae)

Description: Woody shrub 4'–8' tall with 3-nerved, ovate-lanceolate, coarsely toothed leaves averaging 2"–3" long and 1"–2" wide. Pale blue to white flower heads measure about ⅜" wide.

Bloom Season: October to January

Habitat/Range: Hammock margins, canopy gaps, and disturbed sites from Orange, Hillsborough, and Polk Counties south into the Florida Keys, Texas, and the neotropics

Comments: The name *odorata* relates to the fragrant leaves. Although this fast-growing, pretty shrub attracts a dazzling array of butterflies and other pollinators, it spreads aggressively in gardens and can become a weedy pest by producing hundreds of seedlings in a single growing season. The name Jack-in-the-bush is a corruption of Jackney-bush, used in Belize, Jamaica, and Trinidad. The leaves are used as a fish poison in the West Indies and contain toxic compounds used in some medicines.

PURPLE THISTLE
Cirsium horridulum Michx.
Aster family (Asteraceae)

Description: Herbaceous biennial with spiny, lobed, or deeply incised leaves that form a rosette. The basal leaves reach 12" long and 2" wide, becoming shorter up the flowering stem. The stem leaves are clasping and not as deeply cut. The pinkish-purple flower head (white or yellow in parts of its range) reaches 2"–3" across.

Bloom Season: All year

Habitat/Range: Pinelands, prairies, roadsides, and urban landscapes of the eastern United States, Mexico, and the Bahamas

Comments: *Cirsium* means "swollen vein," alluding to members of the genus used medicinally to treat varicose veins. The name *horridulum* means "prickly." The flowers attract butterflies and other pollinators, including beetles. In Greek mythology, thistles appeared on Earth to grieve the loss of Daphnis, a shepherd said to be the inventor of pastoral poetry. It is a larval host plant of little metalmark and painted lady butterflies.

SLENDER GAYFEATHER
Liatris gracilis Pursh
Aster family (Asteraceae)

Description: Herbaceous perennial with hairy stems and 1-nerved, 2"–6" linear to linear-oblanceolate stem (cauline) leaves that gradually become shorter up the stem. Flower heads are in loose, raceme-like arrangements, with the top flowers opening first.

Bloom Season: July to November

Habitat/Range: Pinelands, scrub, and sandhills from South Carolina to Mississippi south through mainland Florida and on Big Pine Key in the Monroe County Keys

Comments: *Liatris* is Greek for "spoon-shaped," alluding to the shape of the tuberous roots of some species. The name *gracilis* means "slender." This is one of only two members of the genus in the Florida Keys, and both appear to be restricted to Big Pine Key. It was first described in 1814 by German American botanist Frederick Traugott Pursh (1774–1820), who studied the plants collected on the Lewis and Clark Expedition between 1803 and 1806.

SHORTLEAF GAYFEATHER
Liatris quadriflora (Chapm.) Bridges & Orzell
Aster family (Asteraceae)

Description: Herbaceous perennial with mostly glabrous stems bearing linear basal leaves 4"–8" long and up to ¼" wide. Flowering stems reach 16"–60" tall and are lined with clusters of star-shaped flowers opening from the top of the stem downward.

Bloom Season: August to December

Habitat/Range: Endemic to pinelands and prairies of Polk, Lee, and Palm Beach Counties south to the Florida Keys

Comments: The name *quadriflora* is for the 4 flowers produced in each cluster. *Flora of Florida* uses *Liatris tenuifolia* var. *quadriflora; Flora of North America* calls it *Liatris laevigata*. A 2017 revision concludes that all three are separate taxa and the plants in the Keys are *Liatris quadriflora*. Other common names are backache root, deer bowl, and blazing-star. Flowering *Liatris* species will attract an array of butterflies and bees.

SCALELEAF ASTER
Symphyotrichum adnatum (Nutt.) G. L. Nesom
Aster family (Asteraceae)

Description: Herbaceous perennial with deciduous basal leaves, usually absent when flowering. Upper leaves are appressed tightly to the brittle, wirelike stems, somewhat resembling scales. Flowering stems reach about 24" tall with flower heads ⅞"–1" wide.

Bloom Season: All year

Habitat/Range: Sandhills, flatwoods, and pinelands across the Florida Panhandle and from Citrus County south along the western peninsula to Miami-Dade and the Monroe County Keys

Comments: *Symphyotrichum* is Greek for "hair junction" and is believed to allude to the basal bristles of a cultivar in Europe that botanist Christian Gottfried Daniel Nees von Esenbeck (1776–1858) used to describe the genus. The name *adnatum* relates to the adnate (appressed) leaves along the stems, which is a diagnostic feature of this species. In the Florida Keys, scaleleaf aster is mostly found on Big Pine Key. The genus *Symphyotrichum* was separated from the old-world genus *Aster* and is taxonomically difficult, partly due to springtime basal leaves disappearing, leaving vastly different shaped stem leaves.

EASTERN SILVERY ASTER

Symphyotrichum concolor (L.) G. L. Nesom
Aster family (Asteraceae)

Description: Herbaceous perennial 12"–24" tall
when flowering, with elliptic-lanceolate stem
leaves that reach up to 2" long and ½" wide. The
oblanceolate basal leaves wither prior to flowering. Silvery hairs cover both sides of the leaves.
The ray flowers are pinkish purple and typically
number 8–12.

Bloom Season: All year

Habitat/Range: Pinelands, roadsides, and other
open habitats across the Coastal Plain east of the
Mississippi River north to southern New England

Comments: The name *concolor* means "one-
colored," in reference to the ray flowers. This
species is more common on the Florida mainland
and only appears on Florida Keys plant lists for Big
Pine Key. Some members of the genus were used
medicinally by Native Americans and as a smoke
or steam bath to treat mental problems.

POTBELLY AIRPLANT

Tillandsia paucifolia Baker
Pineapple family (Bromeliaceae)

Description: Squat, urn-shaped, epiphytic bromeliad with a few short, thick, curved leaves. Small,
scurfy scales cover the leaves, giving the plant a
silvery gray appearance. Plants average about 4"
tall and are either solitary or in small clusters. The
flower spike is 1½"–3" tall with overlapping pink
bracts. Tubular purple flowers emerge from behind
the bracts.

Bloom Season: March to July

Habitat/Range: Cypress and mangrove forests
from Brevard, Osceola, and Sarasota Counties
south through the Florida Keys, West Indies, and
Mexico south into Central America

Comments: *Tillandsia* honors Swedish-born
physician and botanist Elias Tillandz (1640–1693),
who wrote the first botanical work for Finland.
He changed his name from Tillander to Tillandz
(Swedish for "by land") after traveling by ship from
Finland to Sweden and becoming so seasick he
walked the 621 miles back. The name *paucifolia*
refers to the plant bearing few leaves.

WHITEMOUTH DAYFLOWER
Commelina erecta L.
Spiderwort family (Commelinaceae)

Description: Herbaceous perennial with erect or ascending stems to 12" or more, bearing sheathed, linear leaves measuring 1"–6" long and ³⁄₁₆"–½" wide that alternately clasp the stem. Flowers are about 1" wide with 2 showy blue (rarely white) petals above a much smaller white petal.

Bloom Season: All year

Habitat/Range: Dry, open woodlands from North Carolina and Texas south throughout Florida into the West Indies

Comments: *Commelina* honors Dutch botanist Jan (Johannes) Commelin (1629–1692), his physician and botanist nephew Caspar Commelin (1667–1732), and Caspar's physician son, also named Caspar, who are represented by the 2 large petals and the third smaller petal. The name *erecta* refers to the erect growth habit. The name "dayflower" relates to the ephemeral blossoms that open once and congeal by late morning. Water trapped in the inflorescence bracts is used in Mexico and Belize as eye drops.

SLENDER DWARF MORNING-GLORY
Evolvulus alsinoides (L.) L.
Morning-Glory family (Convolvulaceae)

Description: Slender herbaceous perennial with appressed, spreading hairs covering the stems. The stems may be ascending or prostrate with alternate, oblong or elliptic leaves to ⅞" long and ⅜" wide. Flowers are typically pale blue and average ⁷⁄₁₆" wide.

Bloom Season: Mostly September to June

Habitat/Range: Coastal rock barrens and disturbed sites of Lee, Broward, Miami-Dade, and the Monroe County Keys through tropical and subtropical regions of the world

Comments: *Evolvulus* means "to unroll," alluding to the non-twining stems. The name *alsinoides* refers to the plant's resemblance to a species of sandwort in the genus Alsine (Caryophyllaceae). Hairstreaks and other small butterflies visit the flowers. In Mexico it is called *ojitos azules*, or "blue eyes." It has a number of medicinal uses in the Caribbean and tropical America. Also check the "White Flowers" section in this guide for other *Evolvulus* species.

DWARF BINDWEED
Evolvulus convolvuloides (Willd. ex Schult.) Stearn
Morning-Glory family (Convolvulaceae)

Description: Herbaceous perennial with vine-like prostrate stems that ascend near the tips and are lined with alternate, obovate to elliptic or lanceolate leaves averaging ⅜"–¾" long and ¼"–⅜" wide. The stems are glabrous or with scattered, appressed hairs. The flowers are very pale blue or white with a darker blue central ring. Each flower measures about ⅜" across.

Bloom Season: Mostly November to June

Habitat/Range: Salt marshes and coastal rock barrens of the Miami-Dade and Monroe County mainland south into the Florida Keys and through the West Indies to South America

Comments: The name *convolvuloides* relates to the plant's resemblance to members of the related genus Convolvulus. In the Florida Keys, this state-listed endangered species is mostly found from Windley Key to Big Pine Key. It was first described in 1820 as Nama *convolvuloides* from plants collected in Venezuela.

OCEANBLUE MORNING-GLORY
Ipomoea indica (Burm.) Murr.
Morning-Glory family (Convolvulaceae)

Description: Herbaceous twining vine with heart-shaped or 3-lobed, 2"–4" alternate, pubescent leaves and 2"–3" funnel-shaped flowers that range in color from blue, pinkish violet, or purple.

Bloom Season: All year

Habitat/Range: A wide range of coastal and inland habitats in tropical and warm temperate regions of the world

Comments: *Ipomoea* is Greek for "wormlike" and relates to the twining stems of most species. The name indica means "of India" and reveals the extensive global range of this species, one of the most common morning-glory species in Florida. Skippers and other small butterflies crawl down the throat of the flowers to access the nectar; hummingbirds and sphinx moths also visit the flowers. Look for this species in the Florida Keys along hammock margins, canopy gaps, fringes of mangrove habitat, or in disturbed sites, often clambering over other vegetation.

RAILROAD VINE
Ipomoea pes-caprae (L.) R. Br. subsp. *brasiliensis* (L.) Ooststr.
Morning-Glory family (Convolvulaceae)

Description: Trailing herbaceous vine with rounded, 2"–4" leaves that are notched at the tip. The stems can reach 20' long or more and are an important beach dune stabilizer. The pinkish-purple, funnel-shaped flowers are about 3" wide, with darker rose-purple nectar guides radiating out from the throat.

Bloom Season: All year

Habitat/Range: Beach dunes and rocky shorelines of tropical and subtropical regions of the world

Comments: The name *pes-caprae* means "goat foot," alluding to the shape of the leaves; brasil-iensis relates to Brazil, where this variety was first collected in 1693. The name railroad vine refers to the long stems that often run parallel to each other down the beach, like railroad tracks. This species is a global traveler, dispersing its seeds into the sea so currents can transport them across the world's oceans to other beaches. Other common names are bayhops and goat's foot. In ancient Hawaii the flowers were used as a sooth-ing sheath on young boys after circumcision. The plant is widely used medicinally in the Caribbean as a purgative and to treat and bathe sores, relieve insect stings, lower high blood pressure, and cure "weakness in women."

SALTMARSH MORNING-GLORY

Ipomoea sagittata Poir.
Morning-Glory family (Convolvulaceae)

Description: Herbaceous twining vine with very narrow arrowhead-shaped leaves 1½"–4" long and ⅜"–¾" wide. Showy, funnel-shaped axillary flowers measure 2½"–3" wide, ranging from rose-purple to lavender with a darker throat.

Bloom Season: All year

Habitat/Range: Brackish and freshwater marshes of the southeastern United States, Mexico, Guatemala, Bahamas, Cuba, and Jamaica

Comments: The name *sagittata* refers to the sagittate (arrowhead-shaped) leaves. It was first described in 1789 by botanical explorer and clergyman Jean Louis Marie Poiret (1755–1834). This salt-tolerant species can be found in both coastal and inland habitats where there is reliably moist soil, including prairies and cypress swamps. The plant's narrow leaves make it easy to identify when not in flower. Sphinx moths, bees, butterflies (mainly skippers), and hummingbirds visit the flowers.

LITTLEBELL

Ipomoea triloba L.
Morning-Glory family (Convolvulaceae)

Description: Herbaceous twining vine with 3-lobed or heart-shaped leaves ranging from 1"–2" long with a nearly equal width. Flowers are somewhat hexagonal with pointed lobes and reach about ¾" wide.

Bloom Season: All year

Habitat/Range: Invasive in disturbed sites throughout much of Florida. Native to the neotropics.

Comments: The name *triloba* refers to the 3-lobed leaves. The common name relates to the flowers resembling small bells when held upside down. This non-native vine can be a troublesome weed that invades groves, highway and utility corridors, fencerows, and residential landscapes. It was first recorded in Florida in 1891 from the Florida Keys and has since spread north to the Florida Panhandle. It is used as an herbal wash in the American tropics to treat insect stings and sores. The flowers are visited by hummingbirds, sphinx moths, bees, and small butterflies.

SKYBLUE CLUSTERVINE
Jacquemontia pentanthos (Jacq.) G. Don
Morning-Glory family (Convolvulaceae)

Description: Twining vine with heart-shaped leaves that average 1½"–2½" long and 1"–1½" wide. Showy, sky-blue, broadly funnel-shaped flowers are ¾"–1" wide and appear in open clusters from the leaf axils.

Bloom Season: Mostly September to March

Habitat/Range: Hammock margins and coastal habitats from Broward and Collier Counties south through the Florida Keys, Greater Antilles, Mexico, and Central America

Comments: *Jacquemontia* honors French geologist and botanist Victor Jacquemont (1801–1832), who undertook a scientific expedition to India in 1828 to collect plants for the Muséum National d'Histoire Naturelle but contracted a tropical disease and died in Bombay at the age of thirty-one. The name *pentanthos* means "with five stamens." This state-listed endangered species is cultivated by native-plant enthusiasts because of its spectacular display of eye-catching blossoms. It is much more common in the Florida Keys than elsewhere in Florida and, when in flower, can turn the landscape blue.

SPURRED BUTTERFLYPEA
Centrosema virginianum (L.) Benth.
Pea family (Fabaceae)

Description: Herbaceous perennial vine with long, trailing, or twining stems and alternate leaves divided into 3 highly variable ovate to linear-lanceolate leaflets measuring 1"–1½" long and ¼"–⅜" wide. Flowers are solitary or in pairs, each about ¾"–1¼" wide, ranging in color from purplish lavender to nearly white. Fruits are narrowly linear, 2-valved pods 1½"–4" long.

Bloom Season: All year

Habitat/Range: Pinelands, scrubby sandhills, and coastal strand of the southern United States, Bermuda, and the West Indies to Argentina

Comments: *Centrosema* is Greek for "spur" and "standard," in reference to the spurred upper petal (standard). The name *virginianum* means "of Virginia," where this species was first collected in the early 1700s. Swedish botanist Carolus Linnaeus (1707–1778) described it in 1753 and the species was later revised by British botanist George Bentham (1800–1884) in 1837. There is one other native *Centrosema* species in central and northern Florida and two species of *Clitoria*, where this species was once placed. Spurred butterfly pea is a larval host plant of the long-tailed skipper and is sometimes cultivated by native-plant enthusiasts and butterfly gardeners.

BLUE PEA
Clitoria ternatea L.
Pea family (Fabaceae)

Description: Perennial vine with alternate, compound leaves typically with 3–7 ovate or broadly elliptic leaflets measuring ¾"–1½" long and half as wide. Flowers are about 1¾" long and are self-pollinating.

Bloom Season: All year

Habitat/Range: Invasive in disturbed sites and hammock margins in Miami-Dade County and the Monroe County Keys. Probably native to tropical Africa, but its natural range is obscured by naturalizing from widespread cultivation.

Comments: *Clitoria* alludes to the resemblance of the keel of the flower to female genitalia. The name *ternatea* is for Ternate Island in the Maluku chain of islands in Indonesia. The flowers are boiled with white rice to turn the rice blue. It is a larval host plant of the long-tailed skipper. This vine is only sparingly cultivated in Florida; there is also a double-flowered form in the nursery trade. Another common name is Asian pigeonwings.

WILD BUSHBEAN OR PHASEY BEAN
Macroptilium lathyroides (L.) Urb.
Pea family (Fabaceae)

Description: Herbaceous vine with compound leaves divided into 3 somewhat ovate leaflets from 1¼" long and ¾" wide or more. The reddish-purple flowers are on long stems. Pods are linear to 4" long.

Bloom Season: All year

Habitat/Range: Invasive in pinelands, coastal berms, dunes, salt marshes, and disturbed sites through most of Florida. Native to the neotropics.

Comments: *Macroptilium* means "long-winged," referring to the large wing petals that protrude at odd angles. The name *lathyroides* refers to the plant's resemblance to a species of Lathyrus (Fabaceae). Wild bushbean is a Category II invasive species in Florida but is most commonly found colonizing overgrown roadsides, vacant lots, canal banks, and other disturbed sites, where it covers other vegetation. It is grown as a peasant crop in Latin America and is sometimes used by long-tailed skippers as a larval host plant.

SEASIDE GENTIAN OR MARSH GENTIAN

Eustoma exaltatum (L.) Salisb. ex G. Don
Gentian family (Gentianaceae)

Description: Herbaceous annual, 10"–18" tall with elliptic, grayish-green opposite leaves that clasp the stem. The leaves measure ¾"–2½" long and half as wide. The 5-lobed, tulip-like, ¾"–1" flowers are purple or white, always with a dark purple center, and are produced at the top of the stem.

Bloom Season: All year

Habitat/Range: Coastal habitats from Levy and Brevard Counties south along both coasts through the Florida Keys (disjunct in Escambia, Duval, and Putnam Counties), West Indies, and tropical America

Comments: *Eustoma* is Greek for "open mouth," in reference to the cupped flowers. The name *exaltatum* means "lofty," alluding to the upright growth habit. The plant is also called catchfly prairie gentian. In the Florida Keys it often occurs along roadsides that border mangroves, where purple-flowered and white-flowered forms can sometimes be found growing together. In the West Indies the leaves are steeped in water as an eyewash, and the leaves and roots are used medicinally to increase the appetite and aid in digestion. There are only three species in the genus, with *Eustoma grandiflorum*, native to Mexico and the American Midwest, being widely cultivated.

NARROWLEAF BLUE-EYED GRASS
Sisyrinchium angustifolium Mill.
Iris family (Iridaceae)

Description: Herbaceous perennial with glabrous, narrowly linear, grasslike leaves that average 8"–14" long and about ¼" wide on branching stems. The leaf bases do not persist as fibrous tufts, which helps separate this plant from the following species. The 6-lobed, starlike flowers are about ½" wide.

Bloom Season: Mostly January to August

Habitat/Range: Moist, sunny habitats, including roadsides, throughout all of Florida and across much of the United States and Canada

Comments: *Sisyrinchium* is a combination of words used by Greek philosopher Theophrastus (372–287 BC) meaning "pig" and "snout," alluding to pigs grubbing roots with their snouts for food. The name *angustifolium* describes the narrow leaves. This is a taxonomically difficult genus, with four species reported as native to Florida and one non-native naturalized species. This and the following native species are the only members of the genus recorded from the Florida Keys.

NASH'S BLUE-EYED GRASS
Sisyrinchium nashii E. P. Bicknell
Iris family (Iridaceae)

Description: Herbaceous perennial with branching stems and leaf bases that persist as fibrous tufts. The narrowly linear leaves are glabrous, with light blue flowers that are slightly smaller than the previous species.

Bloom Season: All year

Habitat/Range: Pinelands and open sandy habitats from North Carolina across to Mississippi and south through Florida

Comments: The name *nashii* honors American botanist George Valentine Nash (1864–1921), who worked at the New York Botanical Garden and was sometimes joined by noted botanist John Kunkel Small (1869–1938) on collecting trips to South Florida. In the Florida Keys, this species is found in the pine rocklands of Big Pine Key within the National Key Deer Refuge, where it is uncommon. Look for it along the Jack Watson Nature Trail and the nearby Blue Hole Trail off Key Deer Boulevard.

LITTLEWOMAN
Salvia serotina L.
(Also Salvia micrantha Vahl.)
Mint family (Lamiaceae)

Description: Herbaceous perennial to about 18"
tall with opposite, broadly ovate leaves with crenate margins, averaging ¾"–1½" long and ½"–1"
wide. The leaves are squared off at the base and
are very aromatic when crushed. The ¼" flowers
are on terminal spikes.

Bloom Season: All year

Habitat/Range: Locally common in cultivated
grounds and disturbed sites from Central Florida
south to the Florida Keys, Bermuda, West Indies,
and Mexico to Panama

Comments: *Salvia* is taken from the Latin
salvere, "to feel well," and was first used by
Pliny (AD 23–79) for the Mediterranean *Salvia
officinalis*. The name serotina means "late in
coming," referring to the plant's flowering and
fruiting. Some members of this genus, such as
Salvia divinorum, cause hallucinations if smoked or
chewed. Many other species are prized additions
to butterfly gardens.

HAVANA SKULLCAP
Scutellaria havanensis Jacq.
Mint family (Lamiaceae)

Description: Herbaceous perennial with slender
stems averaging 4"–6" tall. Opposite, softly hairy
leaves are ovate, ⅜"–⅝" long, with entire or
slightly toothed margins. The flowers are in the
upper leaf axils and average ⅝" long and ½" wide.

Bloom Season: All year

Habitat/Range: Pinelands of Miami-Dade County
and the Monroe County Keys to the Bahamas and
Greater Antilles

Comments: *Scutellaria* is Latin for "small dish,"
alluding to the prominent pouch on the calyx. The
name *havanensis* means "of Havana," capital
city of Cuba, where plants were collected and
described in 1760 by Holland botanist Nikolaus
Joseph von Jacquin (1727–1817). The name
skullcap is based on the resemblance of the flowers to a type of military helmet worn by American
colonists. The plant is used in Cuba to treat spleen
infections, swelling of the feet, psoriasis, edema,
and sarcoptic mange.

SMALL BUTTERWORT
Pinguicula pumila Michx.
Bladderwort family (Lentibulariaceae)

Description: Herbaceous, insectivorous perennial
with a small rosette of elliptic to ovate leaves
measuring up to ½" long. The leaves feel greasy
when touched. Solitary flowers about ⅜" wide are
blue, violet, white, or rarely yellow and produced
on erect stems averaging 4"–6" tall.

Bloom Season: All year

Habitat/Range: Damp habitats from Walton
County east and south to the Florida Keys and
along the Coastal Plain from North Carolina to
Texas

Comments: *Pinguicula* alludes to the greasy texture of the leaf surface. The name *pumila* means
"little," referring to the tiny rosette of leaves. Like
other species in the genus, the leaves entrap, curl
over, and digest small insects. The species prefers
damp soils but can be found rooted in limestone
crevices. In the Florida Keys it is only known from
Big Pine Key and is the only terrestrial insectivorous species in the Keys.

FLORIDA BLUEHEARTS
Buchnera floridana Gand.
Broomrape family (Orobanchaceae)

Description: Herbaceous, hemiparasitic perennial
with an erect stem, typically less than 10" tall,
with opposite, elliptic to ovate lanceolate basal
leaves averaging ¾"–1½" long to about ¼" wide.
The leaf blades are not conspicuously 3-veined as
on the similar *Buchnera americana*. The 5-lobed
blue or white flowers are about ⅜" across.

Bloom Season: All year

Habitat/Range: Pinelands, flatwoods, and sandhills from South Carolina to Texas south throughout Florida

Comments: *Buchnera* honors German physician
Andreas Elias Büchner (1701–1769) but reported
in error as being named for German botanist
Johann Gottfried Buchner (1605–1749). The name
floridana means "of Florida," where it was first
described in 1919 by French botanist Michel Gandoger (1850–1926). Gandoger is noted for publishing thousands of plant names that are no longer
accepted, and even this species is sometimes
placed under synonymy with *Buchnera americana*.

CAROLINA SEA LAVENDER
Limonium carolinianum (Walter) Britton
Leadwort family (Plumbaginaceae)

Description: Herbaceous, rhizomatous perennial with a basal rosette of elliptic, obovate, or oblanceolate leaves averaging 2"–6" long and ⅝"–1½" wide. The lavender or white ³⁄₁₆" flowers are in airy panicles.

Bloom Season: June to December

Habitat/Range: Salt marshes and salt flats along the Gulf and Atlantic seacoasts east to Bermuda

Comments: *Limonium* is an ancient Greek name for a meadow, relating to plants that inhabit salt marshes. The name *carolinianum* means "of Carolina." British-born American botanist Thomas Walter (1740–1789) first collected this species in South Carolina and described it in 1788 as *Statice caroliniana*. Other common names are seaside thrift, ink root, and marsh rosemary. Significant threats to this plant are the wholesale harvesting of the flowering stems for dried floral arrangements and herbalists gathering the roots in winter to brew a tea as a remedy for colds, fever, and diarrhea.

CHRISTMAS BERRY
Lycium carolinianum Walter
Nightshade family (Solanaceae)

Description: Semiwoody, often thorny shrub to 6' tall with long, flexible, arching branches bearing spatulate, succulent leaves that average ½"–1" long and ¼"–⅜" wide. The 4-lobed flowers reach about ½" wide and are followed by ¼" red berries.

Bloom Season: All year

Habitat/Range: Coastal habitats from South Carolina south through Texas and most of coastal Florida

Comments: *Lycium* is a name used by Pedanius Dioscorides (AD 40–80) and Pliny (AD 23–79) for a prickly shrub that grew around a region in Asia Minor called Lycia. The name *carolinianum* means "of Carolina." Other names are wolfberry and Carolina desert-thorn. The very ornamental red fruits gave rise to the name Christmas berry. Hummingbirds, butterflies, and sphinx moths visit the flowers of this salt-tolerant shrub; songbirds eat the fruits. The related *Lycium barbarum* and *L. chinense* produce the nutritional goji berries of commerce.

BAHAMA NIGHTSHADE

Solanum bahamense L.
Nightshade family (Solanaceae)

Description: Low-branching woody shrub to 8' tall with brittle (sometimes prickly) stems bearing alternate oblong to lanceolate leaves 3"–4" long to 2" wide. Flowers are about ⅜"–½" across with narrowly linear-lanceolate lobes. Round, bright-red berries are about ¼" wide and produced in rows.

Bloom Season: All year

Habitat/Range: Coastal habitats from Central Florida south through the Florida Keys, the Bahamas, Cuba, Hispaniola, and Grand Cayman

Comments: The meaning of *Solanum* is obscure but may come from the Latin *solamen*, meaning "a comfort," or "soothing," relating to the pharmacological uses of psychoactive species. The name *bahamense* refers to the Bahamas, where it was first collected and later described in 1753 by Carolus Linnaeus (1707–1778). It is called cankerberry in the Bahamas. The juice from the fruits has been used to treat a fungal disease called thrush.

BLUE PORTERWEED

Stachytarpheta jamaicensis (L.) Vahl
Verbena family (Verbenaceae)

Description: Herbaceous perennial typically less than 12" tall but with long, low-spreading stems. Opposite, coarsely toothed, broadly ovate leaves measure 1"–4" long and ¾"–1½" wide. A long, quill-like spike bears ⅜" flowers that last a single day.

Bloom Season: All year

Habitat/Range: Pinelands and coastal habitats of Central Florida south through the Florida Keys, Bermuda, West Indies, and tropical America

Comments: *Stachytarpheta* means "thick spike" and relates to the flower spike. The name *jamaicensis* means "of Jamaica," where it was first collected and later described in 1753 as *Verbena jamaicensis* by Carolus Linnaeus (1707–1778). Other common names are joee, Jamaican vervain, and rat tail. The name porterweed is for a porter-like drink brewed from the leaves in the Bahamas. Many butterflies visit the flowers, and it is a larval host plant of the tropical buckeye butterfly.

LIGNUMVITAE

Guaiacum sanctum L.
Caltrop family (Zygophyllaceae)

Description: Small to medium-large tree, 10'–20' tall or more, with opposite, compound leaves bearing 6–10 oblong to obovate leaflets measuring ½"–1" long to ½" wide. Flowers are solitary or in clusters, each measuring about ¾" across. The lobed fruits ripen yellow and split open to reveal seeds covered with a red aril.

Bloom Season: Sporadically all year

Habitat/Range: Tropical hardwood hammocks of the Florida Keys (Miami-Dade and Monroe Counties), West Indies, and tropical America

Comments: *Guaiacum* is taken from *guayacán*, a Hispaniolan Taino name for the tree. The name sanctum means "sacred." Wood from lignumvitae weighs 78½ pounds per cubic foot, but black ironwood (*Krugiodendron ferreum*) and red mangrove (*Rhizophora mangle*) are denser. The sap from lignumvitae was once popular for treating syphilis and is still used against venereal disease in the Caribbean. The wood is used for making self-lubricating bearings and bushing blocks on ships. The former national champion was on Lignumvitae Key but was dethroned in 1997 by a larger specimen discovered on Totten Key within Biscayne National Park. The species is threatened globally by wood harvesters, habitat loss, and a scale insect.

Rose-of-Plymouth (*Sabatia stellaris*)

SHORELINE SEAPURSLANE

Sesuvium portulacastrum (L.) L.
Carpetweed family (Aizoaceae)

Description: Herbaceous perennial with long, succulent stems that spread across the ground, often rooting at the nodes. The succulent, opposite, elliptic to oblanceolate leaves average 1"–1½ long and about ⅜"–⁷⁄₁₆" wide. Star-shaped pink to nearly white flowers are ½" wide.

Bloom Season: All year

Habitat/Range: Coastal dunes, salt flats, and brackish marshes from Pennsylvania to North Carolina and Texas south through coastal Florida, West Indies, tropical America, Europe, Africa, Asia, and Australia

Comments: *Sesuvium* is for the Sesuvii, a Gallic tribe mentioned by Julius Caesar (100–44 BC). The name *portulacastrum* relates to its somewhat fanciful resemblance to the genus *Portulaca*, the purslanes. The leaves are edible but salty, and have been used to treat scurvy (vitamin C deficiency). In the Caribbean the pulverized leaves are used to treat puncture wounds from venomous fish. The leaves are sometimes pickled.

DESERT HORSEPURSLANE

Trianthema portulacastrum L.
Carpetweed family (Aizoaceae)

Description: Herbaceous annual with prostrate pinkish, succulent stems to 36" long. The paired, succulent leaves are suborbicular to obovate and reach 1"–2" long and ¾"–1½" wide, with one leaf in the pair larger than the other. Pink, axillary flowers are solitary or in clusters of 3 per axil, measuring about ½" wide.

Bloom Season: All year

Habitat/Range: Coastal habitats and disturbed sites throughout tropical and temperate regions of the world

Comments: *Trianthema* is Greek for "three flowers." The name *portulacastrum* relates to the plant's resemblance to the genus *Portulaca*, the purslanes. Young leaves are eaten in parts of its range, but health warnings include diarrhea and paralysis. The leaves have been used medicinally in Africa and Asia to treat jaundice, dropsy, high blood pressure, and rheumatism; the roots have been used as an abortifacient. It is found from Long Key to Big Pine Key.

MADAGASCAR PERIWINKLE
Catharanthus roseus (L.) G. Don
Dogbane family (Apocynaceae)

Description: Herbaceous perennial to 12" tall or more with opposite, oblong leaves averaging 1"–2" long and half as wide, with a pale midrib. The 5-lobed flowers are rosy pink with a darker center, but white-flowered forms are common. Flowers average 1¼" across.

Bloom Season: All year

Habitat/Range: Invasive in open, sunny habitats (including beach dunes) throughout much of Florida. Endemic to Madagascar.

Comments: *Catharanthus* is Greek for "pure flower," and the name *roseus* relates to the rose-pink flowers. This species is commonly cultivated and is naturalized in tropical and warm temperate regions worldwide. The flowers are pollinated by butterflies and moths, and although the seeds are explosively dehiscent, they are also dispersed by ants. This species is widely used medicinally and is the source of drugs used to treat cancer, but all parts are extremely toxic if eaten raw.

ROSY CAMPHORWEED
Pluchea baccharis *(Mill.) Pruski*
(Also *Pluchea rosea* R. K. Godfrey)
Aster family (Asteraceae)

Description: Herbaceous perennial, typically less than 12" tall with alternate, sessile leaves ¾"–2½" long and ¼"–1¼" wide, covered with short, soft hairs. The leaves smell strongly of camphor when crushed. Rose-pink disk flowers are in compact terminal heads.

Bloom Season: All year

Habitat/Range: Wet pinelands and seasonally flooded habitats of the southeastern United States, West Indies, and tropical America

Comments: *Pluchea* honors French clergyman, naturalist, and professor Noël-Antoine Pluche (1688–1761). In this case, the name *baccharis* comes from the New Latin *bacchar*, for a plant having a fragrant root. Another common name is marsh fleabane, which relates to early settlers of the southeastern United States placing the leaves in their bedding to deter fleas. Butterfly gardeners sometimes cultivate the plant, but it requires reliably moist soil.

SWEETSCENT
Pluchea odorata (L.) Cass.
Aster family (Asteraceae)

Description: Herbaceous annual or short-lived perennial to 4' tall, with alternate, aromatic, ovate to ovate-lanceolate leaves measuring 2"–4" long and 1"–2" wide, becoming smaller above. Flower heads are in flat-topped cymes, each head measuring about ³⁄₁₆" across. Seeds are wind dispersed.

Bloom Season: All year

Habitat/Range: Marshes, wet depressions, edges of flooded prairies, and salt marshes across the southeastern United States, West Indies, and tropical America

Comments: The name *odorata* relates to the aromatic leaves. Another common name is saltmarsh fleabane, but the species also occurs in inland freshwater habitats. It is not often cultivated, even though a flowering plant will be surrounded by nectar-seeking butterflies. Medical studies indicate this species possesses terpenes with antifungal, antimicrobial, and antibacterial properties. It also has been used to expel parasitic worms, repel fleas, and treat venomous snakebite.

FLORIDA IRONWEED
Vernonia blodgettii Small
Aster family (Asteraceae)

Description: Herbaceous perennial to 24" tall or more with alternate, sessile, linear or narrowly lanceolate leaves 2"–4" long and up to ½" wide. Rayless flower heads are few to many in open clusters and average about ½" across.

Bloom Season: All year

Habitat/Range: Pinelands and prairie margins of Central and South Florida into the northern Bahamas

Comments: *Vernonia* was created by German botanist Johann Christian Daniel von Schreber (1739–1810) to commemorate British bryologist and entomologist William Vernon (1666–1711). The name *blodgettii* honors botanist John Loomis Blodgett (1809–1853), who first discovered this species on Big Pine Key; it was later described in 1903 by botanist John Kunkel Small (1869–1938). Florida ironweed was once thought to be endemic to Florida until it was determined that plants identified as *Vernonia insularis* on Andros Island, Bahamas, actually were this species.

PITCHAPPLE OR AUTOGRAPH TREE
Clusia rosea Jacq.
Mangosteen family (Clusiaceae)

Description: Tree to 20' or more with opposite, thick obovate leaves that average 4"–6" long and 2½"–4" wide. The white, waxy flowers reach 3" wide, with pink markings at the base of the petals. White globose fruits average 2"–2½" wide.

Bloom Season: All year

Habitat/Range: Reported from Key West and Big Pine Key in the mid-1800s and on Sugarloaf Key in 1935 but later extirpated from Florida. Its current native range includes the West Indies and tropical America.

Comments: *Clusia* honors French botanist Charles de l'Écluse (1526–1609), who latinized his name to Carolus Clusius. The name *rosea* alludes to the rosy-pink markings on the flowers. The name autograph tree relates to the use of a sharp object to etch words onto the leaf surface, where they will remain even after the leaf falls. Travelers on foot would use the leaves to pass messages to others following the same route. The plant is also called Scotch attorney, alluding to its habit of growing epiphytically and killing the host tree with strangling roots. Although this tree was apparently native to the Florida Keys, it was long ago extirpated but remains a popular tall hedge or landscape tree in Florida. It is treated as an invasive species by resource managers because trees in the nursery trade were imported from elsewhere, often escaping cultivation and found growing epiphytically on palms and rough-barked trees in hammocks.

OGDEN'S KEYS SPURGE
Euphorbia ogdenii K. A. Bradley & Sadle
Spurge family (Euphorbiaceae)

Description: Herbaceous annual, 3"–10" tall, with opposite, linear-elliptic, typically 1-veined leaves measuring ¼"–¾" long and half as wide. Pinkish axillary flowers measure about ¹⁄₁₆" wide.

Bloom Season: All year

Habitat/Range: Endemic to coastal rock barrens and pine rocklands from Plantation Key to Key West

Comments: *Euphorbia* honors Trojan War hero Euphorbus, physician to King Juba II of the ancient kingdom of Numidia in northwest Africa. The name *ogdenii* honors ornithologist John C. Ogden (1938–2012), who played a key role in saving the California condor from extinction and was the senior scientist overseeing the Comprehensive Everglades Restoration Plan. The species was named in 2021 by botanists Keith Bradley (1971–) and Jimi Sadle (1972–) after *Chamaesyce scoparia* was moved to *Euphorbia*; the name *Euphorbia scoparia* was already in use as a synonym of *Euphorbia tirucalli*, therefore requiring a new species name.

BAYBEAN
Canavalia rosea (Sw.) DC.
Pea family (Fabaceae)

Description: Trailing or twining vine with leathery, alternate leaves that are divided into 3 large leaflets. Each leaflet is nearly orbicular, averaging 2"–4" wide. Flowers are in axillary racemes with 2–3 rosy ¾" flowers produced at each node. The pods are 5"–6" long and 1"–1½" wide.

Bloom Season: All year

Habitat/Range: Beaches and rocky shorelines of tropical and warm temperate regions worldwide

Comments: *Canavalia* is believed to have come from *kanavali* or *kavavali*, a local name for this species in the Malabar region of India. The name *rosea* is for the rose-colored flowers. The seeds are toxic, but the leaves are cooked and eaten in Asia. Ocean currents transport the seeds, which are common drift seeds on beaches around the world. The species is a larval host plant of the red-white-and-blue, day-flying faithful beauty moth.]

SOUTH FLORIDA MILKPEA
Galactia austrofloridensis A. R. Franck
Pea family (Fabaceae)

Description: Herbaceous twining vine with appressed hairs on the stems or somewhat glabrous. The leaves are divided into 3 linear-oblong leaflets that measure about 1¼" long and ⁵⁄₁₆" wide. Flowers measure about ⅜" long on 1"–1½" stalks (peduncles).

Bloom Season: All year

Habitat/Range: Pine rocklands, coastal berms, and disturbed sites of Miami-Dade County, the Monroe County Keys, and the Bahamas

Comments: *Galactia* means "milk-yielding" and is a name first used in 1756 to describe a species with milky sap. The name *austrofloridensis* combines *austro*, or "south," and *floridensis*, relating to Florida. Florida International University botanist Alan Franck (1980–) described this species in 2017 to distinguish it from *Galactia volubilis* by its characteristic narrow leaflets, and from *Galactia grisebachii* and *G. parvifolia* by its long peduncles (flower stalks).

FLORIDA HAMMOCK MILKPEA
Galactia striata (Jacq.) Urb.
Pea family (Fabaceae)

Description: Herbaceous twining vine with leaves divided into 3 ovate-elliptic leaflets, each measuring 1½"–2½" wide. The ⅜" flowers differ from other species by the thin white stripes on the standard. Pods split open to reveal bright red seeds.

Bloom Season: All year

Habitat/Range: Forest margins, canopy gaps, and disturbed sites from Manatee County south along Florida's west coast to Miami-Dade County through the Florida Keys, the Bahamas, and Greater Antilles

Comments: The name *striata* refers to the striations on the standard (also called a banner). This species is common in the Florida Keys, especially along hammock margins, and was a larval host plant of the zestos skipper, a butterfly that is presumed extirpated from Florida because there have been no sightings since 2004, perhaps the result of aerial spraying for mosquito control.

EASTERN MILKPEA
Galactia volubilis (L.) Britton
Pea family (Fabaceae)

Description: Slender vine with strongly twining, hairy stems and with leaves divided into 3 ovate leaflets averaging ½"–1¾" long and half as wide (the terminal leaflet is longest). Flowers measure about ½"–⅝" long.

Bloom Season: All year

Habitat/Range: Sandhills, scrub, and coastal swales of the eastern United States and the West Indies

Comments: The name *volubilis* relates to the twining habit of the stems. This and other species serve as larval hosts for the cassius blue, ceraunus blue, gray hairstreak, silver spotted skipper, and zarucco duskywing butterflies. However, it is not purposely cultivated, nor are any other milkpea species in Florida, except occasionally by local native-plant and butterfly enthusiasts. This species was used medicinally by the Seminole to treat "baby sickness," "Cow Creek sickness," appetite loss, diarrhea, fever, headaches, and as an aid in childbirth.

BAHAMA BLACKBEAD
Pithecellobium bahamense Northrop
Pea family (Fabaceae)

Description: Woody shrub 4'–6' tall with alternate, compound leaves divided into 2 to 4 obovate leaflets, each about 1"–1½" long and ½" wide, with short, sharp, stipular spines in the leaf axils. Bright pink to crimson flower heads measure about ¾" in diameter and produce coiled or curved pods to about 4" long.

Bloom Season: Mostly September to December

Habitat/Range: Pinelands of the Florida Keys (Big Pine Key), the Bahamas, and Cuba

Comments: *Pithecellobium* alludes to the contorted pods. The name *bahamense* relates to the Bahamas, where the species was first collected in 1890 by American botanist Alice Rich Northrop (1864–1922) with her husband, John Isaiah Northrop (1861–1891), who was killed in a laboratory explosion nine days before their son was born. This state-listed endangered species was first vouchered in Florida on Big Pine Key in 2007 by botanist Keith Bradley (1971–), who reported more than 200 plants in a spreading colony.

KEYS BLACKBEAD
Pithecellobium keyense Britton ex Britton & Rose
Pea family (Fabaceae)

Description: Woody shrub or small tree to 18' tall. The alternate, evenly bipinnate leaves have 2 or 4 obliquely obovate leaflets that reach 1"–1½" long and ½"–⅝" wide. Pale pink or white flower heads measure about ¾" in diameter and produce coiled pods to 4" long and split open to reveal black seeds with a red aril.

Bloom Season: September to December

Habitat/Range: Pinelands and hammocks from Martin County south to Miami-Dade and Monroe Counties (both mainland and Keys), the Bahamas, Cuba, and Mexico

Comments: The name *keyense* alludes to the Florida Keys. This state-listed threatened species is a larval host of the large orange sulphur and cassius blue butterflies and is one of the most ubiquitous flowering shrubs of the Florida Keys. According to the ancient Greek doctrine of signatures, it was believed that plants that produced leaves, fruits, or seeds shaped like human body parts were a sign from the gods that they could be used to treat ailments of those body parts. Because the seeds of *Pithecellobium* species are kidney-shaped, they were used to treat kidney problems.

ROSE-OF-PLYMOUTH OR MARSH PINK
Sabatia stellaris Pursh
Gentian family (Gentianaceae)

Description: Herbaceous annual with opposite ovate basal leaves 1"–1½" long and ¼" wide, with smaller upper leaves. The branched stems are topped by 1"–1½" flowers with 5–6 rose-pink, white, or two-toned petals. The center of the flower is yellow, bordered by a red, jagged line.

Bloom Season: All year

Habitat/Range: Freshwater wetlands and pinelands of the eastern United States, Bahamas, Cuba, and Mexico

Comments: *Sabatia* honors Italian physician and botanist Liberato Sabbati (1714–1778), curator of the Rome Botanical Garden. The name *stellaris* means "starlike," alluding to the flower shape. The name rose-of-Plymouth came about because it was believed by English Puritans that the genus *Sabatia* was named for the Sabbath. It is common on the southern mainland but local in the Keys, appearing on plant lists for Key Largo and Big Pine Key.

AMERICAN BEAUTYBERRY
Callicarpa americana L.
Mint family (Lamiaceae)

Description: Woody shrub 4'–6' tall, with opposite ovate to elliptic toothed leaves covered with coarse hairs. The leaves average 2"–4" long and 1¼"–2¼" wide. Pink (rarely white) clusters of axillary flowers produce showy clusters of pinkish-purple (rarely white) fruits.

Bloom Season: All year

Habitat/Range: Pinelands, hammock margins, and open sandy habitats of the southern United States, Bermuda, Cuba, Mexico, and the Bahamas

Comments: *Callicarpa* translates to "beautiful fruit"; the name *americana* means "of America." This pretty shrub is commonly cultivated for its colorful clusters of bird-attracting fruits, but also to make jams and pies. The fragrant leaves can be wiped on skin to repel mosquitoes, which may work on an outdoor patio but not in summertime swarms of salt marsh mosquitoes. The species has a long history of medicinal uses for such ailments as edema, malaria, colic, and venereal disease.

WEST INDIAN PINKROOT
Spigelia anthelmia L.
Logania family (Loganiaceae)

Description: Herbaceous annual to 16" tall or less. The broadly lanceolate leaves are prominently veined, 3"–6" long, and up to 3" wide. Terminal flower spikes bear pink or white tubular flowers with dark pink stripes, each about ¼" wide.

Bloom Season: All year

Habitat/Range: Pinelands and coastal disturbed sites of South Florida, the Bahamas, and tropical America

Comments: *Spigelia* honors Flemish physician and botanist Adriaan van den Spiegel (1578–1625), who latinized his name to Adrianus Spigelius. In 1606 he published the first work on preparing dried herbarium specimens. The name *anthelmia* refers to the medicinal use of this species to expel intestinal worms. The leaves contain spigeline, which is effective against intestinal worms but toxic if taken in quantity. The leaves are toxic to grazing livestock. The plant is called wormgrass and pink in the Bahamas.

SCARLET AMMANNIA
Ammannia coccinea Rottb.
Loosestrife family (Lythraceae)

Description: Herbaceous annual with opposite, sessile leaves set at right angles to the ones above and below. The lower leaves are mostly oblong-elliptic, becoming linear-lanceolate up the square stem, with the leaf base broadly lobed. Upper leaves reach about 3" long and ¼"–⅜" wide. Dark pink ¼" flowers, each with 4 or 5 petals, are in small axillary clusters.

Bloom Season: April to October

Habitat/Range: Wet or flooded soils of short hydroperiod glades, pond margins, depressions, and sinks across much of North America, the West Indies, and tropical America

Comments: *Ammannia* commemorates German physician and botanist Paul Ammann (1634–1691). The name *coccinea* means "red" and alludes to the color of the stems on most plants. The species is also called scarlet toothcups and valley redstem. Pink redstem (*Ammannia latifolia*), with smaller leaves and flowers, also occurs in the Florida Keys, but both are uncommon.

LOCUSTBERRY
Byrsonima lucida (Mill.) DC.
Malpighia family (Malpighiaceae)

Description: Locustberry can become a tree to 18' in hammocks but is kept shrubby in pinelands by fire. The obovate leaves average ½"–1" long and up to about ½" wide. The flowers reach ⅜" wide and open white, turning pink and then red as they age, forming multicolored clusters. The round, brownish-orange fruits are about ⅜" wide.

Bloom Season: Periodically all year

Habitat/Range: Pinelands and hammocks of Miami-Dade and the Monroe County Keys through much of the West Indies

Comments: *Byrsonima* is taken from a Greek word for leather, alluding to the bark of some species used in tanning hides. The name *lucida* means "shiny," relating to the glossy leaves. The flowers are self-incompatible and require cross-pollination, so more fruits are set when trees grow close together. The flowers produce oils from glands and are dependent on specific oil-collecting bees for pollination. Locustberry is a state-listed threatened species due to habitat loss and its limited range in Florida. The edible fruits are savored by birds, and the leaves serve as larval food for the Florida duskywing butterfly, making it popular among bird and butterfly enthusiasts in southern Florida. It is the only native member of the Malpighiaceae in Florida.

SOUTHERN BEEBLOSSOM

Oenothera simulans (Small) W. L. Wagner & Hoch
(Also *Gaura angustifolia* Michx.)
Evening Primrose family (Onagraceae)

Description: Herbaceous biennial to 5' tall, branched at the top with narrowly oblanceolate basal leaves and narrowly lanceolate stem leaves 1"–2½" long and ¼"–³⁄₁₆" wide, becoming narrower up the stem. The flowers can appear white to pinkish.

Bloom Season: All year

Habitat/Range: Pinelands and other open habitats, including roadsides, from North Carolina to Mississippi south throughout Florida

Comments: *Oenothera* is Greek for "wine" and "wild animal," alluding to the belief that soaking the roots in wine would tame wild animals. The name *simulans* means "similar," for the plant's similarity to the genus *Gaura*. Bees are attracted to the blossoms, and the plant serves as a larval host for proud (gaura) sphinx and clouded crimson moths. The leaves were used in herbal folk medicine in the Southern states.

PINE PINK

Bletia purpurea (Lam.) DC.
Orchid family (Orchidaceae)

Description: Terrestrial orchid with longitudinally pleated, linear-lanceolate leaves that arise from hard, round pseudobulbs. The leaves reach 18" long and 2" wide, resembling seedling palm leaves. Pink to purplish-pink (rarely white) flowers are on tall, branched spikes and measure about ¾" wide.

Bloom Season: Mostly December to July

Habitat/Range: Pinelands, prairies, scrubby flatwoods, or rarely on stumps and floating logs in swamps of southern Florida, into the West Indies and tropical America

Comments: *Bletia* commemorates eighteenth-century Spanish pharmacist and botanist Don Luis Blet. The name *purpurea* alludes to the pinkish-purple flower color. In the Florida Keys, this state-listed threatened species is found in the National Key Deer Refuge on Big Pine Key. The pseudobulbs enable it to survive in fire-prone habitats. Some populations become self-pollinated in bud (cleistogamy), so the flowers never open—a discouraging trait for wildflower photographers.

MONK ORCHID
Oeceoclades maculata (Lindl.) Lindl.
Orchid family (Orchidaceae)

Description: Terrestrial orchid with mottled two-toned green, lanceolate leaves measuring 4"–8" long and about 2" wide, with a hard, ovoid pseudobulb at the base. The erect flower spike is topped by 6–12 flowers, each measuring about ½" wide.

Bloom Season: September to October

Habitat/Range: Invasive in shady forests, groves, and urban areas from north-central Florida south into the Florida Keys, West Indies, and tropical America. Native to Africa.

Comments: *Oeceoclades* means "private branch," in reference to the species' separation from the genus *Angraecum*. The name *maculata* relates to the mottled leaves. The species was first discovered in Florida in Matheson Hammock (Miami-Dade County) in 1974 and has since spread rapidly south through the Florida Keys and north into north-central Florida. It is self-pollinated by rain (rain-assisted autogamy). Although invasive in natural areas, it is not a listed species because it does not adversely affect the function of native habitats.

BEACH FALSE FOXGLOVE
Agalinis fasciculata (Elliott) Raf.
Broomrape family (Orobanchaceae)

Description: Loosely branched, hemiparasitic annual to about 3' tall, with pubescent stems branched above the middle. Narrowly linear, pubescent leaves measure ¾"–1½" long and occur in fascicles (bundles). Flowers are about 1" wide in terminal racemes.

Bloom Season: All year

Habitat/Range: Pinelands, beaches, and sandhills from New York to Kansas south to Texas, Florida, Cuba, and Puerto Rico

Comments: *Agalinis* relates to the resemblance of the type species to a *Linum* (flax). The name *fasciculata* alludes to the fascicled, or bundled, leaves. Seedling roots of false foxgloves must attach to the roots of grasses or other herbaceous plants in order to survive, although they also photosynthesize (hemiparasitic). This is the most common false foxglove in Florida, but in the Florida Keys it is only recorded in the National Key Deer Refuge on Big Pine Key. It is a larval host plant of the common buckeye butterfly.

SALTMARSH FALSE FOXGLOVE

Agalinis maritima (Raf.) Raf. var. *grandiflora*
(Benth.) Pennell
Broomrape family (Orobanchaceae)

Description: Herbaceous annual with tight clusters of short, leafy branches averaging 12"–18" tall bearing broadly linear leaves to about 1¼" long. Rose-pink flowers are about ⅝" wide.

Bloom Season: All year

Habitat/Range: Coastal wetlands and tidal swamps from Texas to Florida, north to Nova Scotia, and into Mexico, the Bahamas, and Greater Antilles

Comments: The name *maritima* is for the species' coastal, or maritime, habitat; the name *grandiflora* alludes to the flowers being larger than other varieties of this species. The common buckeye butterfly uses members of this genus as larval host plants. There are seventeen *Agalinis* species in Florida; five are reported from the Florida Keys, with this species being the most frequent in the Keys, found in nearly all the state parks and the National Key Deer Refuge on Big Pine Key.

HERB-OF-GRACE

Bacopa monnieri (L.) Pennell
Plantain family (Plantaginaceae)

Description: Mat-forming herbaceous perennial with succulent, creeping stems that root along the nodes. Succulent, somewhat spatulate leaves reach about ½" long and ¼" wide. The 5-lobed, pale pink flowers are about ⅜" wide.

Bloom Season: All year

Habitat/Range: Freshwater and brackish wetlands through the southeastern United States and tropical regions worldwide

Comments: *Bacopa* is an aboriginal name among indigenous people of French Guiana. The name *monnieri* honors French botanist Louis-Guillaume le Monnier (1717–1799). This is a staple plant in holistic medicine practiced in India, where it is used to treat Alzheimer's disease, anxiety, attention deficit disorder, mental fatigue, and other ailments but lacks scientific research to support its effectiveness. Look for it in open, sunny habitats where there is reliably moist soil. It is a favored larval host of the white peacock butterfly, whose larvae can devour large patches of plants.

SHOWY MILKWORT

Asemeia violacea (Aubl.) J. F. B. Pastore & J. R. Abbott
(Also *Polygala grandiflora* Walter; *Asemeia grandiflora* [Walter] Small)
Milkwort family (Polygalaceae)

Description: Herbaceous perennial 8"–16" tall, with narrow, oblanceolate to elliptic, alternate leaves that exude milky sap when broken. The leaves average ½"–1½" long and ¼"–⅜" wide. The flowers have 3 petals that are fused together to form a tube, with 2 violet to rose-pink petallike sepals appearing like wings.

Bloom Season: All year

Habitat/Range: Pinelands, prairies, and other open habitats across the southeastern United States to the Bahamas

Comments: *Asemeia* is believed to mean "without a sign," in reference to the absence of brush-like teeth on the keel petal that is present in members of the genus *Polygala*, and one reason it was separated from that genus. The name *violacea* relates to the violet-colored flowers. This species is common throughout Florida.

KISS-ME-QUICK OR PINK PURSLANE

Portulaca pilosa L.
Purslane family (Portulacaceae)

Description: Succulent, herbaceous annual or short-lived perennial with alternate, sessile, cylindrical leaves to about ⅜" long with dense, soft, spreading (pilose) hairs in the leaf axils. Flowers appear at the tips of the branches and measure about ⅜" wide or slightly wider.

Bloom Season: All year, but mostly October to March

Habitat/Range: Pinelands, coastal strand, and rock barrens of the southeastern United States, West Indies, and tropical America

Comments: *Portulaca* means "little door," referring to the lid of the capsule. The name *pilosa* alludes to the pilose hairs in the leaf axils. The name kiss-me-quick alludes to the ephemeral flowers. Of the four species of *Portulaca* in the Florida Keys, this is the only one with purplish-pink flowers (see the "Yellow Flowers" section in this guide) and is known from Elliott Key, Bahia Honda, Indian Key, and Lignumvitae Key.

COKER'S GOLDEN CREEPER
Ernodea cokeri Britton ex Coker
Madder family (Rubiaceae)

Description: Mounding or spreading perennial with opposite, sessile, narrowly linear leaves that measure ½"–1½" long and ¼" wide or less. A key characteristic that separates it from the following species is the presence of a single, longitudinal nerve on narrower leaves. Tubular flowers are dark pink with 4 curled lobes, each measuring about ½" long. Oval, ¼" fruits are golden yellow.

Bloom Season: All year

Habitat/Range: Pine rocklands of Miami-Dade County, Monroe County Keys, and the Bahamas

Comments: *Ernodea* is Greek for "offshoot," alluding to the many leafy branches produced along the stem. The name *cokeri* honors American botanist and mycologist William Chambers Coker (1872–1953), who became a professor at the University of North Carolina, where he established the Coker Arboretum in 1903. This state-listed endangered species was thought to be endemic to the Bahamas before specimens collected in Florida as early as 1914 were correctly identified. It had previously been referred to as *Ernodea littoralis* var. *angustifolia*. It is sparingly propagated in South Florida for the native-plant nursery trade.

BEACH CREEPER
Ernodea littoralis Sw.
Madder family (Rubiaceae)

Description: Mounding or spreading perennial with lanceolate leaves 1"–1½" long and ⅜"–½" wide with 3–5 longitudinal nerves. Tubular, ½"–⅝" flowers are usually reddish pink with curled lobes that reveal the white inner tube. The oval ⅜" fruits are golden yellow.

Bloom Season: All year

Habitat/Range: Coastal habitats from Volusia and Hillsborough Counties south along both coasts into the Florida Keys and the neotropics

Comments: The name *littoralis* refers to the species' coastal habitat, the littoral zone. Native-plant enthusiasts sometimes grow this species as a drought- and salt-tolerant landscape plant for border plantings or as a mounding ground cover. Hummingbirds will visit the flowers if the plant is elevated in a hanging basket. A solid pink–flowered form of this species in the pine rocklands on Big Pine Key is sold by Florida native-plant nurseries as "Big Pine Pink."

LARGEFLOWER MEXICAN CLOVER
Richardia grandiflora (Cham. & Schltdl.) Steud.
Madder family (Rubiaceae)

Description: Low-spreading herbaceous perennial with narrowly elliptic, coarsely hairy leaves averaging ½"–¾" long and ⅜"–½" wide. Numerous, paired, 6-lobed flowers are about ½" across, lightly blushed with lilac.

Bloom Season: All year

Habitat/Range: Invasive in road swales, lawns, trail margins, and other disturbed sites, mostly across Central Florida south through the Florida Keys. Native to South America.

Comments: *Richardia* honors British physician and botanist Richard Richardson (1663–1741). The name *grandiflora* alludes to the large flowers compared to other members of the genus. This is a Category II invasive species that can form blankets of flowers along roadsides, giving rise to a local name, "Florida snow." It was first described in 1828 as *Richardsonia grandiflora* by German botanists Ludolf Karl Adelbert von Chamisso (1781–1838) and Diederich Franz Leonhard von Schlechtendal (1794–1866). Bees and butterflies visit the flowers.

PRIDE OF BIG PINE
Strumpfia maritima Jacq.
Madder family (Rubiaceae)

Description: Woody shrub to 2' tall in saline habitats or to 6' or more in upland habitats. The fleshy, revolute leaves reach about 1" long and ⅛" wide, congested near the branch tips. The small, white to pinkish, 5-lobed flowers are produced in few-flowered racemes that are shorter than the leaves. Small subglobose fruits are white.

Bloom Season: All year

Habitat/Range: Pine rocklands and coastal habitats of the Lower Florida Keys to the West Indies and tropical America

Comments: *Strumpfia* honors German chemistry and botany professor Christoph Karl Strumpff (1700–1779), who edited Carolus Linnaeus's Genera *Plantarum*, published in 1753. The name *maritima* relates to the species' coastal, or maritime, habitat. This state-listed endangered species is the only member of the genus and is restricted in Florida to the Lower Florida Keys, with most populations on Big Pine Key.

VERDOLAGA-FRANCESA
Talinum fruticosum (L.) Juss.
(Also *Talinum triangulare* Willd.)
Talinum family (Talinaceae)

Description: Short-lived perennial averaging 12"–24" tall, with fleshy, alternate, obovate to oblanceolate leaves 1"–3" long and ½"–1½" wide. Flowers are about ⅝" wide.

Bloom Season: April to October

Habitat/Range: Naturalized in disturbed sites of Pinellas, Polk, Lee, Miami-Dade, and Monroe County Keys. Native to the West Indies, tropical America, and West Africa.

Comments: *Talinum* is believed to be an aboriginal name of an African species. The name *fruticosum* means "shrubby." This species is commonly grown in many parts of the world as a leaf vegetable and potherb, with common names like Ceylon spinach, waterleaf, and Surinam purslane. The name *verdolaga-francesa* translates to "French purslane." The plant is rich in vitamins but also high in oxalic acid and should be avoided by people suffering from kidney problems, gout, and rheumatoid arthritis.

RED AND ORANGE FLOWERS

Coastal indigo (*Indigofera miniata*)

SIXANGLE FOLDWING

Dicliptera sexangularis (L.) Juss.
Acanthus family (Acanthaceae)

Description: Herbaceous, much-branched annual to about 36" tall, with ovate to oblong-lanceolate basal leaves to 4" long and 2" wide, becoming much smaller up the stems. The curved flowers are flattened and measure ¾"–1" long.

Bloom Season: All year

Habitat/Range: Coastal and inland habitats, including trail margins, edges of salt marshes and mangroves of north-central Florida south through the Florida Keys, West Indies, and tropical America

Comments: *Dicliptera* is Greek for "folding" and "wing," for the structure of the capsule. The name *sexangularis* means "six-angled," alluding to the stems. Hummingbirds and butterflies visit the flowers, and it is a larval host plant of the Cuban crescent. Cultivated by native-plant enthusiasts, it is weedy in garden settings, spreading from seed wherever there is bare soil. Quite pretty in flower, it is worth tolerating as a "weed" in home landscapes.

BRAZILIAN PEPPER

Schinus terebinthifolia Raddi
Cashew family (Anacardiaceae)

Description: Tree to 24' tall with alternate, compound leaves bearing 3–9 elliptic leaflets averaging 2"–3" long and ¾"–1" wide. Small, white, unisexual flowers are in terminal clusters; female trees bear large clusters of ⅛" red fruits.

Bloom Season: October to March

Habitat/Range: Invasive in a variety of habitats, including pinelands, hammock margins, fringes of mangroves, and coastal strand. Native to South America.

Comments: *Schinus* is Greek for the mastic tree (*Pistacia lentiscus*) and alludes to the similarity of the resinous sap. The name *terebinthifolia* is for the resemblance of the leaves to the terebinth tree (*Pistacia terebinthus*). This is an aggressive Category I invasive species that negatively alters native habitats. The sap can cause a skin rash on sensitive people. The dried fruits are the pink peppercorns of commerce, but consumption can cause mild to serious health issues.

SCARLET MILKWEED OR TROPICAL MILKWEED
Asclepias curassavica L.
Dogbane family (Apocynaceae)

Description: Herbaceous annual 12"–24" tall, with lanceolate leaves averaging 3"–5" long and ½"–¾" wide. Flowers are two-toned red and yellow or solid yellow, produced in terminal clusters. The fusiform fruits split open to reveal seeds attached to silky hairs that allow them to drift in the wind.

Bloom Season: All year

Habitat/Range: Invasive in residential landscapes, fencerows, canal banks, along trails, and other disturbed sites. Native to tropical America.

Comments: *Asclepias* honors the legendary Greek physician and deity Aesculapius. The name *curassavica* means "of Curaçao." It is a larval host plant of monarch and queen butterflies, as well as the milkweed tussock moth, but the plant also can host a protozoan parasite that can kill monarch and queen larvae. Its perennial growth disrupts monarch migration, so planting it in cold-temperate regions is controversial. Monarch populations in South Florida are resident.

BLANKET FLOWER
Gaillardia pulchella Foug.
Aster family (Asteraceae)

Description: Herbaceous annual with entire or lobed, oblong, linear, or spatulate leaves covered with coarse hairs. The rays are often variously two-toned red and yellow with purple or brown disks. The flower heads average 2"–2½" across.

Bloom Season: All year

Habitat/Range: Naturalized in open sandy habitats, including beach dunes and disturbed sites throughout Florida. Native to the southwestern United States and Mexico.

Comments: *Gaillardia* honors eighteenth-century French magistrate and patron of botany Gaillard de Charentonneau. The name *pulchella* means "beautiful." Blanketflower has long been regarded as a Florida native but has recently been determined to not be native anywhere east of the Mississippi River, where it had not been reported by early botanists until 1878, when it showed up in ship ballast at an Alabama seaport. Other names are firewheel and Indian blanket. It is used for roadside beautification projects in Florida.

GEIGER TREE
Cordia sebestena L.
Borage family (Boraginaceae)

Description: Deciduous tree to 18' tall, with broadly ovate to ovate-elliptic, scabrous leaves averaging 4"–6" long and 3"–4" wide. Bright orange, clustered flowers measure about 1" wide, producing white, ovoid, fleshy fruits ¾"–1½" long.

Bloom Season: All year

Habitat/Range: Rocky coastal strand in Lee, Miami-Dade, and Monroe (mainland and Keys) Counties, West Indies, and tropical America

Comments: *Cordia* honors German physician and botanist Valerius Cordus (1515–1544). The name *sebestena* is an Arabic name originally applied to another plant. Its nativity in Florida is disputed based on there being no reports of it by early botanists. Also, a well-known wrecker, Captain John Henry Geiger (1807–1875), reported bringing specimens from Cuba to his home in Key West in the mid-1800s. However, the species is native to the nearby Bahamas and Cuba, and the fruits not only float in seawater and travel in ocean currents but are eaten by white-crowned pigeons, which migrate from the islands to South Florida each spring. It is also uncommon to rare in the Florida Keys, growing in the same habitat where it occurs in other parts of its range. It was given the name geiger tree by famed naturalist John James Audubon (1785–1851) when he painted white-crowned pigeons perched on the boughs of a tree in Geiger's yard for his classic book, *Birds of America*. Geiger's Key West home is now the Audubon House. Hummingbirds and butterflies visit the flowers.

REFLEXED WILD-PINE
Tillandsia balbisiana Schult. and Schult. f.
Bromeliad family (Bromeliaceae)

Description: Epiphytic bromeliad averaging 5"–8" tall with leaves in a bulbous rosette, often curving and twisting downward. The erect, slender scape is red and topped by red floral bracts with purple, tubular flowers. Seeds are wind-dispersed.

Bloom Season: All year

Habitat/Range: Epiphytic on various species of trees and shrubs from Central Florida south through the Florida Keys, West Indies, and tropical America

Comments: *Tillandsia* honors Swedish-born physician and botanist Elias Tillandz (1640–1693), who wrote the first botanical work for Finland. He changed his name from Tillander to Tillandz (Swedish for "by land") after traveling by ship from Finland to Sweden and becoming so seasick he walked the 621 miles back. The name *balbisiana* honors Italian botanist and politician Giovanni-Batista Balbis (1765–1831). It is a state-listed threatened species, called "cuttlefish" in the Bahamas.

CARDINAL AIRPLANT OR STIFF-LEAVED WILD-PINE
Tillandsia fasciculata Sw.
Bromeliad family (Bromeliaceae)

Description: Epiphytic bromeliad that forms a dense rosette of somewhat stiff, pointed leaves. The flower spikes are branched at the top, typically with bright red and yellowish bracts enclosing cylindrical purple flowers. Some populations have pinkish bracts and purple flowers; albino forms bear yellowish-green bracts and white flowers.

Bloom Season: All year

Habitat/Range: Epiphytic on trees in mangrove forests, hammocks, wooded swamps, and inland hardwood forests throughout Central and South Florida, West Indies, and from Central America south to northern South America.

Comments: The name *fasciculata* means "formed into a bundle," alluding to the rosette of leaves. The name "wild-pine" references its relative, the pineapple. In the Bahamas it is called "dog-drink-water," for dogs that drink water collected in plants that have fallen to the ground. It is a state-listed endangered species due to an imported Mexican weevil with larvae that kill the plants.

SEMAPHORE CACTUS
Consolea corallicola Small
Cactus family (Cactaceae)

Description: Spiny cactus to 6' tall, with a trunk armed with many sharp spines that angle downward. Oblong stem segments (cladodes) spread on a single plane from the top of the trunk, measuring 6"–10" long and 2½"–4" wide, copiously armed when young. Flowers are red to orange-red, functionally male, and measure about ⅝" across. Seedless, yellow fruits abort if produced.

Bloom Season: All year

Habitat/Range: Endemic to coastal habitats of the Florida Keys (Miami-Dade and Monroe Counties)

Comments: *Consolea* honors Italian botanist Michelangelo Console (1812–1897) of the Palermo Botanical Garden. The name *corallicola* means "growing on coral," in this case the coralline reef rock of the Florida Keys. There are only two extant wild populations of this federal- and state-listed endangered cactus, but there are currently six state and federal preserves in the Florida Keys where it is being cultivated or has been reintroduced. It is also being cultivated at Fairchild Tropical Botanic Garden in Coral Gables for their endangered species reintroduction program. All populations are clonal because the flowers are functionally male. The species was first collected by botanist John Kunkel Small (1869–1938) on Big Pine Key in 1919 and is now critically imperiled due to hurricanes, sea level rise, its inability to produce seeds, and the presence of an introduced moth (*Cactoblastis cactorum*), whose larvae can kill cacti. A large population was discovered on an island within Biscayne National Park during a floristic inventory conducted following Hurricane Andrew in 1992.

COCHINEAL CACTUS

Opuntia cochenillifera (L.) Mill.
Cactus family (Cactaceae)

Description: Multibranch treelike cactus to 12' or more with oblong, mostly spineless pads due to selective breeding by growers, but still producing clusters of tiny bristles that break off in the skin and are irritating and difficult to remove. The flowers produce red, conical fruits.

Bloom Season: All year

Habitat/Range: Endemic to Mexico but cultivated in Florida and sometimes found growing along margins of preserves where pads have been discarded and become established

Comments: *Opuntia* is a name given to a plant that grew around the city of Opus in ancient Greece. The name *cochenillifera* relates to the cochineal insect (*Dactylopius coccus*), a type of scale that feeds on the plant and is harvested to produce a red dye called carmine or cochineal. The pads (called nopales) are peeled, cooked, and eaten in Mexico, Jamaica, and other countries, often served with eggs.

KEYS PRICKLY PEAR

Opuntia keyensis Britton ex Small
Cactus family (Cactaceae)

Description: Erect, much-branched cactus to 9' tall with elliptic, oval, or obovate pads averaging 5"–7" long and 3"–4" wide, with small clusters of very short, sharp bristles. Peach- to salmon-colored flowers are 2"–2½" wide.

Bloom Season: All year

Habitat/Range: Coastal rock barrens and margins of hammocks and mangroves of the Florida Keys

Comments: The name *keyensis* means "of the Florida Keys." This species was first described by botanist Nathaniel Lord Britton (1859–1934) from plants collected on Boot Key in 1909. When Britton described the species, he did not satisfy the rules of botanical nomenclature, so it was corrected and validly published in 1919 by botanist John Kunkel Small (1869–1938). This species is sometimes sunk under synonymy with the yellow-flowered *Opuntia stricta* but has recently been resurrected as a distinct species, partly based on flower color and larger growth habit.

CINNAMON BARK
Canella winterana (L.) Gaertn.
Canella family (Canellaceae)

Description: Small tree, typically 20' tall or less, with leathery, obovate to spatulate leaves 2"–4" long and ¾"–2" wide, spicy-fragrant when crushed. Flowers are in axillary clusters and are followed by red to purplish, ⅜" globose fruits.

Bloom Season: All year

Habitat/Range: Coastal hammocks of Miami-Dade and Monroe Counties (mainland and Keys), West Indies, and South America

Comments: *Canella* means "a reed," alluding to the bark, which forms a roll, or quill, when dried. The name *winterana* relates to when Carolus Linnaeus (1707–1778) placed it in the genus *Winteranus*. Biting a leaf of cinnamon bark will cause a burning sensation. The rolled bark was commonly used as a substitute for cinnamon as early as the thirteenth century, but the source of true cinnamon is members of the genus *Cinnamomum*. The bark of *Canella* is macerated in rum and used as a remedy to reduce fever and as a gargle for sore throat. The bark was once exported from the United States to Europe for pharmaceutical uses. Butterflies (especially hairstreaks) visit the flowers.

PINELAND QUAILBERRY

Crossopetalum ilicifolium (Poir.) Kuntze
Staff-tree family (Celastraceae)

Description: Somewhat woody perennial with nearly prostrate or ascending branches and mostly opposite ovate to elliptic, holly-like toothed leaves averaging ½" long and slightly narrower. The tiny flower petals are red, followed by bright red, ¼" fruits.

Bloom Season: All year

Habitat/Range: Pinelands of Collier, Miami-Dade, and the Monroe County Keys, the Bahamas, and Cuba

Comments: *Crossopetalum* means "fringed petals"; the name *ilicifolium* alludes to the resemblance of the leaves to an Ilex, or holly. Other common names for this state-listed threatened species are Christmasberry and ground holly. The name quailberry relates to quail being attracted to the red fruits. A decoction made from the roots of this and the following species has been used in the West Indies to expel kidney stones, treat kidney infections, and counteract inflammation of the bladder and kidneys.

MAIDENBERRY

Crossopetalum rhacoma Crantz
Staff-tree family (Celastraceae)

Description: Woody shrub or small tree to 10' tall but usually half that height. Angular branches bear opposite, ½"–1", linear-lanceolate to obovate leaves with crenulate margins. Tiny flowers are tinged red and clustered in the leaf axils. Subglobose fruits ripen red.

Bloom Season: All year

Habitat/Range: Hammocks, margins of mangroves, and coastal scrublands in Sarasota and Miami-Dade Counties, the Monroe County Keys, West Indies, and Colombia

Comments: The name *rhacoma* was used by Pliny (AD 23–79) for an old-world plant. This state-listed threatened species is more common in the Florida Keys than on the mainland, where it can be found along road edges that bisect mangrove-buttonwood associations. It is very ornamental when in fruit but is seldom seen in cultivation. In the West Indies the roots and bark are boiled and used as a medicinal bath to relieve pain from dysentery and burning eyes.

PAINTED LEAF
Euphorbia cyathophora Murray
(Also *Poinsettia cyathophora* [Murray] Bartl.)
Spurge family (Euphorbiaceae)

Description: Herbaceous annual 6"–30" tall with mostly opposite leaves ranging from linear-lanceolate to narrowly obovate and somewhat fiddle-shaped, often with red bases on the upper leaves. The leaves average 2"–4" long and ¼"–2" wide. Stems and leaves exude milky sap when broken. Inconspicuous flowers are terminal, with a single involucral gland.

Bloom Season: All year

Habitat/Range: Open disturbed sites, rocky flats, and pinelands of the eastern and southern United States, throughout Florida, the West Indies, and tropical America

Comments: *Euphorbia* honors Trojan War hero *Euphorbus*, physician to King Juba II of the ancient kingdom of Numidia in northwest Africa. The name *cyathophora* means "cuplike," in reference to the cup-shaped involucre of fused bracts, the cyathia. This is a common weedy species of disturbed sites, including residential landscapes. Another name is fire-on-the-mountain.

PINELAND SPURGE
Euphorbia pinetorum (Small) G. L. Webster
(Also *Poinsettia pinetorum* Small)
Spurge family (Euphorbiaceae)

Description: Herbaceous perennial typically less than 18" tall with linear-lanceolate leaves averaging 2"–4" long and ⅛"–³⁄₁₆" wide, usually with red at the base. Tiny yellowish flowers are in terminal, irregular clusters, with 3–4 involucral glands.

Bloom Season: All year

Habitat/Range: Endemic to pine rocklands of southern Miami-Dade County and the Monroe County Keys

Comments: The name *pinetorum* means "of pinelands." This state-listed endangered species was first described as *Poinsettia pinetorum* in 1904 by botanist John Kunkel Small 1869–1938) from plants he collected between Homestead and Camp Jackson in southern Miami-Dade County. Look for it in pine rockland habitat in the National Key Deer Refuge on Big Pine Key. It can be confused with narrow-leaved forms of *Euphorbia cyathophora*, which is an annual with a single involucral gland.

CORAL BEAN OR CHEROKEE BEAN
Erythrina herbacea L.
Pea family (Fabaceae)

Description: Deciduous, soft-wooded shrub 6'–8' tall. Compound leaves are divided into 3 leaflets that are widest at the base and average about 3" long and wide. Tubular, 1½"–3" flowers are on erect, 4"–8" spikes, often produced when the plant is leafless. Seedpods are 3"–4" long, constricting around each seed, opening at maturity to reveal hard, bright red seeds.

Bloom Season: January to October

Habitat/Range: Hammock margins, pinelands, and coastal strand from North Carolina to Texas south through Florida

Comments: *Erythrina* is Greek for "red." The name *herbacea* means "not woody." The seeds are poisonous and have been crushed and used to poison rats. Tea brewed from the leaves has sleep-inducing properties and has been used to treat hysteria, but many home remedies have resulted in grave poisoning. Hummingbirds visit the flowers.

COASTAL INDIGO
Indigofera miniata Ortega
Pea family (Fabaceae)

Description: Herbaceous perennial with appressed hairs that give the leaves a grayish appearance. The ¾"–1¼" leaves are compound with 5–9 narrow leaflets. Reddish or salmon-pink flowers appear in the leaf axils, each measuring about ⅜" long.

Bloom Season: All year

Habitat/Range: Sandy and rocky pinelands from Florida and Georgia, west to Texas and Oklahoma

Comments: *Indigofera* is Latin meaning "to bear indigo," in reference to the dye extracted from some species, but indigo dye is now mostly produced synthetically. It had been described as *Indigofera miniata* var. *floridana* in 1981 by botanist Duane Isely (1918–2000) and regarded as endemic to Florida. It occurs in the National Key Deer Refuge on Big Pine Key and is reportedly a larval host plant of the ceraunus blue and zarucco duskywing butterflies. It is quite attractive in flower but, surprisingly, is seldom cultivated.

FLORIDA KEYS INDIGO
Indigofera oxycarpa Desv.
(Also *Indigofera keyensis* Small; *Indigofera trita* L. f. subsp. *scabra* [Roth] de Kort & Thijsse; *Indigofera mucronata* Spreng. ex DC. var. *keyensis* [Small] Isely)
Pea family (Fabaceae)

Description: Mounding or scrambling perennial with appressed hairs on the stems and compound leaves bearing mostly 5 opposite, ovate or elliptic leaflets to ¾" long and ½" wide. The pink flowers are about ¼" long, producing narrowly linear cylindrical seedpods to 1" long and about ⅟₁₆" wide.

Bloom Season: Mostly September to April

Habitat/Range: Coastal hammock margins and rocky coasts of Cuba, Jamaica, Central America, Brazil, and the Florida Keys (extirpated from Collier and Miami-Dade Counties)

Comments: The name *oxycarpa* means "sharply pointed fruit." In 1913 botanist John Kunkel Small (1869–1938) described plants in the Florida Keys as a new, endemic species, which he named *Indigofera keyensis*. In 1984 it was relegated as a subspecies of the globally widespread *Indigofera trita*, but in 1992, Louisiana State University botanist Alan Wayne Lievens determined that *Indigofera oxycarpa* is the correct name for plants in the New World. It is a state-listed endangered species and a larval host plant of the ceraunus blue and zarucco duskywing butterflies.

TRAILING INDIGO
Indigofera spicata Forssk.
Pea family (Fabaceae)

Description: Trailing perennial with compound leaves bearing 3–5 ovate leaflets to ⅝" long and ⅜" wide. Coral-colored flowers are on erect spikes 1"–1½" tall. Linear-oblong pods are numerous, each about ¾" long.

Bloom Season: All year

Habitat/Range: Invasive in pinelands and disturbed sites throughout much of Florida. Native to the Old World.

Comments: The name *spicata* means "spiked," in reference to the inflorescence. This species can be fatal to horses if it amounts to 50 percent or more of the ingested feed; even pet food made from animals that have grazed on it can cause severe liver damage if consumed. This is a pernicious weed in lawns, pastures, and roadsides in South Florida and is difficult to eradicate due to a long taproot. It is a larval host plant of the ceraunus blue and zarucco duskywing butterflies.

ANIL DE PASTO
Indigofera suffruticosa Mill.
Pea family (Fabaceae)

Description: Much-branched shrub to 6' tall with alternate, odd-pinnate, compound leaves bearing 9–17 oblong to oblong-obovate, opposite leaflets ½"–1" long. Flowers are in few- to many-flowered racemes, with flowers ranging from vermillion to pale crimson, each about ¼" long.

Bloom Season: All year

Habitat/Range: Weedy thickets and disturbed sites across the southern United States, Bermuda, West Indies, and tropical America. Not native to Florida

Comments: The name *suffruticosa* means "shrub-like." The common name is Portuguese for "pasture indigo," alluding to its habit of growing in pastures. In the Florida Keys it tends to invade coastal rock barrens and hammock margins. It differs from other species in this guide by being an upright shrub. Consumption of the seeds can cause severe liver damage and alteration of chromosome numbers in humans, as well as serious health issues in dogs.

TRUE INDIGO
Indigofera tinctoria L.
Pea family (Fabaceae)

Description: Much-branched, mounding perennial shrub to about 6' tall with alternate, odd-pinnate compound leaves bearing 9–15 oval to obovate leaflets averaging ⅜"–¾" long. Flowers are in racemes and range from salmon-red to rose-pink, each about ¼" long. Pods are linear-cylindric to 1¼" long, often numerous.

Bloom Season: All year

Habitat/Range: Invasive in coastal habitats and disturbed sites, with vouchered specimens from Hillsborough and Miami-Dade Counties and the Monroe County Keys. Native to India and Malaysia.

Comments: The name *tinctoria* means "to dye or color," referring to the indigo dye produced from this species that is one of the oldest dyes known to humankind. The plant is used medicinally to treat epilepsy, syphilis, liver disorders, and kidney stones; a tincture made from the seeds is used in India to kill head lice. Consumption of the seeds can cause liver problems and other health issues.

POEPPIG'S ROSEMALLOW
Hibiscus poeppigii (Spreng.) Garcke
Mallow family (Malvaceae)

Description: Perennial shrub to 5' tall with ovate, coarsely toothed, rough-textured leaves ¾"–2" long and half as wide. Pendent flowers are solitary from the leaf axils, each averaging ¾" long.

Bloom Season: All year

Habitat/Range: Hammocks and coastal rock barrens of southern Florida, West Indies, and Mexico

Comments: *Hibiscus* is an ancient Greek name for a mallow. The name *poeppigii* honors German botanist, zoologist, and explorer Eduard Friedrich Poeppig (1798–1868), who has also had an angiosperm, orchid, monkey, snake, and toad named in his honor. This state-listed endangered species is known in Florida only from Miami-Dade County and the Monroe County Keys and is sometimes cultivated for its attractive flowers. Hummingbirds eat the pollen and conduct aerial acrobatics to access the floral nectar from the pendent flowers. The species occurs in John Pennekamp, Windley Key, Lignumvitae Key, and Long Key State Parks.

STRANGLER FIG

Ficus aurea Nutt.
Mulberry family (Moraceae)

Description: Large, usually deciduous tree to 60'
or more with stout aerial roots; often seen growing
on other trees and palms. The leaves average
4"–5" long and 2"–3" wide, with short petioles.
Tiny flowers are produced on the inside wall of the
figs. The figs are nearly sessile to about ⅜" wide,
ripening to reddish purple.

Bloom Season: All year

Habitat/Range: Hammocks of Central and South
Florida to tropical America

Comments: *Ficus* is Latin for "fig." The name *aurea*
alludes to the yellowish twigs. The common name
relates to the "strangling" roots that entwine
the trunk of the host tree when it grows as an
epiphyte, often killing its host after many years
by shading it to death. This species is a larval
host plant of the ruddy daggerwing butterfly and
Edwards' wasp moth. The small figs are a favorite
food of many birds.

SHORTLEAF FIG

Ficus citrifolia Mill.
Mulberry family (Moraceae)

Description: Large, usually deciduous tree (sometimes growing on other trees and palms) to 50' tall
or more with stout aerial roots. The leaves average
2½"–5" long and 1½"–3" wide, with long petioles
and often with a slightly cordate base. The small
figs are on ⅜" stalks, differentiating this species
from the strangler fig.

Bloom Season: All year

Habitat/Range: Hammocks of South Florida and
tropical America

Comments: The name *citrifolia* alludes to the
leaves resembling a *Citrus* (Rutaceae). Birds, especially cedar waxwings and white-crowned pigeons,
savor the ripe figs. The leaves are larval food of
the ruddy daggerwing butterfly, Edwards' wasp
moth, fig sphinx, and a striking blue-and-orange
moth, *Hemerophila diva*. This is a handsome shade
tree for large property but must be kept far away
from underground plumbing, septic tanks, drain
fields, roads, driveways, and sidewalks due to its
aggressive roots.

WORMVINE
Vanilla barbellata Rchb. f.
Orchid family (Orchidaceae)

Description: Vining orchid with narrow, bract-like leaves that abort, leaving smooth, ½"-thick, green or orange stems that root to trees at the nodes. Fragrant flowers are about 2"–2½" wide with green sepals and petals and a lip that is white above, red below. Pendent pods are about 3" long and ⅜" wide.

Bloom Season: April to July

Habitat/Range: Coastal hammocks, mangrove-buttonwood associations, and rarely pine rocklands of Miami-Dade County and the Monroe County mainland and Keys through the West Indies

Comments: *Vanilla* is from the Spanish *vainilla*, or "small pod," in reference to the bean-like seed capsules. The name *barbellata* means "little beard," alluding to the small bristles on the lip. This state-listed endangered species is local around the Flamingo area and mangrove backcountry of Everglades National Park and from Elliott Key in Biscayne National Park to Big Pine Key in the Florida Keys. It is related to *Vanilla planifolia*, the principal vanilla orchid grown commercially for production of vanilla extract.

FLORIDA FIREBUSH

Hamelia patens Jacq. var. *patens*
Madder family (Rubiaceae)

Description: Large, rounded shrub or small tree to 16' tall with green or red-tinged, elliptic to obovate-elliptic leaves, mostly in groups of 3 along the stem. The leaves average 2"–4" long and 1"–2" wide. Terminal clusters of red to orange-red tubular flowers are followed by ellipsoid fruits that ripen to black.

Bloom Season: All year

Habitat/Range: Hammocks of Florida and the neotropics

Comments: *Hamelia* honors French botanist Henri Louis Duhamel du Monceau (1700–1782). The name *patens* means "spreading" and alludes to the branches. Firebush attracts a variety of butterflies, sphinx moths, bees, and hummingbirds. The fruits are eaten by birds; the leaves are larval food of the pluto and tersa sphinx moths. A yellow-flowered variety (var. *glabra*) with leaves mostly in groups of 4 is naturalized in Florida. The species is native to tropical America and widely cultivated in Florida.

GRAYTWIG

Schoepfia schreberi J. F. Gmelin
(Also *Schoepfia chrysophylloides* [A. Rich.] Planch.)
Whitewood family (Schoepfiaceae)

Description: Small, hemiparasitic tree averaging 10'–14' tall with whitish, corky, fissured bark. Glossy leaves are lanceolate to elliptic, averaging 1"–2" long and about ½" wide. The axillary flowers measure about ⅛" wide. Small, ellipsoid fruits ripen orange or red, with a persistent rim of the corolla at the tip.

Bloom Season: October to April

Habitat/Range: Hammocks and coastal forests from Volusia County south along the east coast to Martin County and then across all of southern Florida through the Florida Keys, West Indies, and northern South America

Comments: *Schoepfia* honors German physician and botanist Johann David Schoepf (1752–1800). The name *schreberi* honors German naturalist and professor Johann Christian Daniel von Schreber (1739–1810). This species parasitizes the roots of other trees, and a 1979 study found root parasitism on ten different host species.

Erect pricklypear (*Opuntia stricta*)

POISONWOOD

Metopium toxiferum (L.) Krug & Urb.
Cashew family (Anacardiaceae)

Description: Large tree to 40' or more with compound leaves bearing 3–7 (usually 5) ovate to obovate leaflets averaging about 3" long and 2" wide. The midrib divides the leaflets equally. Large panicles of yellowish flowers, each about ¼" wide, produce oblong, ⅜" orangish fruits.

Bloom Season: All year

Habitat/Range: Hammocks and pinelands from Martin and Collier Counties south through the Florida Keys, the Bahamas, and Greater Antilles

Comments: *Metopium* refers to the gum of an unknown African tree. The name *toxiferum* relates to the tree's toxic sap. The sap contains urushiol, the same toxin in poison ivy (*Toxicodendron radicans*), which causes a mild to severe blistering rash on sensitive people. The fruits are a favorite of the endangered white-crowned pigeon and other birds. The leaves resemble the unrelated gumbo limbo (*Bursera simaruba*), but its leaflets are divided inequilaterally with up to 9 leaflets per leaf (usually 7).

PINELAND GOLDEN TRUMPET

Angadenia berteroi (A. DC.) Miers
Dogbane family (Apocynaceae)

Description: Herbaceous perennial 6"–30" tall, often branching near the top. Opposite leaves are linear-oblong with curled-under margins, measuring 1"–2" long and ⅜"–½" wide. Flowers are near the branch tips, usually 1–3 open at a time, each measuring about 1" across.

Bloom Season: All year

Habitat/Range: Pinelands of Miami-Dade County and the Monroe County Keys, Bahamas, Cuba, and Hispaniola

Comments: *Angadenia* is a combination of the Greek words ang, for "box," or "case," and *aden*, for "gland," presumably referring to the enclosed stigma. The name *berteroi* honors Italian physicist, physician, and botanist Carlo Luigi Giuseppe Bertero (1789–1831), who changed his name from Santa Vittoria d'Alba. The sap can cause severe eye irritation, and sensitive people may develop a skin rash from contact with the sap. This is a state-listed threatened species.

WILD ALLAMANDA
Pentalinon luteum (L.) B. F. Hansen & Wunderlin
Dogbane family (Apocynaceae)

Description: Twining vine with opposite, obovate to elliptic, glossy leaves averaging 2"–3" long and 1"–1¼" wide. The stems and leaves exude milky sap if broken. Showy, bright yellow trumpet-shaped flowers reach about 2" across.

Bloom Season: May to November

Habitat/Range: Mangroves and coastal hammocks from St. Lucie and Lee Counties south through the Florida Keys and the West Indies to Central America

Comments: *Pentalinon* alludes to the narrow threads at the tip of the 5 anthers. The name *luteum* means "yellow," in reference to the flowers. The plant also has an unusual common name, hammock viperstail, in parts of its range, perhaps alluding to the long, wispy new growth at the tip of the stems. Skippers and native bees crawl down the floral tube to access nectar. The species is in the native-plant nursery trade and can be grown on a fence, arbor, or tall trellis. Outbreaks of voracious larvae of the polka-dot wasp moth (oleander moth) can entirely defoliate the vine. It also serves as larval food for the alope sphinx moth.

SEA OXEYE OR BAY MARIGOLD
Borrichia arborescens (L.) DC.
Aster family (Asteraceae)

Description: Perennial shrub with dark green, glossy, oblanceolate to spatulate, opposite leaves that average 1"–2" long and ¼"–½" wide, with entire or slightly toothed margins. Flower heads are about 1"–1¼" across.

Bloom Season: All year

Habitat/Range: Rocky shorelines, dunes, and coastal marshes of Miami-Dade and Monroe Counties (both mainland and Keys), West Indies, and Bermuda

Comments: *Borrichia* honors Danish physician, scientist, and professor Ole Borch (1626–1690), who latinized his name to Olaus Borrichius. The name *arborescens* means "treelike," alluding to its upright growth habit even though the shrub does not come close to becoming a tree. The flowers of this salt-tolerant shrub attract butterflies, and it is sometimes used in coastal landscapes. It may hybridize with the following species to form a fertile hybrid called *Borrichia* x *cubana*, but back-crosses with either parent are infertile.

OXEYE DAISY OR SEASIDE TANSY
Borrichia frutescens (L.) DC.
Aster family (Asteraceae)

Description: Perennial shrub with ascending stems to 3' tall or more, forming rhizomatous colonies. Grayish-green, elliptic to oblanceolate, opposite leaves average 1"–2" long and ½"–¾" wide. The mid-stem leaves have dentate to serrate margins. Flower heads are solitary or rarely paired, each about 1"–1¼" across.

Bloom Season: All year

Habitat/Range: Rocky shorelines, beaches, and brackish marshes along the Atlantic and Gulf coastlines from Maryland to Texas, West Indies, Bermuda, and coastal Yucatán

Comments: The name *frutescens* means "shrubby." This species is cultivated for coastal landscapes where salt tolerance is required. The flowers attract butterflies, and the seeds are eaten by buntings, sparrows, cardinals, and grosbeaks. This is the most common of the two species in Florida and is often found growing in association with the previous species. Growth habit and the color of the leaves help separate them.

STRAGGLER DAISY
Calyptocarpus vialis Less.
Aster family (Asteraceae)

Description: Herbaceous perennial with stems that often root at the nodes to form large colonies. Toothed, hairy leaves are opposite along the stem and average about 1" long and ¾" wide. Flower heads are about ¼" across.

Bloom Season: All year

Habitat/Range: Invasive weed in disturbed sites, including roadsides, trail margins, and residential landscapes. Native to tropical America.

Comments: *Calyptocarpus* is Greek for "covered fruit," alluding to the fruits inside the phyllary cup. The name *vialis* relates to growing along a roadside. The plant is called *hierba del caballo* (horse herb) in Spanish-speaking countries due to it being a favorite of grazing horses. Although not native, it is often tolerated as a ground cover that can withstand foot traffic. It was first described in 1832 by German botanist Christian Friedrich Lessing (1809–1862) from plants collected in Mexico.

LEAVENWORTH'S TICKSEED
Coreopsis leavenworthii Torr. & A. Gray
Aster family (Asteraceae)

Description: Herbaceous perennial 12"–24" tall with narrow, opposite leaves that become smaller up the stem, measuring ½"–6" long to ⅛"–¼" wide. Flower heads are solitary or in few-flowered clusters terminating the stem, each measuring 1"–1¼" across with lobed rays.

Bloom Season: All year

Habitat/Range: Pinelands, wet flatwoods, and roadsides of southern Alabama throughout all of Florida

Comments: *Coreopsis* means "tick-like," alluding to the seeds' resemblance to ticks. The name *leavenworthii* honors American botanist Melines Conklin Leavenworth (1796–1862). All native species of Coreopsis are Florida's official state wildflower; this species is the most common statewide and was once regarded as a Florida endemic. Botanists with the *Flora of North America* believe this species should be placed under synonymy with Coreopsis tinctoria, a species that is common and widely cultivated across much of North America.

COASTAL PLAIN YELLOWTOPS
Flaveria linearis Lag.
Aster family (Asteraceae)

Description: Profusely branched herbaceous perennial with narrowly linear, sessile, 1-veined leaves to about 4" long and ¼" wide. Flowers are in flat-topped, dense clusters at the top of the stems.

Bloom Season: All year

Habitat/Range: Open, coastal and inland habitats from Florida, the West Indies, and Mexico's Yucatán Peninsula

Comments: *Flaveria* means "yellow," alluding to the yellow dye extracted from some species. The name *linearis* refers to the narrowly linear leaves. Butterflies and bees are common sights around flowering plants, making it popular among gardeners in Florida. Four members of this genus are native to Florida, but this is by far the most commonly seen species, especially in recently burned prairies and along roadsides that border open, sunny habitats. It occurs in virtually all of the state parks in the Florida Keys as well as the National Key Deer Refuge on Big Pine Key.

CLUSTERED YELLOWTOPS
Flaveria trinervia (Spreng.) C. Mohr
Aster family (Asteraceae)

Description: Herbaceous annual with widely divergent, 4-angled stems with sessile, toothed, lanceolate leaves averaging 2"–3" long to about ½" wide. Small clusters of flowers appear in the leaf axils along the stem.

Bloom Season: All year

Habitat/Range: Sandy pinelands and disturbed sites throughout tropical and warm temperate regions of the neotropics

Comments: The name *trinervia* relates to the 3 nerves, or veins, in the leaf blade. A medicinal tea brewed from the leaves and flowers of this and related species has been used to "soothe and quiet the nerves" and to cure bed-wetting in children. Small butterflies visit the flowers, but the plant is not purposely cultivated by gardeners. It is on the plant lists for Dagney Johnson, John Pennekamp, Long Key, and Bahia Honda State Parks, as well as the National Key Deer Refuge on Big Pine Key.

SANDDUNE CINCHWEED OR TEA BLINKUM

Pectis glaucescens (Cass.) D. J. Kell
Aster family (Asteraceae)

Description: Mat-forming herbaceous perennial with leaves that emit a lemonlike fragrance when crushed. The opposite, sessile, narrowly linear leaves average ½"–1" long, with 2 rows of glands on the lower surface. The stalked flower heads are solitary with 5 small, yellow rays surrounding the disk.

Bloom Season: All year

Habitat/Range: Pinelands, beaches, and disturbed sites of central and southern Florida through the West Indies

Comments: *Pectis* is Latin for "comb," alluding to the comblike bristles at the tip of the dry, 1-seeded achenes of some species. The name *glaucescens* means "blue-green" and relates to the leaf color. Spreading cinchweed (*Pectis prostrata*) also occurs in the Keys but has wider leaves and sessile flower heads. This and other species are used medicinally in the West Indies to treat diarrhea, venereal disease, colds, and tuberculosis, and to increase menstrual flow and stop flatulence.

TRACY'S SILKGRASS

Pityopsis tracyi Small
(Also *Heterotheca graminifolia* [Michx.] Shinners var. *tracyi* [Small] R. W. Long)
Aster family (Asteraceae)

Description: Herbaceous perennial 12"–20" tall with alternate leaves. The linear-lanceolate basal leaves average 4"–8" long, with fewer and much smaller, narrowly linear stem leaves. The flower heads are about ¾" across.

Bloom Season: All year

Habitat/Range: Endemic to pinelands of peninsular Florida and the Florida Keys

Comments: *Pityopsis* alludes to the similarity of the leaves to pine needles. The name *tracyi* honors botanist Samuel Mills Tracy (1847–1920) who worked on the flora of Missouri and Mississippi. Some botanists place this species under synonymy with the more widespread *Pityopsis graminifolia*, but in 1933, botanist John Kunkel Small (1869–1938) described *Pityopsis tracyi* as shorter in stature and having narrowly linear upper stem leaves, with the lower leaves being greatly elongated. This description fits plants on Big Pine Key.

CAMPHOR DAISY
Rayjacksonia phyllocephala (DC.) R. L. Hartman & M. A. Lane
Aster family (Asteraceae)

Description: Erect or sprawling herbaceous perennial to 24" tall or more. Alternate, linear to lanceolate, aromatic leaves are covered with sticky glands with coarse, widely spaced teeth along the margins. The showy flower heads are in branched arrays, each measuring about 1"–1¼" across. Seeds are wind-dispersed.

Bloom Season: September to June

Habitat/Range: Sandy soils typically in or near estuaries, salt flats, beaches, and dunes and along waterways of Colorado, Texas, Louisiana, Florida, and Mexico

Comments: *Rayjacksonia* honors American botanist and plant geneticist Raymond Carl Jackson (1928–2008), who was a professor of botany at Texas Tech University and recognized for his plant collections in Mexico. The name *phyllocephala* means "leaf head," alluding to the leaves that continue up the stem to the base of the flower heads. This species is local and sporadic in Florida, and has been vouchered in Manatee and Lee Counties and the Lower Florida Keys (Monroe County). Although very attractive, this species is virtually absent in the Florida native-plant nursery trade. It is the only member of the genus in Florida and can be confused with *Heterotheca subaxillaris*.

FLORIDA KEYS GOLDENROD

Solidago chrysopsis Small
Aster family (Asteraceae)

Description: Herbaceous perennial bearing a simple, straight flowering stem with narrowly linear basal leaves and almost scalelike upper stem leaves. The flower spike is uniformly unbranched.

Bloom Season: All year

Habitat/Range: Limestone soils from Martin County south to Miami-Dade County and the Monroe County Keys

Comments: *Solidago* means "become whole," presumably in reference to the plant's healing properties. The name *chrysopsis* alludes to the yellow-gold flowers. In 2016, University of Waterloo professor John C. Semple conducted a study of the *Solidago stricta* complex and determined that the narrow-leaved plants in the Florida Keys and southeastern mainland were distinct enough to relegate back to *S. chrysopsis*, a species described by John Kunkel Small (1869–1938) in 1898. Surprisingly, of the twenty-one species in Florida, this is the only goldenrod in the Florida Keys. Goldenrods are maligned as causing allergies, but they do not have airborne pollen.

CREEPING OXEYE OR WEDELIA

Sphagneticola trilobata (L.) Pruski
(Also *Wedelia trilobata* [L.] Hitchc.)
Aster family (Asteraceae)

Description: Herbaceous perennial with prostrate or ascending branches, often rooting at the nodes, with opposite, sessile, 3-lobed leaves averaging 2"–3½" long and 1½"–2" wide. The yellow to orangish-yellow flower heads typically measure 1¼"–1½" across. The ray flowers are notched at the tip.

Bloom Season: All year

Habitat/Range: Invasive on beaches, rocky shorelines, and disturbed sites throughout much of Florida. Native to the neotropics.

Comments: *Sphagneticola* is Latin for "dwelling in *Sphagnum*," in reference to the type species growing in wet habitats where sphagnum moss occurs. The name *trilobata* means "three-lobed," referring to the leaves. This popular landscape plant is now a Category II invasive species. The trailing stems can form a dense ground cover to the exclusion of native species and are difficult to eradicate.

ORIENTAL FALSE HAWKSBEARD
Youngia japonica (L.) DC.
Aster family (Asteraceae)

Description: Herbaceous biennial with lobed, glabrous or pubescent leaves averaging 2"–4" long and ¾"–1½" wide. Flowers are on erect stems 3"–6" tall. Flower heads are about ⅜" wide with wind-dispersed seeds.

Bloom Season: All year

Habitat/Range: Invasive in open, sunny habitats, but especially lawns, gardens, and other disturbed sites throughout Florida; native from Japan to India and Pacific Islands in the Far East

Comments: *Youngia* honors English poet Edward Young (1683–1765) and English physician, physicist, and Egyptologist Thomas Young (1773–1829). The name *japonica* means "of Japan." This ubiquitous weed should be well-known to Florida gardeners. Extracts from the plant have been shown to have anticancer and antiviral properties. Young leaves are cooked and eaten as a potherb in Asia. Hairstreaks, crescents, and other small butterflies visit the flowers.

PINELAND HELIOTROPE
Euploca polyphylla (Lehm.) J. I. M. Melo & Semir
(Also *Heliotropium polyphyllum* Lehm.)
Borage family (Boraginaceae)

Description: Herbaceous perennial 5"–10" tall or more, with linear-lanceolate to narrowly elliptic leaves reaching 1" long and ¼" wide. Yellow or white flowers are in terminal, scorpioid cymes and arranged in 2 ranks.

Bloom Season: All year

Habitat/Range: Wet flatwoods and other moist, sunny habitats from Taylor and Flagler Counties south to the Florida Keys (disjunct in Escambia County), through the West Indies into South America

Comments: *Euploca* alludes to the plicate folds (folded like a fan) in the corolla of the type species. The name *polyphylla* means "with many leaves." The word "heliotrope" refers to "turning toward the sun," but the sunflower is more dramatically heliotropic than members of *Euploca* or *Heliotropium*. Earlier botanists separated the white-flowered plants as *Heliotropium polyphyllum* and the yellow-flowered plants as *Heliotropium leavenworthii*. Butterflies visit the flowers.

SPANISH LADY
Opuntia abjecta Small ex Britton & Rose
Cactus family (Cactaceae)

Description: Clump-forming cactus with ascending stems that are typically about 4"–6" tall, with round to obovate or elliptic pads (cladodes) averaging 2"–2½" across. The wickedly sharp, dark reddish-brown spines turn white with age. Yellow flowers are about 2½" wide. Fruits ripen purple or yellow-green.

Bloom Season: March to May

Habitat/Range: Endemic to coastal rock barrens of the Middle and Lower Florida Keys

Comments: *Opuntia* is a name given to a plant that grew around the city of Opus in ancient Greece. The name *abjecta* relates to "small," alluding to the small stature of this species. This state-listed endangered species is threatened by habitat destruction, sea level rise, and an introduced moth (*Cactoblastis cactorum*), whose larvae bore into and kill Opuntia species. This moth is native to South America and first appeared in Florida in 1989, where it has become a threat to native *Opuntia* and *Consolea* species. The spines on this species have recurved barbs that make their removal both difficult and painful. Barely touching a spine with your foot or ankle can cause the entire pad (cladode) to dislodge and may cause other pads to seemingly jump onto your ankle as well, giving rise to the names Keys jumping cactus and Keys joe-jumper. This species is closely allied to *Opuntia millspaughii* in the West Indies.

BULLSUCKERS
Opuntia ochrocentra Small ex Britton & Rose
Cactus family (Cactaceae)

Description: Spiny cactus to 20" tall with elliptical pads (cladodes) measuring 4"–7" long and up to 3½" wide. There are 1–5 long, sharp, barbed spines per cluster. The spines are yellow to dark yellow when young and flattened at the base. The flower buds are reddish with yellow, waxy flowers averaging 2½" across. Conical fruits ripen red to reddish purple.

Bloom Season: April to June

Habitat/Range: Endemic to coastal rock barrens of Big Pine Key and Big Munson Island in the Lower Florida Keys; historically on Cape Sable (Monroe County) and Cape Romano (Collier County)

Comments: The name *ochrocentra* translates to "yellow centers." This critically imperiled cactus is threatened by habitat destruction, sea level rise, collectors, and the larvae of an introduced moth (*Cactoblastis cactorum*). The flowers open in late morning and close in late afternoon and are visited by bees, butterflies (skippers), and beetles. Fertile fruits are only produced when the flowers are outcrossed, as observed by University of Florida cacti taxonomist Lucas Majure (1981–). This cactus was first discovered in 1921 by botanist John Kunkel Small (1869–1938) on the southeastern end of Big Pine Key.

ERECT PRICKLYPEAR

Opuntia stricta (Haw.) Haw.
Cactus family (Cactaceae)

Description: Erect, much-branched cactus to 6' tall with spatulate, obovate, or elliptic pads (cladodes) to about 12" long and 5" wide. Spines are solitary or 2–3 together. Waxy yellow flowers are about 2½" wide. Conical fruits are reddish purple.

Bloom Season: April to August

Habitat/Range: Shell mounds, middens, mangroves, and coastal barrens from southeastern Georgia south to the Florida Keys and West Indies

Comments: The name *stricta* means "upright," in reference to the species' growth habit. It is locally common in the Florida Keys and can sometimes be seen along roadsides that border coastal hammocks. Spanish explorers wrote that the Calusa and Tequesta tribes in southern Florida peeled and ate the pads of this species and also cured them, like figs, to eat when traditional food was scarce. It is known to hybridize with *Opuntia abjecta* in the Florida Keys.

CRABWOOD OR OYSTERWOOD

Gymnanthes lucida Sw.
Spurge family (Euphorbiaceae)

Description: Tree to 20' tall bearing alternate, glossy leaves with scalloped margins, measuring 2"–3" long and about 1" wide. Axillary flower spikes produce many male flowers overtopping a few female flowers. Some trees only produce male flowers. Green, 3-lobed fruits are on long stems.

Bloom Season: April to September

Habitat/Range: Hammocks of Miami-Dade and Monroe Counties (mainland and Keys), West Indies, and Central America

Comments: *Gymnanthes* means "naked flower," alluding to the lack of sepals and petals on the flowers. The name *lucida* refers to the shiny leaves. It is a larval host plant of the Florida purplewing butterfly, and the wood was once used for walking canes and cuff buttons. The common name oysterwood alludes to the sheen of polished wood resembling that of the inside of an oyster shell; "crabwood" may be a corruption of *carapo*, the French Guiana name for the wood.

BIG PINE PARTRIDGE PEA

Chamaecrista keyensis Pennell
(Also *Chamaecrista lineata* [Sw.] Greene var. *keyensis* [Pennell] H. S. Irwin & Barneby)
Pea family (Fabaceae)

Description: Herbaceous perennial to 30" tall with compound leaves bearing up to 9 pairs of narrow leaflets covered with short hairs. The axillary flowers reach about 1" wide with reddish-purple anthers.

Bloom Season: All year

Habitat/Range: Endemic to pine rockland habitat on Big Pine Key but with early collections on No Name, Ramrod, and Cudjoe Keys and reported from Little Pine Key

Comments: *Chamaecrista* is a pre-Linnaean name that has been translated to mean "low crest" or "peacock crest." The name *keyensis* means "of the Florida Keys," and the species was named in 1917 by American botanist Francis Whittier Pennell (1886–1952) of the New York Botanical Garden. This endemic, state-listed endangered species is restricted to the Lower Florida Keys, likely occurring only on Big Pine Key at present, where it is locally common. It is a larval host plant of the cloudless sulphur, little yellow, gray hairstreak, and ceraunus blue butterflies.

SENSITIVE PEA

Chamaecrista nictitans (L.) Moench var. *aspera*
(Muhl. ex Elliott) H. S. Irwin & Barneby
Pea family (Fabaceae)

Description: Herbaceous annual with soft, shaggy hairs along the stems that average 18"–24" tall. The compound leaves measure 1¼"–2¾" long to about ¾" wide with 7–32 linear, hairy leaflets. The flowers reach ⅜" wide.

Bloom Season: Mostly July to September

Habitat/Range: Pinelands and flatwoods throughout much of Florida north to South Carolina

Comments: The name *nictitans* means "blinking" or "moving" and alludes to the leaflets that close at night. The name *aspera* means "rough" and refers to the coarse hairs on the stems and pods. It can be found growing in association with the previous species on Big Pine Key. It is a larval host plant of the cloudless sulphur, little yellow, gray hairstreak, and ceraunus blue butterflies. *Chamaecrista nictitans* var. *nictitans* has hairless stems, but only ranges south to Collier County.

BIG PINE RABBITBELLS

Crotalaria linaria Small
Pea family (Fabaceae)

Description: Herbaceous perennial with prostrate or ascending hairy stems bearing linear to linear-elliptic pubescent leaves measuring ½"–1" long and ¼"–⅜" wide. The ½" flowers are often solitary. The narrow leaves and small purple calyx are distinctive.

Bloom Season: All year

Habitat/Range: Endemic to coastal habitats from Pinellas and Palm Beach Counties south along both coasts and on Big Pine Key in the Florida Keys.

Comments: *Crotalaria* means "to rattle" and was taken from the rattlesnake genus *Crotalus* for the loose seeds that rattle in the pods. The name *linaria* refers to the linear leaves. Botanist John Kunkel Small (1869–1938) described this species in 1913 from plants he found on Big Pine Key. This species has long been placed under synonymy with *Crotalaria rotundifolia*, a widespread species that ranges from Central Florida north to Louisiana and Virginia south through the neotropics.

LOW RATTLEBOX
Crotalaria pumila Ortega
Pea family (Fabaceae)

Description: Herbaceous perennial, often decumbent but with ascending stems to about 10" tall with alternate leaves divided into 3 oblong to obovate leaflets averaging ¼"–⅜" long. Usually 1- to 5-flowered with an oval standard decorated with thin red lines and the keel bent at a sharp right angle. Each flower is about ⅜" wide.

Bloom Season: All year

Habitat/Range: Pinelands of peninsular Florida to the Florida Keys, West Indies, and the southwestern United States through tropical America

Comments: The name *pumila* means "little," for the plant's small stature. This species is known from Dagny Johnson, John Pennekamp, and Windley Key State Parks, plus the National Key Deer Refuge on Big Pine Key. It is a larval host plant of the day-flying bella moth, with its orangish-pink forewings marked with white bands and black spots. The pink hind wings create a flash of color when the moth takes flight.

FEWFLOWER HOLDBACK
Denisophytum pauciflorum (Griseb.) Gagnon & G. P. Lewis
(Also *Caesalpinia pauciflora* [Griseb.] C. Wright)
Pea family (Fabaceae)

Description: Woody shrub to 6' tall with bipinnately compound leaves bearing 3–5 pairs of leaflets, each with 5 pairs of elliptic sub-leaflets. Sharp, ¼" spines appear in the leaf axils. The flowers are about ½" wide, opening in midafternoon. Flattened pods are ¾"–1½" long.

Bloom Season: All year

Habitat/Range: Pinelands of the Lower Florida Keys and West Indies

Comments: *Denisophytum* was created by French botanist René Viguier (1880–1931) to honor his botanist friend Marcel Denis (1897–1929). The name *pauciflorum* means "few flowers." This is a state-listed endangered species apparently restricted to Big Pine Key in Florida, especially along roadsides that bisect its habitat. It was first described in 1866 as *Libidibia pauciflora* by German botanist August Heinrich Rudolf Grisebach (1814–1879) from plants collected in Cuba.

GRAY NICKER OR NICKERBEAN
Guilandina bonduc (L.)
(Also *Caesalpinia bonduc* [L.] Roxb.)
Pea family (Fabaceae)

Description: Large sprawling vine with thick, spiny stems often reclining on nearby shrubs. Alternate leaves are evenly bipinnate with recurved, often paired, wickedly sharp thorns on the petioles. Ovate to elliptic leaflets are in 4–8 pairs, each measuring ¾"–1½" long and ½"–¾" wide. Conspicuous stipules at the base of the petioles resemble incised leaflets. Flowers with broadly oblong petals are congested on erect spikes. Spiny, suborbicular pods split open to reveal 1–3 hard, marble-size gray seeds.

Bloom Season: All year

Habitat/Range: Margins of mangrove forests, beaches, and other coastal habitats from Levy and Volusia Counties south along both coasts into the Florida Keys; also in the tropics and subtropics worldwide

Comments: *Guilandina* honors German physician and botanist Melchior Wieland (1519–1589), who "Italianized" his last name to Guilandini after moving to Italy. He collected plants in North Africa, where he was taken captive and enslaved for several years. The name *bonduc* is French, from the Arabic *bunduq*, or hazelnut, in apparent reference to the seeds. This plant is exceptionally spiny, including the seedpods. Very sharp, hooked thorns on the bottom of the petioles make thickets of the plant impenetrable. It is a larval host plant of the martial scrub-hairstreak, ceraunus blue, and critically imperiled Miami blue butterflies.

YELLOW NICKER

Guilandina major (Medik.) Small
(Also *Caesalpinia major* [Medik.] Dandy & Exell)
Pea family (Fabaceae)

Description: Perennial vine with stout, prickly stems. Alternate leaves are evenly bipinnate with prickly petioles and ovate-oblong leaflets in 4 to 7 pairs, each measuring about 1"–2" long and ½"–¾" wide. Dull yellow flowers are in spikes, usually with only 1 or 2 open at a time. Spiny, suborbicular pods bear 1 or 2 yellow, marble-size seeds.

Bloom Season: All year

Habitat/Range: Coastal habitats from Martin County south along the east coast into the Florida Keys and in the tropics and subtropics worldwide

Comments: The name *major* alludes to the species' wide global range. This species resembles gray nicker but is not as wickedly armed and is much less common. It is a larval host plant of the martial scrub-hairstreak and ceraunus blue butterflies and possibly the critically imperiled Miami blue.

TROPICAL PUFF

Neptunia pubescens Benth.
Pea family (Fabaceae)

Description: Mat-forming, berbaceous perennial with ascending or reclining stems that may reach 30" long or more. The evenly bipinnate leaves produce up to 60 opposite pairs of tiny, narrowly linear leaflets. Flower clusters are on long-stalked terminal spikes.

Bloom Season: April to November

Habitat/Range: Pinelands, flatwoods, margins of salt marshes, and disturbed sites from Florida to Texas and Mexico south to Brazil

Comments: *Neptunia* honors Neptune, the Roman god of fresh water and the sea, and relates to members of the genus that grow near water. The name *pubescens* alludes to the pubescence (soft hairs) covering the stems and leaves. It is also called sensitive pea because the leaflets close when touched and also close on their own at night. It is a larval host plant of the ceraunus blue butterfly but is very seldom seen in cultivation. Some species are eaten as potherbs in Asia.

BROWNHAIR SNOUTBEAN
Rhynchosia cinerea Nash
Pea family (Fabaceae)

Description: Perennial vine with trailing or twining stems reaching 36" long and covered with coarse gray hairs. Alternate leaves are divided into 3 broadly obovate leaflets, averaging 1"–1¼" long and ½"–1" wide, with a smooth upper surface and hairy below. Flowers are tightly clustered in axillary racemes.

Bloom Season: All year

Habitat/Range: Endemic to pinelands, scrub, sand-hills, and other open habitats of peninsular Florida and the Florida Keys

Comments: *Rhynchosia* is Greek for "a beak," alluding to the keel petals. The name *cinerea* means "ashy" or "gray" and relates to the stiff gray hairs on the stems. The species was first described in 1895 by American botanist George Valentine Nash (1864–1921) from plants collected near Eustis in Lake County, Florida. In the Florida Keys it is found in the pine rocklands of the National Key Deer Refuge on Big Pine Key.

LEAST SNOUTBEAN
Rhynchosia minima (L.) DC.
Pea family (Fabaceae)

Description: Perennial vine with long, trailing or twining stems lined with downward-angled hairs. Leaves are divided into 3 ovate to obovate leaflets, each averaging ¾"–1" long with an equal width. Small flowers are on a long axillary stem, yellow with thin red lines on the standard.

Bloom Season: All year

Habitat/Range: Pinelands, flatwoods, sand-hills, and disturbed sites throughout Florida and from Georgia to Texas, Arkansas, and Missouri; pantropical

Comments: The name *minima* means "least," referring to the plant's small stature compared to other species. Essential oils extracted from the plant exhibit significant antimicrobial, antifungal, and antioxidant activities. The plant also can harbor a golden mosaic virus that can infect other plants. This species is common in the Florida Keys, often found growing on fences or scrambling across other plants along hammock margins.

SWARTZ'S SNOUTBEAN OR BONANEY-BEAN

Rhynchosia swartzii (Vail) Urb.
Pea family (Fabaceae)

Description: Perennial vine with trailing or twining stems lined with alternate compound leaves divided into 3 rhombic-ovate leaflets that are pubescent on both sides. The terminal leaflet is 1"–2" long and has a longer stem than the slightly smaller lateral leaflets. Flowers are in few-flowered racemes, followed by pods that split open to reveal red seeds.

Bloom Season: January to May, but sporadically all year

Habitat/Range: Hammock margins of Miami-Dade County and the Monroe County Keys, the Bahamas, Cuba, and Mexico

Comments: The name *swartzii* honors Swedish botanist Olof Peter Swartz (1760–1818), who became the first specialist in orchid taxonomy and sailed to the West Indies to collect plants. In the Florida Keys, this state-listed endangered species is very local and occurs only on plant lists for Key Largo (Monroe County) and Elliott Key (Miami-Dade County).

BAHAMA SENNA

Senna mexicana (Jacq.) H. S. Irwin & Barneby var. *chapmanii* (Isely) H. S. Irwin & Barneby
(Also *Cassia chapmanii* Isely)
Pea family (Fabaceae)

Description: Woody shrub to about 4' tall with alternate, compound leaves divided into 3–5 pairs of lanceolate or elliptic leaflets averaging ¾"–1" long and ⅜"–½" wide. The flowers reach ¾" wide.

Bloom Season: All year

Habitat/Range: Pinelands and coastal strand of Miami-Dade County and the Monroe County Keys, the Bahamas, and Cuba

Comments: *Senna* is from the Arabic *sana* or *sanna*, meaning "brilliance" or "radiance." The name *mexicana* means "of Mexico"; *chapmanii* honors botanist Alvan Wentworth Chapman (1809–1899). This state-listed threatened species was first collected in 1912 by botanist John Kunkel Small (1869–1938) on Big Pine Key. Members of this genus serve as larval hosts for the silver-spotted skipper, cloudless sulphur, orange-barred sulphur, and sleepy orange butterflies and the lunate zale moth.

VALAMUERTO

Senna pendula (Humb. & Bonpl. ex Willd.) H. S. Irwin & Barneby var. *glabrata* (Vogel) H. S. Irwin & Barneby
Pea family (Fabaceae)

Description: Woody shrub bearing evenly pinnate, alternate, compound leaves with a gland between the lowermost pair of leaflets. The oblong leaflets average 1" long and ½" wide. Flowers are about ¾" wide and produce cylindrical pods that reach 4" long and ⅜" wide, with seeds embedded in a sticky aril.

Bloom Season: All year

Habitat/Range: Invasive along hammock margins and disturbed sites of southern Florida. Native to South America.

Comments: The name *pendula* alludes to the pendulous pods; *glabrata* is for the nearly glabrous leaves. This is a Category I invasive species that invades undisturbed native plant communities. This and other species are responsible for poisoning grazing livestock; the seeds can be fatal to humans if eaten raw, giving rise to the Spanish name *valamuerto*, or "dead man."

DANGLEPOD

Sesbania herbacea (Mill.) McVaugh
Pea family (Fabaceae)

Description: Erect herbaceous perennial reaching 12' tall with compound leaves bearing numerous oblong leaflets measuring ⅜"–1" long and ⅛"–¼" wide, closing at night. Axillary flowers are about ⅝" long and ½" wide, opening only once in the afternoon. Linear seedpods average 4"–6" long and ¼" wide.

Bloom Season: All year

Habitat/Range: Open, moist habitats, disturbed sites, croplands, and roadsides across much of the United States, Mexico, and Central America

Comments: *Sesbania* is from *saysaban*, the Arabic name for *Sesbania sesban*. The name *herbacea* means "not woody." Ants and wasps feed on sugars produced by glands, and the seeds are an important food source for quail, wild turkeys, doves, ducks, and limpkins. The plant has reputedly poisoned cattle in Florida and Texas but is grown as cattle fodder in the American tropics. It is a larval host plant of the zarucco duskywing butterfly.

YELLOW NECKLACEPOD
Sophora tomentosa (L.) var. *truncata* Torr. & A. Gray
Pea family (Fabaceae)

Description: Multi-trunk shrub to 10' tall with odd-pinnate, opposite leaves, pubescent when young, with 11–19 oblong to oval leaflets averaging 1" long and ½" wide. Terminal racemes bear bright yellow, pealike flowers ⅝"–¾" long, followed by pendent pods that constrict around each seed, like beads.

Bloom Season: All year

Habitat/Range: Coastal habitats and rocky flats in coastal Central Florida south through the Florida Keys, the Bahamas, Puerto Rico, and the Virgin Islands

Comments: *Sophora* is Arabic for "yellow," relating to the flower color. The name *tomentosa* means "densely woolly," alluding to the pubescence on the leaves and young stems of the species. The varietal name *truncata* refers to the squared-off (truncate) base of the calyx. Hummingbirds frequent the flowers, but a cautionary word for parents: The seeds are toxic to eat and are produced in necklace-like pods that may be attractive to young children. The non-native, naturalized var. *occidentalis* from tropical America is distinguished by persistent, silky pubescence covering the leaves (especially the new growth). It has become popular in the Florida nursery trade, often mistakenly sold as a Florida native.

EVERGLADES KEY PENCIL-FLOWER
Stylosanthes calcicola Small
Pea family (Fabaceae)

Description: Herbaceous perennial with low-spreading or erect branches and alternate leaves divided into 3 glabrous, lanceolate to ovate, toothed leaflets, each bearing 3–5 pairs of conspicuous veins. Small, pealike flowers are about ¼" wide. The jointed pods have a straight or slightly curved beak and produce a single fertile seed.

Bloom Season: All year

Habitat/Range: Pine rocklands and rocky flats of Miami-Dade County and the Monroe County Keys to the Bahamas, Cuba, Guatemala, and Mexico

Comments: *Stylosanthes* is Greek for "column-flower," alluding to the column-like calyx tube. The name *calcicola* relates to growing on limestone. This state-listed endangered species is only known in the Florida Keys from the National Key Deer Refuge on Big Pine Key. It is a larval host plant of the barred yellow, a common small butterfly found statewide. Look for larvae to be present between February and November.

CHEESYTOES
Stylosanthes hamata (L.) Taub.
Pea family (Fabaceae)

Description: Herbaceous much-branched perennial with spreading or ascending stems that form mats, but can reach up to 36" tall. Alternate, compound leaves are divided into 3 lanceolate to elliptic leaflets averaging ½"–1" long and ¼" wide. Flowers are about ⁵⁄₁₆" wide.

Bloom Season: All year

Habitat/Range: Open sandy sites and roadsides of central and southern Florida, West Indies, and tropical America

Comments: The name *hamata* means "hooked tip," alluding to the jointed pods that are hooked at the tip. This weedy species is used medicinally throughout the West Indies to treat fevers, kidney problems, and colds; it is often used as a forage crop for livestock. A related species in Australia produces toxins capable of immobilizing and killing ticks on cattle. The plant is a larval host of the barred yellow butterfly but is seldom purposely cultivated.

CINNECORD OR TAMARINDILLO
Vachellia choriophylla (Benth.) Seigler & Ebinger
(Also *Acacia choriophylla* Benth.)
Pea family (Fabaceae)

Description: Woody tree to 18' tall or more with alternate, bipinnate, dark green leaves bearing 4–10 pairs of oblong leaflets, each about ½" long and ⅜" wide. Round, ⅜" flower heads are in branched clusters. Woody pods measure up to 3" long and ⅝" wide.

Bloom Season: April to August

Habitat/Range: Disturbed sites of the Florida Keys and pinelands of the Bahamas and Cuba

Comments: *Vachellia* honors English clergyman George Harvey Vachell (1799–1839), who collected plants in China. The name *choriophylla* means "having separate leaves." A single tree was discovered on Key Largo in 1967 by botanist Taylor Alexander (1915–2005), but it was later killed by a fire. Wild specimens are currently known to exist on Key Largo and at Old Settler's Park on Tavernier. Although it is state-listed as endangered, the species' native status is debatable.

SWEET ACACIA
Vachellia farnesiana (L.) Wright & Arn.
(Also *Acacia farnesiana* [L.] Willd.)
Pea family (Fabaceae)

Description: Perennial shrub or small tree to 16' tall or more with sharp spines ¾"–1" long. Compound leaves bear many small leaflets to about ¼" long. Fragrant flowers are in globose heads to about ⅜" across. Seedpods reach 2½" long and ⅝" wide with a rounded tip.

Bloom Season: All year

Habitat/Range: Pinelands, coastal hammocks, and shell mounds in warm temperate and tropical regions of the world

Comments: *Vachellia* honors Reverend George Harvey Vachell (1798–1839), who collected plants in China. The name *farnesiana* honors Italian nobleman Odoardo Farnese (1573–1626). Some regard this species as native to the Old World and naturalized elsewhere. It is farmed in France and elsewhere for "violet" perfume production. In the Florida Keys it is not as common as the smaller but similar pineland acacia (*Vachellia peninsularis*).

PORKNUT

Vachellia macracantha (Humb. & Bonpl. ex Willd.) Seigler & Ebinger
Pea family (Fabaceae)

Description: Tree to 20' or more with pubescent twigs and sharp spines 1½"–3" long. The alternate, bipinnate leaves have up to 30 pairs of oblong-linear leaflets. The globose flower heads measure about ⁷⁄₁₆" wide on clustered, ¾" axillary stems.

Bloom Season: June to November

Habitat/Range: Historically in coastal berms and along fringes of mangrove habitat of the Lower Florida Keys; also the West Indies and tropical America

Comments: The name *macracantha* means "with large spines." This species was first discovered on Vaca Key in 1952 by botanist Ellsworth Paine Killip (1890–1968); botanist George Newton Avery (1922–1983) found a colony of fifteen trees on Ramrod Key in 1963. The species no longer exists on Vaca Key. Some botanists regard it as a waif, arriving naturally in a tropical storm or hurricane winds but not persisting.

PINELAND ACACIA

Vachellia peninsularis Small
(Also *Acacia pinetorum* F. J. Herm.; *Vachellia farnesiana* [L.] Wright & Arn. var. *pinetorum* [F. J. Herm.] & Ebinger)
Pea family (Fabaceae)

Description: Woody shrub, typically 3'–5' tall with straight, sharp spines ½"–¾" long. The alternate leaves are divided into tiny leaflets measuring ³⁄₁₆" long or less. The fragrant flowers are in globose heads to about ⅜" across. Seedpods reach 2" long and ⅜" wide, with a hooked tip.

Bloom Season: All year

Habitat/Range: Endemic to pinelands of Central Florida south to the Florida Keys

Comments: The name *peninsularis* alludes to peninsular Florida. There are unsubstantiated reports of this species being found in the Bahamas, but without the existence of voucher specimens, it is being regarded as endemic to Florida. It is locally common on Big Pine Key and is a larval host plant of the nickerbean blue butterfly.

HAIRYPOD COWPEA
Vigna luteola (Jacq.) Benth.
Pea family (Fabaceae)

Description: Herbaceous trailing or climbing vine, often with entwined stems bearing alternate, compound leaves with 3 ovate to lanceolate leaflets averaging 1½"–2½" long and ¾"–1" wide. Flowers are about ¾" across and are in few-flowered clusters on tall, angled stems that stand well above the leaves.

Bloom Season: All year

Habitat/Range: Open, sunny habitats and disturbed sites across the southern United States, the Bahamas, Bermuda, tropical America, and the old-world tropics

Comments: *Vigna* honors Italian professor Dominicus Vigna (1581–1647), who wrote a commentary on Theophrastus in 1625. The name *luteola* means "yellow," in reference to the flowers. It is a larval host plant of the Dorantes skipper, long-tailed skipper, and gray hairstreak butterflies. The plant is used in Polynesia to cure "ghost sickness," an ailment believed to be supernaturally induced. The common name originated from the Chickasaw name, *waakimbala*, meaning "cow bean."

BRISTLESEED YELLOW STARGRASS
Hypoxis wrightii (Baker) Brackett
Stargrass family (Hypoxidaceae)

Description: Herbaceous perennial with linear leaves 5"–7" long arranged in a basal rosette arising from an underground corm. Basal, star-shaped flowers are solitary or sometimes paired, measuring about ½" wide.

Bloom Season: Mostly December to August

Habitat/Range: Pinelands of Florida, the Bahamas, and Greater Antilles

Comments: *Hypoxis* alludes to the pointed bases of the ovaries. The name *wrightii* honors American botanist Charles Wright (1811–1885). The species was first described as *Hypoxis juncea* var. *wrightii* in 1878 by English botanist John Gilbert Baker (1834–1920), but given species status in 1923 as *Hypoxis wrightii* by American botanist Amelia Ellen Brackett (1896–1926), who died suddenly of appendicitis as she was preparing to present her research for her doctorate. In the Florida Keys this species is found in pine rockland habitat on Big Pine Key and is one of the first plants to flower after a fire.

HUMPED BLADDERWORT

Utricularia gibba L.
Bladderwort family (Lentibulariaceae)

Description: Mat-forming, carnivorous, aquatic perennial with delicate creeping or floating stems. Leaves are in filiform segments with numerous, or few, bladderlike traps. Flowers have an oblong-conic spur and are produced on 1- to 4-flowered erect scapes.

Bloom Season: All year

Habitat/Range: In ponds, lakes, roadside canals, and marshes throughout Florida; widespread across North and South America, the West Indies, tropical Africa, and Asia

Comments: *Utricularia* is Latin for "little bag," alluding to the small, bladderlike traps on the leaves of all species in this genus. The name *gibba* means "a pouchlike enlargement," alluding to the shape of the spur on the flower. When the bladderlike traps are triggered, they instantly expand and the suction entraps small aquatic life, such as rotifers and water fleas. This is the only bladderwort in the Florida Keys and is known from freshwater habitats on Big Pine Key.

SAND FLAX

Linum arenicola (Small) H. J. P. Winkler
Flax family (Linaceae)

Description: Herbaceous perennial with very slender stems that average 8"–12" tall with widely spaced, narrow leaves that reach about ⅜" long and ¹⁄₁₆" wide. Solitary, 5-petaled flowers are about ⅜" across.

Bloom Season: All year

Habitat/Range: Endemic to pine rocklands of Miami-Dade County and the Monroe County Keys

Comments: *Linum* is an ancient Latin name for flax. The name *arenicola* means "sand dweller." In the Florida Keys, this state-listed endangered species is only found in pine rockland habitat on Big Pine and Upper Sugarloaf Keys. Two important products, linen and linseed oil, are derived from the stems and seeds of several European and Mediterranean species of flax. Spun fibers of flax have been found in burial sites in Switzerland that date back 10,000 years. Another species, *Linum medium* var. *texanum*, historically occurred on Big Pine Key but is believed to be extirpated.

POORMAN'S PATCH
Mentzelia floridana Nutt. ex Torr. & A. Gray
Loasa family (Loasaceae)

Description: Spreading, herbaceous perennial with ascending branches lined with alternate to ovate or triangular leaves that are covered with short, barbed hairs measuring ¾"–2" long and half as wide. Flowers are solitary in the upper leaf axils and average 1"–1¼" across.

Bloom Season: Mostly January to April

Habitat/Range: Beaches, dunes, shell middens, roadsides, and disturbed coastal habitats of Florida and the Bahamas

Comments: *Mentzelia* honors German physician and botanist Christian Mentzel (1622–1701), who studied Sinology, an academic discipline that focuses on the study of Chinese philosophy, language, literature, culture, and history. The name *floridana* means "of Florida." The plant is also called Florida stickleaf due to its leaves, which cling tightly to clothing; also called poorman's patch, for downtrodden people walking through colonies of the plants and getting their pantlegs covered with leaves, like patches. Removing the leaves is difficult. In the Florida Keys it is known from Elliott, Indian, and Long Keys.

COASTAL INDIAN MALLOW
Abutilon permolle (Willd.) Sweet
Mallow family (Malvaceae)

Description: Shrubby perennial to 6' tall with velvety pubescence covering the leaves. The heart-shaped leaves measure 2½"–4" long with a nearly equal width. The yellow flowers are mostly solitary, averaging about 1" wide. The fruits are cup-shaped, flat on top, with seeds in tight chambers.

Bloom Season: All year

Habitat/Range: Coastal habitats, including hammock margins, of southern Florida, West Indies, and Mexico

Comments: *Abutilon* was adapted from an Arabic word for a mallow-like plant. The name permolle means "very softly pubescent." Some species are important fiber plants and are also noted for the production of mucilage and the sweetener first used to produce marshmallows. The mucilage from this species has been used to cleanse wounds; the heated leaves are used in the Bahamas to treat boils. The fruits are used in the Bahamas to make decorative impressions in butter.

YUCATAN FLYMALLOW
Cienfuegosia yucatanensis Millsp.
Mallow family (Malvaceae)

Description: Herbaceous perennial to 20' tall with alternate, linear-oblong to lanceolate leaves (seedling leaves are 3-lobed) averaging 1"–2" long and ¼"–⅜" wide. Axillary flowers are solitary on long stems, measuring about ¾" across with 5 overlapping petals.

Bloom Season: All year

Habitat/Range: Brackish and freshwater marshes, coastal rock barrens, and disturbed sites of the Florida Keys, Mexico, Cuba, and the Bahamas

Comments: *Cienfuegosia* commemorates Spanish physician and botanist Bernardo de Cienfuegos (1580–1640), who authored the seven-volume *Historia de las Plantas* (History of Plants). The name *yucatanensis* is for the Yucatán Peninsula of Mexico, where the species was first collected in 1899 by botanist Charles Frederick Millspaugh (1854–1923). This state-listed endangered species is restricted to the Florida Keys in Florida. The flowers open only once, for several hours beginning in late morning.

WILD COTTON
Gossypium hirsutum L.
Mallow family (Malvaceae)

Description: Woody shrub 6'–12' tall with alternate, usually 3-lobed, orbicular leaves 2"–6" long and nearly equal in width. Flowers average 2"–3" wide and are typically pale yellow (aging pinkish), usually with a crimson spot at the base of each petal. Seeds are nestled in thick, fluffy white or tan hairs.

Bloom Season: All year

Habitat/Range: Coastal habitats of central and southern Florida, the Bahamas, Cayman Islands, Hispaniola, and coastal Mexico

Comments: *Gossypium* is Latin for "cotton tree." The name *hirsutum* means "hairy," alluding to the hairy young branches and petioles. Wild cotton was once targeted for eradication in Florida out of concern that it could harbor boll weevils and infect cotton crops in the Southern states. It is now a state-listed threatened species and illegal to cultivate in Florida. Cotton seeds contain gossypol, a substance used as a male contraceptive in China because it interferes with sperm production. The substance is also used to treat HIV/AIDS, uterine disorders, and cancer, without evidence that it is effective. Cotton was cultivated in the Middle East as early as 1800 BC and would become a controversial crop in the southeastern United States due to the use of enslaved Africans to harvest the cotton bolls. It is a larval host plant of the yellow scallop moth.

BLADDERMALLOW
Herissantia crispa (L.) Brizicky
Mallow family (Malvaceae)

Description: Herbaceous perennial, often with long stems. Alternate, velvety, ovate leaves are deeply cordate at the base, averaging ¾"–2" long and ½"–1" wide. The axillary flowers are about 1" wide, producing inflated, globose capsules with thin, fluted, papery walls.

Bloom Season: All year

Habitat/Range: Coastal and sandy inland habitats of central and southern Florida, Texas, Arizona, New Mexico, California, West Indies, and tropical America

Comments: *Herissantia* honors French poet, physician, and naturalist Louis Antoine Prosper Hérissant (1745–1769). The name *crispa* means "curled," alluding to the capsule margins. It is a larval host plant of the gray hairstreak and mallow scrub-hairstreak butterflies in Florida. The species is found in every state park in the Florida Keys plus the National Key Deer Refuge on Big Pine Key, and it is often found along hammock margins bisected by US 1 and other roadways in the Keys.

SPREADING FANPETALS
Sida abutifolia Mill.
Mallow family (Malvaceae)

Description: Herbaceous perennial with softly hairy, mostly prostrate stems. The toothed leaves are soft to the touch and measure ⅜"–1" long and ¼"–½" wide. The flowers open in the afternoon and reach ⅜" wide, with petals that range from pale yellow to nearly white.

Bloom Season: All year

Habitat/Range: Coastal rock barrens and disturbed sites, including roadsides, of the Southern United States, West Indies, and tropical America

Comments: *Sida* is an adaptation of an ancient Greek plant name. The name *abutifolia* alludes to the leaves resembling a species of *Abutilon* (Malvaceae). This species is local in the Keys and is known from Lignumvitae Key, Long Key, Curry Hammock, and Fort Zachary Taylor State Parks, plus the National Key Deer Refuge on Big Pine Key. It is also found along roadsides on other keys, such as Grassy Key and Crawl Key.

FRINGED FANPETALS

Sida ciliaris L.
Mallow family (Malvaceae)

Description: Herbaceous perennial with mostly prostrate stems, sometimes ascending to 14" tall. Alternate, ⅜"–⅝" leaves are glabrous above, pubescent below, shallowly toothed above the middle, and congested near the branch tips. The petioles are lined with hirsute-ciliate hairs. The ⅜" flowers are yellow or a peachy-salmon color.

Bloom Season: All year

Habitat/Range: Mostly found in disturbed soils in Pinellas, Hillsborough, Broward, Miami-Dade, and the Monroe County Keys to Texas, West Indies, and South America

Comments: The name *ciliaris* means "fringed with hairs," alluding to the petioles. This is a common species along roadsides and other disturbed sites throughout the Florida Keys. Some members of this genus produce strong fibers; others produce secretions that are used to kill ants and cockroaches. There are five native members of this genus in Florida; six other introduced species are naturalized in the state.

COMMON WIREWEED OR COMMON FANPETALS

Sida ulmifolia Mill.
(Also *Sida acuta* Burman; misapplied)
Mallow family (Malvaceae)

Description: Herbaceous perennial 12"–36" tall with alternate, toothed leaves that average ¾"–1" long and ½"–¾" wide. The solitary, ½"–⅝" flowers are on short stalks.

Bloom Season: All year

Habitat/Range: Pinelands and disturbed sites of the southeastern United States; circumtropical

Comments: The name *ulmifolia* refers to the resemblance of the leaves to an *Ulmus*, or elm (Ulmaceae). This ubiquitous weed is a larval host plant of the gray hairstreak, mallow scrub-hairstreak, common checkered-skipper, white checkered-skipper, and tropical checkered-skipper butterflies, which is the principal reason it is sometimes tolerated in gardens. Cuban jute or Indian hemp (*Sida rhombifolia*) also occurs in the Florida Keys and is very similar but with rhomboid leaves and flowers on ½" stalks (peduncles). It produces a strong fiber (*wallis*) that is used for cordage and coarse fabric, especially in the Philippines.

SEA HIBISCUS OR MAHOE

Talipariti tiliaceum (L.) Fryxell
(Also *Hibiscus tiliaceus* L.)
Mallow family (Malvaceae)

Description: Spreading tree to 30' tall or more with broadly ovate leaves that are palmately 7- to 9-veined with a deeply cordate base, measuring up to 5" long and wide. Two varieties occur in Florida—var. *tiliaceum* has yellow flowers with a red center; the flowers of var. *pernambucensis* are uniformly yellow.

Bloom Season: All year

Habitat/Range: Invasive in coastal and inland habitats, including mangroves, from St. Lucie and Manatee Counties south through the Florida Keys. Native to Asia and Pacific islands.

Comments: *Talipariti* was taken from the Malayan thaali ("shampoo") and *paruthi* ("cotton") for its use as a shampoo and its floral resemblance to a species of Gossypium, the source of cotton. The name *tiliaceum* is for its resemblance to a species of *Tilia* (Malvaceae). The plant is a Category II invasive species in Florida.

PORTIA TREE

Thespesia populnea (L.) Sol. ex Corrêa
Mallow family (Malvaceae)

Description: Multi-trunk tree to 20' or more with ovate-orbicular leaves, cordate at the base, on long petioles and measuring about 4" long and 3" wide. Each flower lasts one day, opening yellow early in the morning then turning orange in the afternoon.

Bloom Season: All year

Habitat/Range: Invasive in coastal and inland habitats, including mangroves, from Brevard and Manatee Counties south through the Florida Keys. Native to the Old World tropics.

Comments: *Thespesia* is Greek for "marvelous" or "divine." The name *populnea* alludes to the plant's resemblance to a species of *Populus* (Salicaceae). It is a Category I invasive species in Florida and can overwhelm coastal habitats. Seeds are buoyant and can be dispersed long distances by ocean currents. Other common names are seaside mahoe, Spanish cork, Pacific rosewood, and Indian tulip tree. In Hawaii it is often planted around places of worship.

SLEEPY MORNING
Waltheria indica L.
Mallow family (Malvaceae)

Description: Subshrub 3'–6' tall with alternate, toothed, tomentose, ovate to oblong leaves that average 1"–2" long and ½"–1" wide. Flowers are about ⅛" wide, crowded in mostly sessile, axillary inflorescences.

Bloom Season: All year

Habitat/Range: Pinelands, sandhills, and disturbed sites of Central and South Florida, West Indies, and tropical America

Comments: *Waltheria* honors German anatomist, physician, and botanist Augustin Friedrich Walther (1688–1746), who was a professor at the University of Leipzig and director of the Leipzig Botanical Garden. The name *indica* means "of India," where the plant was first collected. The common name sleepy morning relates to the flowers that open in mid- to late morning. It is a larval host of the mallow scrub-hairstreak and martial scrub-hairstreak in Florida but is seldom purposely cultivated by gardeners. It was formerly placed in the Sterculiaceae, or chocolate family.

DEVIL'S CLAWS OR PULLBACK
Pisonia aculeata L.
Four O'clock family (Nyctaginaceae)

Description: Large, woody shrub with long branches that reach high into trees by the use of stout, very sharp, recurved thorns. Opposite leaves range from elliptic-oval to suborbicular and average 1½"–2½" long and ⅝"–1½" wide. Small, very fragrant, flowers are in round clusters, followed by dry, 5-angled fruits that cling to hair, feathers, and clothing.

Bloom Season: February to June

Habitat/Range: Hammocks of central and southern Florida

Comments: *Pisonia* honors Dutch physician and naturalist Willem Piso (1611–1678), who latinized his name to Guilielmus Piso and was regarded as one of the leaders in tropical medicine. The name *aculeata* refers to the recurved thorns on the stem branches. The thorns are wickedly sharp and will grab skin and clothing. The clusters of fruits can kill small birds that become helplessly entangled in them. Bees swarm on the flowers.

DOLLAR ORCHID

Prosthechea boothiana (Lindl.) W. E. Higgins var. *erythronioides* (Small) W. E. Higgins
(Also *Encyclia boothiana* [Lindl.] Dressler)
Orchid family (Orchidaceae)

Description: Epiphytic orchid recognized by its round, flattened pseudobulbs that are the size of a silver dollar. The 1–3 glossy, lanceolate leaves measure 2"–4" long and about 1" wide. The flowers reach ⅝"–⅞" wide, with spreading greenish-yellow sepals and petals with irregular brownish-maroon spots.

Bloom Season: August to October

Habitat/Range: Coastal hammocks and mangroves of southern Florida, the Bahamas, and the neotropics

Comments: *Prosthechea* refers to the appendage on the back of the column. The name *boothiana* honors British botanist William Beattie Booth (1804–1874); *erythronioides* apparently refers to the similarity of the 3 anthers to those of *Erythronium americanum* (Liliaceae). This state-listed endangered species has a preference for growing on buttonwood (*Conocarpus erectus*) trees in coastal forests.

COMMON YELLOW WOODSORREL

Oxalis corniculata L.
Woodsorrel family (Oxalidaceae)

Description: Herbaceous annual with leaves divided into 3 leaflets that somewhat resemble a shamrock. The creeping stems root at the nodes, forming extensive colonies. Flowers are about ½" wide and produce cylindrical capsules that forcibly discharge seeds long distances.

Bloom Season: All year

Habitat/Range: Disturbed sites and moist habitats, including lawns and gardens, throughout much of the United States, West Indies, and tropical America

Comments: *Oxalis* refers to the oxalic acid (calcium oxalate) in the leaves. The name *corniculata* means "with small horns," alluding to the projections on the seeds. This is a common weedy species in residential lawns and landscapes. The sour leaves are edible but can inhibit calcium intake if eaten in quantity and can cause kidney stones and other kidney ailments. Also called creeping woodsorrel, it is the only member of the genus in the Florida Keys.

95

MEXICAN PRICKLYPOPPY

Argemone mexicana L.
Poppy family (Papaveraceae)

Description: Wickedly spiny herbaceous annual
1'–3' tall with deeply lobed, alternate leaves
ranging 3"–8" long with sharp tips terminating
each lobe and short, sharp spines lining the bottom
of the midvein. The petals form a tulip-like cup to
about 1½" across. Stems and leaves exude yellow
sap if broken.

Bloom Season: January to June

Habitat/Range: Disturbed sites of the United
States and Mexico

Comments: *Argemone* means "cataract," a name
given to another poppy-like plant believed to cure
cataracts of the eyes. The name *mexicana* means
"of Mexico." The seeds and latex are toxic to
grazing animals. The plant is used medicinally to
remove warts and to treat malaria and headaches,
also to cleanse the body after childbirth. Poisoning
from ingesting the latex causes extreme swelling
of the feet and legs. This species is in the same
family as the opium poppy (*Papaver somniferum*).

TINY PURSLANE

Portulaca minuta Correll
Purslane family (Portulacaceae)

Description: Herbaceous perennial with opposite,
succulent, obovate to obovate-elliptic, red to
reddish-green leaves ⅛"–³⁄₁₆" long and ¹⁄₁₆"–³⁄₃₂"
wide. The entire plant spreads to ¾"–2" across,
with flowers to about ⅛" wide.

Bloom Season: All year

Habitat/Range: Pine rocklands of Big Pine Key,
Lower Sugarloaf Key, No Name Key, and the
Bahamas

Comments: *Portulaca* means "little door" and
refers to the lid of the capsule. The name *minuta*
means "very small." This species was first
described as a Bahamas endemic in 1979 by botanist Donovan Stewart Correll (1908–1983), but it
was discovered on Big Pine Key in September 2013
by botanist Keith Bradley (1971–). It was later
found on Lower Sugarloaf and No Name Keys,
and because it is easily overlooked, it likely occurs
elsewhere in the Lower Florida Keys.

FIELD PURSLANE
Portulaca oleracea L.
Purslane family (Portulacaceae)

Description: Prostrate herbaceous annual or short-lived perennial with flattened, obovate or spatulate leaves on typically red stems. The leaves can be green or red, averaging ⅜"–⅝" long and ¼"–⅜" wide. Flowers are about ⅜" across.

Bloom Season: All year

Habitat/Range: Open, sunny habitats in tropical and warm temperate regions worldwide, including disturbed sites

Comments: The name *oleracea* means "vegetable" or "herbal" and alludes to both its use as an edible vegetable and its medicinal uses. Although the new-world nativity of this species has been questioned, taxonomists believe there is ample evidence of its pre-Columbian existence in the Americas to regard it as a native species, and there is evidence that it was eaten by Native Americans. The leaves contain the richest source of an Omega-3 fatty acid (alpha-linolenic acid) of any leafy vegetable studied to date. The plant is used medicinally to treat cardiovascular disease and is fed to chickens to reduce cholesterol in eggs. This species has a wide global distribution and has been used as food for centuries, especially in the Mediterranean region.

REDSTEM PURSLANE

Portulaca rubricaulis Kunth
Purslane family (Portulacaceae)

Description: Herbaceous perennial with red, spreading or ascending stems lined with linear, hemispheric leaves averaging ⅜"–½" long and no more than ⅛" wide. The flowers are ½"–⅝" across.

Bloom Season: All year

Habitat/Range: Coastal rock barrens, dunes, salt marshes, and shell mounds from Pinellas and Charlotte Counties south along the Gulf coast into Miami-Dade and the Monroe County Keys through the West Indies into tropical America

Comments: The name *rubricaulis* alludes to the red stems. This species was first described in 1823 by German botanist Karl Sigismund Kunth (1788–1850) from plants collected in Venezuela. Redstem purslane is found from John Pennekamp Coral Reef State Park on Key Largo to the Key West National Wildlife Refuge. Flowers of this species in the Caribbean may be red, orange, or salmon colored, but all plants in Florida have yellow flowers.

RED MANGROVE

Rhizophora mangle L.
Mangrove family (Rhizophoraceae)

Description: Tree to 50' tall or more with arching prop roots produced from the trunk. Elliptic, leathery leaves are opposite and measure 3"–6" long and 1"–2" wide. The ½" flowers produce leathery fruits to about 1" long, with a solitary seed that germinates on the tree to produce an elongated, brown-tipped, green propagule.

Bloom Season: All year

Habitat/Range: Muddy shores and estuarine swamps (rarely inland) from Florida, the West Indies, tropical America, West Africa, and Pacific Islands

Comments: *Rhizophora* means "root-bearing." *Mangle* is an Arawak name for a swamp. The maze of prop roots provides critical habitat for countless marine organisms; the tree canopy offers prime nest sites for ospreys, bald eagles, herons, egrets, cormorants, brown pelicans, and other birds. The species is a larval host for the mangrove skipper butterfly. Tannic acid in the bark has been used to tan leather.

HAMMOCK SNOWBERRY

Chiococca alba (L.) Hitchc.
Madder family (Rubiaceae)

Description: Climbing or scrambling shrub with somewhat 4-angled branches and opposite, glossy, ovate to lanceolate leaves averaging 1½"–2" long and ¾"–1" wide. Bell-shaped flowers measure about ⅜" long and face downward. Round fruits are white and measure ¼" across.

Bloom Season: All year

Habitat/Range: Hardwood forests from Dixie and Duval Counties continuously south along both Florida coasts to the Monroe County Keys and the West Indies

Comments: *Chiococca* is Greek for "snowberry." The name *alba* means "white" and alludes to the fruits. It is called milkberry in parts of its range. Members of the genus serve as larval host plants for Grote's sphinx and pluto sphinx moths in southern Florida. Two other species, *Chiococca parvifolia* (hammock margins) and *Chiococca pinetorum* (pine rocklands), also occur in the Florida Keys.

KEYS HOPBUSH

Dodonaea elaeagnoides Rudolph ex Ledeb. & Alderst.
(Also *Dodonaea viscosa* Jacq. subsp. *elaeagnoides* [Rudolph ex Ledeb. & Alderst.] *Acevedo-Rodriguez)*
Soapberry family (Sapindaceae)

Description: Small, shrubby tree typically 8'–12' tall, with glossy, obovate leaves that are notched at the tip, measuring ½"–1" long and about ½" wide. Clustered flowers are followed by papery, 3-winged fruits that turn pink as they mature.

Bloom Season: August to December

Habitat/Range: Hammock margins and thickets of the Florida Keys and the West Indies

Comments: *Dodonaea* honors Flemish botanist Rembert Dodoens (1516–1585), who latinized his name to Rembertus Dodonaeus. The name *elaeagnoides* alludes to the plant's resemblance to a species of *Elaeagnus*. This state-listed endangered species is only known in Florida from the Florida Keys. Another species, *Dodonaea viscosa*, is native to mainland Florida, and its fruits were used by early colonists as a substitute for hops to make beer and as a wash to "ward off evil influences."

WILD LIME
Zanthoxylum fagara (L.) Sarg.
Citrus family (Rutaceae)

Description: Spiny, dioecious shrub or small tree to 16' tall with compound, aromatic leaves and small wings between the leaflets. The crenulate, elliptic leaflets average ¼"–⅜" long and wide. Fragrant flowers are in axillary clusters; females bear small, round fruits that split open to reveal small, shiny black seeds.

Bloom Season: February to July

Habitat/Range: Hammocks from Citrus, Marion, and Volusia Counties south through the Florida Keys, Texas, Mexico, Central America, and the West Indies

Comments: *Zanthoxylum* means "yellow wood," alluding to the color of the sapwood of some species. The name *fagara* means "a cursed tree," referring to the sharp thorns on the branches. In the Florida Keys, this is a larval host of the giant swallowtail, the endangered Schaus swallowtail, and the rare Bahamian swallowtail. It is sometimes cultivated by butterfly enthusiasts despite the wicked thorns. Birds eat the seeds.

YELLOWWOOD
Zanthoxylum flavum Vahl
Citrus family (Rutaceae)

Description: Dioecious, unarmed tree to 30' tall with alternate, odd-pinnate, compound leaves composed mostly of 5–7 lanceolate to elliptic leaflets averaging 2"–3" long and ¾"–1½" wide. Terminal panicles bear many-flowered, small, very fragrant blossoms. Female trees produce small, obovoid fruits with black seeds.

Bloom Season: Mostly May to August, but periodically all year

Habitat/Range: Hammocks, dunes, and coastal scrub of the Florida Keys, Bermuda, and the West Indies

Comments: The name *flavum* means "yellow" and alludes to the wood. In Florida, this state-listed endangered tree is only known from Bahia Honda State Park and the Key West National Wildlife Refuge in the Lower Florida Keys. It is sparingly cultivated in nurseries that specialize in Florida native plants, both in the Florida Keys and on the southern mainland. Giant swallowtail and possibly Schaus swallowtail butterflies use it as larval food.

FALSE MASTIC
Sideroxylon foetidissimum Jacq.
(Also *Mastichodendron foetidissimum* [Jacq.] H.
J. Lam)
Sapodilla family (Sapotaceae)

Description: Tree to 80' tall or more with a
buttressed trunk and bark that flakes off in thick,
squarish patches. Alternate, wavy-margined leaves
are oblong-obovate to elliptic, reaching 6" long and
2" wide. Flowers are numerous in axillary clusters
along the branches. Oblong fruits are about 1¼"
long and ¾" wide, ripening yellow.

Bloom Season: March to December

Habitat/Range: Hammocks from Volusia and
Manatee Counties south to the Monroe County
Keys and the West Indies

Comments: *Sideroxylon* is Greek for "iron wood,"
alluding to the dense wood. The name *foetidissimum* relates to the fetid odor of the flowers,
reminiscent of something decomposing. Raccoons,
bears, opossums, and squirrels feed on the copious
fruits that cover the ground beneath mature trees.
The hard wood has been used in cabinetry, for
cooking tools such as mortars and pestles, and in
boatbuilding.

PARADISE TREE
Simarouba glauca DC.
Quassia family (Simaroubaceae)

Description: Dioecious tree, rarely to 40' tall,
with alternate, compound leaves bearing 10–20
narrowly oblong, glossy leaflets averaging 1½"–2"
long and ¾"–1¼" wide. Small flowers are in long,
open panicles. Female trees produce oblong-oval,
mostly ¾"-long red fruits that ripen purplish black.

Bloom Season: February to June

Habitat/Range: Hammocks of Brevard and Collier
Counties south through the coastal counties to the
Florida Keys, West Indies, Cuba, southern Mexico,
and Central America

Comments: *Simarouba* is a name of Arawak origin
in French Guiana. The name *glauca* means "bluish
gray," alluding to the glaucescent undersides of
the leaflets. Oils from the fruits have been used for
cooking and making margarine and soap. Gluco-
sides have been extracted from the bark and used
medicinally to treat chronic dysentery, diarrhea,
colic, leukemia, and gonorrhea. In El Salvador, the
fruits are processed into a liqueur taken as a cure
for stomachache.

WALTER'S GROUNDCHERRY
Physalis walteri Nutt.
Nightshade family (Solanaceae)

Description: Herbaceous perennial 6"–20" tall with ovate to lanceolate leaves measuring 1½"–4" long and ⅜"–¾" wide. Trumpet-shaped flowers are pendent to about ¾"–1" wide, producing round, yellow fruits encased in a lantern-like, papery calyx.

Bloom Season: All year

Habitat/Range: Coastal strand and pinelands across the southeastern United States and throughout most of Florida

Comments: *Physalis* is Greek for "a bladder," alluding to the inflated calyx. The name *walteri* honors American botanist Thomas Walter (1740–1789). The species is found from Long Key to Big Pine Key in the Florida Keys. The Carolina sphinx moth, tobacco hornworm, tomato hornworm, and tobacco budworm all use it as a larval host plant. It is closely related to the tomatillo (*Physalis philadelphica*), popular in Mexican cuisine and the main ingredient in salsa verde. *Physalis angulata* and *P. pubescens* also occur in the Florida Keys.

BAY CEDAR
Suriana maritima L.
Bay Cedar family (Surianaceae)

Description: Woody shrub typically less than 6' tall with alternate, light green, linear-spatulate to linear-oblanceolate, densely pubescent leaves averaging 1"–1½" long and ¼" wide. The 5-petaled flowers are small but conspicuous, reaching about ⁵⁄₁₆" wide.

Bloom Season: All year

Habitat/Range: Beach dunes and coastal shell mounds from Pinellas and Brevard Counties south along both coasts to the Florida Keys, West Indies, and tropical America

Comments: *Suriana* honors French physician and botanist Joseph-Donat de Surian (1650–1691), who traveled to the West Indies with famed botanist Charles Plumier (1646–1704). The name *maritima* relates to "growing near the sea," for its maritime habitat. This very attractive shrub is only sparingly cultivated by native-plant enthusiasts in coastal central and southern Florida. The young leaves and flowers serve as larval food for the martial scrub-hairstreak and mallow scrub-hairstreak butterflies.

ROCKLAND STRIPESEED
Piriqueta viridis Small
Turnera family (Turneraceae)

Description: Glabrous, herbaceous perennial 4"–16" tall with linear to linear-spatulate leaves 1"–3" long and ¼"–⅜" wide. The flowers are about 1" wide.

Bloom Season: All year

Habitat/Range: Pinelands from Collier County to Lake Okeechobee south to the Florida Keys and the West Indies

Comments: *Piriqueta* is taken from *piriquette*, the French Guiana name for a related species. The name *viridis* means "green," alluding to the dark green leaves described by botanist John Kunkel Small (1869–1938) in 1904. This narrow-leaved species has recently been separated from the widespread *Piriqueta caroliniana*, with which it hybridizes. According to a recent revision, *Piriqueta caroliniana*, *P. glabra*, and *P. viridis* all occur in Florida, and all are larval host plants of the gulf fritillary butterfly. Oddly, the Turneraceae was recently included in the Passifloraceae (passion-flower family) but has since been separated again.

RAMGOAT DASHALONG OR YELLOW ALDER
Turnera ulmifolia L.
Turnera family (Turneraceae)

Description: Perennial shrub to 2'–3' tall with coarsely toothed leaves from 2"–2½" long and 1"–1¼" wide. Very showy 5-lobed flowers are about 1½" across.

Bloom Season: All year

Habitat/Range: Considered invasive in coastal habitats, pinelands, and roadsides from Volusia and Pasco Counties south along both coasts to the Florida Keys, West Indies, and tropical America

Comments: *Turnera* honors English physician and naturalist William Turner (1508–1568), who was called the Father of English Botany because of herbals he published from 1551 to 1558. The name *ulmifolia* alludes to the similarity of the leaves to an Ulmus (elm). The common name ramgoat dashalong comes from Jamaica, where they believe that male goats get sexually frisky after eating the plant. A Key West collection in 1896 by noted American botanist Allen Hiram Curtiss (1845–1907) indicates this species may actually be native to Florida.

HEARTLEAF LANTANA
Lantana strigocamara R. W. Sanders
(Also *Lantana camara* L., misapplied)
Verbena family (Verbenaceae)

Description: Bushy shrub 4'–6' tall with prickly branches and opposite, ovate to broadly ovate toothed leaves with a rounded or cordate base. Leaves average 2"–3" long and 1"–2" wide. Tubular flowers are ¼" across and appear in two-toned yellow-orange or yellow-violet clusters, with the yellow flowers in the center. The clustered ⅛" fruits ripen from green to bluish black.

Bloom Season: All year

Habitat/Range: Invasive in a wide variety of habitats, especially pinelands throughout Florida; of cultivated origin

Comments: The genus *Lantana* was named because of the resemblance of the type species to *Viburnum lantana*. The name *strigocamara* refers to the strigose hairs on the leaves, combined with the species name of the related *Lantana camara*, which had been misapplied to Florida plants. The name heartleaf lantana was suggested by botanist Roger Sanders (1950–2018) when he described this species in 2006. It is a Category I invasive species in Florida and has contaminated the gene pool of the endangered Florida endemic *Lantana depressa* entities through hybridization. Regardless, cultivars and hybrids of *Lantana strigocamara* continue to be popular in the Florida nursery trade. *Lantana camara* has the distinction of being in the top ten most noxious weeds in the world, and leaf consumption is a leading cause of cattle and sheep fatalities.

MAHOGANY MISTLETOE
Phoradendron rubrum (L.) Griseb.
Mistletoe family (Viscaceae)

Description: Herbaceous, hemiparasitic perennial with 4-angled, slender branches to 12" long or more. The leathery, opposite leaves are oblanceolate to broadly elliptic, measuring ¾"–2" long and ½"–¾" wide. Small greenish-yellow flowers are followed by ⅛" round yellow, orange, or red fruits.

Bloom Season: October to December

Habitat/Range: Parasitic on West Indian mahogany (*Swietenia mahagoni*) trees on Elliott Key and Key Largo, in the Bahamas, and in Cuba

Comments: *Phoradendron* combines two Greek words meaning "thief" and "tree," referring to the parasitic trait of deriving nutrients from its host tree. The name *rubrum* means red, alluding to the color of the fruits on some plants. This is a state-listed endangered species, and resource managers sometimes fly in helicopters over the Upper Florida Keys during the winter dry season when West Indian mahogany trees are leafless, making it easier to locate this rare mistletoe.

MARINEVINE OR SORRELVINE
Cissus trifoliata (L.) L.
Grape family (Vitaceae)

Description: Herbaceous perennial vine with flexible stems and compound leaves divided into 3 leaflets opposite tendrils. The succulent leaflets are coarsely toothed on the upper half and measure ½"–¾" long and wide. Flowers are greenish yellow in axillary corymbs, producing small, ovoid fruits that ripen bluish black.

Bloom Season: All year

Habitat/Range: Hammock margins, pinelands, fencerows, and coastal thickets across the southern United States through the Florida Keys to the West Indies and tropical America

Comments: *Cissus* is Greek for "ivy," alluding to the climbing habit of these vines. The name *trifoliata* refers to the 3 leaflets. This species is found in the Florida Keys from Key Largo to Key West but is only on plant lists for John Pennekamp Coral Reef State Park, Windley Key Fossil Reef Geological State Park, and the National Key Deer Refuge.

POSSUM GRAPE

Cissus verticillata (L.) Nicolson & C. E. Jarvis
Grape family (Vitaceae)

Description: Perennial vine, often climbing into trees and sending thin, flexible, aerial roots all the way to the ground, even if severed from its base. Alternate, usually asymmetric, ovate to ovate-oblong leaves average 2"–4" long and 1½"–2½" wide. Leaves may be densely pubescent or glabrous. Axillary flowers are in cymes and produce globose, bluish-black fruits to about ¼" wide.

Bloom Season: All year

Habitat/Range: Hammock margins and disturbed sites, often climbing over fences, trees, and shrubs in residential landscapes of central and southern Florida, West Indies, and tropical America

Comments: The name *verticillata* means "whorled," alluding to the whorled stems of a "witches' broom" caused by a smut fungus (*Mykosyrinx cissi*) on the plant, which Linnaeus mistakenly described as a mistletoe (*Viscum verticillatum*). Glabrous forms with bluish-gray leaves may be introduced.

MUSCADINE OR SCUPPERNONG

Muscadinia rotundifolia (Michx.) Small var. *munsoniana* (J. H. Simpson ex Planchon) Weakley & Gandhi
(Also *Vitis munsoniana* J. H. Simpson ex Planchon; *Vitis rotundifolia* Michx. var. *munsoniana* [J. H. Simpson ex Planchon] M. O. Moore)
Grape family (Vitaceae)

Description: Woody vine with unbranched tendrils and prominent lenticels on mature stems. Glabrous leaves are coarsely toothed, averaging 2"–4" wide with axillary flower clusters. Edible berries ripen purple.

Bloom Season: April and May, or sporadic all year

Habitat/Range: Hammock margins and pinelands from Alabama and Georgia south throughout Florida

Comments: *Muscadinia* is probably an alteration of muscatel. The name *rotundifolia* relates to the round leaves; *munsoniana* honors grape horticulturist Thomas Volney Munson (1843–1913). It is a larval host plant of the pandorus sphinx moth but is seldom purposely cultivated. Some botanists favor the name *Vitis munsoniana* for plants found in South Florida, based partly on the smaller and more numerous fruits. Of the six grape species native to Florida, this is the only species vouchered from the Florida Keys.

GREATER CALTROP

Kallstroemia maxima (L.) Hook & Arn.
Caltrop family (Zygophyllaceae)

Description: Prostrate, herbaceous annual with spreading, succulent stems and compound leaves with 6–8 oblong to elliptic leaflets, the terminal pair of leaflets usually largest. Flowers average ⅝" across.

Bloom Season: All year

Habitat/Range: Weedy habitats and disturbed sites from South Carolina to Texas, south through Florida, West Indies, and tropical America

Comments: *Kallstroemia* honors Swedish botanist and gardener Anders Kallström (1733–1812). The name *maxima* alludes to the species' wide geographical range. The plant is cooked and eaten in the tropical Americas when nothing else is available, but it has laxative properties. A caltrop is a round metal ball armed with sharp spikes used as a weapon of war in the 1300s to halt the advance of foot soldiers and war elephants. The common name caltrop was given to the plant due to its armed fruits that can puncture feet.

PUNCTURE VINE OR JAMAICAN FEVERPLANT

Tribulus cistoides L.
Caltrop family (Zygophyllaceae)

Description: Herbaceous perennial with hairy, prostrate to ascending stems and softly hairy compound leaves bearing 4–10 pairs of elliptic leaflets to about ½" long. The 5-petaled flowers are 1"–1½" wide and are followed by ⅝" fruits armed with 4 stout ¼" spines.

Bloom Season: All year

Habitat/Range: Invasive in coastal habitats and roadsides of the southeastern United States, including central and southern Florida. Native to southern Africa.

Comments: *Tribulus* is from the Latin *tribolos*, or "caltrop," and relates to the spiny fruits. The name *cistoides* alludes to the resemblance of the flowers to a *Cistus* (Cistaceae). Another common name is burrnut. When in flower, this species is conspicuous along roadsides of the Florida Keys, often forming spreading colonies. The spiny fruits can puncture feet, rubber sandals, and bicycle tires. The plant is used medicinally in Jamaica to treat fevers.

BROWN AND GREEN FLOWERS

Spanish moss (*Tillandsia usneoides*)

FLORIDA AGAVE OR FALSE SISAL
Agave decipiens Baker
Agave family (Agavaceae)

Description: Perennial species maturing with a trunk 3'–9' tall, topped by a rosette of stiff, sharp-tipped, linear-lanceolate leaves measuring 24"–36" long and 3"–4" wide with evenly spaced, hooked teeth along the margins. An erect scape to 20' tall or more is topped by green flowers in clusters of a dozen or more. The plant may take up to 20 years to flower, produce seeds, and die.

Bloom Season: October to March

Habitat/Range: Endemic to coastal habitats from Manatee and Martin Counties south through the Florida Keys

Comments: *Agave* is Greek for "noble" or "admirable." The name *decipiens* means "deceptive," for its similarity to other species. *Agave decipiens* may be of hybrid origin and introduced into Florida from Latin America by pre-Columbian indigenous people. Its high chromosome count indicates a history of human cultivation, but it is currently regarded as a Florida endemic. The related non-native invasive *Agave sisalana* in the Florida Keys has leaf margins that are smooth or with a few small, unevenly spaced teeth. It was described by physician and horticulturist Henry Perrine (1797–1840) and introduced to Cape Sable from Mexico as a fiber-producing plant. Perrine moved to the Florida Keys and was killed there in 1840 during a Seminole raid on the island that is now Indian Key Historic State Park.

PERENNIAL GLASSWORT
Salicornia ambigua Michx.
Amaranth family (Amaranthaceae)

Description: Herbaceous perennial forming extensive colonies by underground rhizomes. The branches are formed of fleshy joints that are mostly erect along the main, horizontal stem, with leaves reduced to minute scales. Minuscule ioflowers appear on the upper jointed stems.

Bloom Season: June to November

Habitat/Range: Coastal, saline habitats from New Hampshire to Mississippi south through coastal Florida, West Indies, and Africa

Comments: *Salicornia* means "salt horn," alluding to the salty, hornlike branches. The name *ambigua* means "doubtful" or "uncertain," described by French botanist André Michaux (1746–1802) and apparently named thus because he was uncertain of its identity; the name was published the year after his death. It is also called Virginia glasswort. The plant is a larval host of the eastern pygmy-blue butterfly. Annual glasswort (*Salicornia bigelovii*) grows in the same habitat but has shorter and thicker stems and is not rhizomatous.

SEA BLITE
Suaeda linearis (Elliott) Moq.
Amaranth family (Amaranthaceae)

Description: Herbaceous perennial (annual in cold temperate regions) 10"–30" tall, with green to red stems and with green or red, narrowly linear leaves 1"–2" long. Bisexual flowers are usually dense on branched spikes.

Bloom Season: All year

Habitat/Range: Salt marshes, beaches, and coastal wetlands along the Atlantic coast from Maine around the coast of Florida to the Gulf coast of Texas, West Indies, and the Yucatán Peninsula

Comments: *Suaeda* is taken from suwed mullah, the Arabic name for a species in the Middle East. The name *linearis* alludes to the linear leaves. In cold temperate regions the plant is commonly called annual seepweed. In the Caribbean it is cooked and eaten after a few changes of water to reduce the saltiness; the leaves are added to soups, stews, and salsa in lieu of salt. Land crabs eat the black seeds.

CRESTED SALTBUSH OR SEASHORE ORACH

Atriplex pentandra (Jacq.) Standl.
Amaranth family (Amaranthaceae)

Description: Herbaceous perennial with angled stems (often red) with broadly obovate or rhombic-ovate leaves averaging 1"–1½" long and ⅜"–½" wide, typically with wavy margins. Male flowers are in dense terminal spikes; female flowers are clustered in the leaf axils.

Bloom Season: All year

Habitat/Range: Salt marshes, beaches, and other coastal habitats from North Carolina discontinu-ously to Texas south through coastal Florida, West Indies, and northern South America; disjunct in Connecticut and Massachusetts

Comments: *Atriplex* is an ancient Latin name used by Pliny (AD 23–79) for the Mediterranean orach (*Atriplex hortensis*). The name *pentandra* means "with five stamens." This is an infrequent but locally common species on shelly and sandy shore-lines of the Florida Keys. Other common names for members of this genus are pretty woman, good woman, and broth-of-the-sea.

EASTERN POISON IVY

Toxicodendron radicans (L.) Kuntze
Cashew family (Anacardiaceae)

Description: Woody, high-climbing vine with leaves divided into 3 leaflets, either entire or with 1 or 2 lobes on each leaflet. The forward leaflet has a long petiole and the 2 side leaflets have very short petioles, with each leaflet averaging 1"–4" long and ½"–2" wide. Flowers are about ¼" wide in axillary clusters. Round, ⅛" fruits ripen white.

Bloom Season: January to July

Habitat/Range: Hardwood forests, wooded swamps, and pinelands across eastern North America

Comments: *Toxicodendron* means "poison tree." The name *radicans* refers to the species' habit of forming roots along the stems that attach to trees, buildings, and whatever else they contact. The sap contains urushiol, which causes a blistering rash on sensitive people, usually after a twenty-four-hour delay, and may require hospitalization. Smoke from burning poison ivy can cause respiratory distress. Birds eat the fruits with impunity.

GREEN ANTELOPEHORN
Asclepias viridis Walter
Dogbane family (Apocynaceae)

Description: Herbaceous perennial, typically less than 10" tall. The long, narrowly oblong leaves measure 4"–6" long and ½"–⅝" wide, with a yellow or red midrib and prominent venation. Flowers are congested in a terminal cluster, with each flower measuring about ½" across with 5 petals that are not reflexed as in most all other species in Florida. The pods are about 3½" long, splitting open to release wind-dispersed seeds.

Bloom Season: February to September

Habitat/Range: Sandy pinelands from Tennessee to Nebraska south to Texas and Florida; occurs in two counties in the Florida Panhandle, five counties in north-central Florida, and then appears in Miami-Dade County and on Big Pine Key in the Monroe County Keys

Comments: *Asclepias* honors the legendary Greek physician and deity Aesculapius. The name *viridis* means "green" and relates to the flower color. A word of warning: All members of the genus Asclepias produce sap that is toxic to humans and pets, and can be fatal if eaten in quantity. However, they are preferred larval host plants for monarch, queen, and soldier butterflies.

KEYS SILVER PALM

Coccothrinax argentata (Jacq.) L. H. Bailey subsp.
argentata
Palm family (Arecaceae)

Description: Solitary palm reaching 14' tall or
more with palmate leaves, green above, silvery
below, having more segments and wider petioles
than those on the mainland. The leaf segments are
lax, and the base of the petiole is not split. Flowers
are pale yellow to white and are visited mostly by
bees. Globose ¼" fruits are purplish black.

Bloom Season: All year

Habitat/Range: Pinelands and coastal strand of
the Florida Keys and West Indies

Comments: *Coccothrinax* combines "berry" and
the genus *Thrinax*. The name *argentata* alludes
to the silvery undersides of the leaves. A 2018
taxonomic revision relegates the Florida mainland
population as subsp. *garberi*, citing shorter stature,
fewer leaves, narrower petioles, and the leaf segments being shorter, narrower, and less numerous
than the subspecies in the Florida Keys. It is a
state-listed threatened species.

KEY THATCH PALM

Leucothrinax morrisii (H. Wendl.) C. Lewis & Zona
Palm family (Arecaceae)

Description: Solitary palm 8'–14' tall or more.
Palmate leaves are bluish green above and pale
gray below, 24"–36" across. Petioles are split
basally. Flowers are creamy white, producing
white, globose, ¼" fruits.

Bloom Season: All year

Habitat/Range: Pinelands, hammocks, and coastal
strand of Miami-Dade and Monroe Counties (mainland and Keys) into the West Indies

Comments: *Leucothrinax* combines "white"
with the genus *Thrinax*, alluding to the pale gray
undersides of the leaves. The name *morrisii* honors
British botanist Daniel Morris (1844–1933). This
state-listed threatened species is common in
parts of the Florida Keys, especially Big Pine Key.
It is also called brittle thatch palm in Florida and
buffalo-top in the Bahamas. Because the fronds
are used to sweep floors, it is called broom palm
in Anguilla and *palma de escoba* (broom palm) in
Puerto Rico.

BUCCANEER PALM OR SARGENT'S CHERRY PALM

Pseudophoenix sargentii H. Wendl. ex Sarg.
Palm family (Arecaceae)

Description: Solitary palm reaching 12'–24' tall with arching pinnate leaves measuring 4'–9' long with the leaf segments held at divergent angles. Branching inflorescences of small, yellowish flowers produce ¾" red fruits.

Bloom Season: All year

Habitat/Range: Coastal hammocks of Elliott Key and Long Key in the Florida Keys into Mexico, Belize, Cuba, Hispaniola, and the Bahamas

Comments: *Pseudophoenix* is Greek for "false" and *Phoenix*, the genus of the date palm. The name *sargentii* honors botanist Charles Sprague Sargent (1841–1927), who discovered more than 200 specimens of this palm on Long Key in the Florida Keys in 1886. It would later become such a popular landscape palm that those not toppled by hurricanes were eventually removed and sold. Fairchild Tropical Botanic Garden has reintroduced it on Elliott and Long Keys. Seeds are dispersed by raccoons and ocean currents.

CABBAGE PALM

Sabal palmetto
Palm family (Arecaceae)

Description: Thick-trunked palm to 45' tall with costapalmate leaves, often with persistent leaf bases on the trunk, and with long, unarmed petioles. Leaf blades are curved downward and measure 3'–4' wide with lax leaf segments. Fragrant flowers are yellowish in dense panicles. Globose fruits ripen black and average ⅜" wide.

Bloom Season: All year

Habitat/Range: Pinelands, wooded swamps, and hardwood forests of the southeastern United States, the Bahamas, and Cuba

Comments: *Sabal* is believed to be a South American name. The name *palmetto* means "a small palm." This is the state tree of Florida and is often called "sabal palm" even though there are sixteen species of *Sabal*, with three in Florida plus a hybrid. The central bud, or "heart," is edible, and the fronds are popular as thatch for roofs of chickees (open-sided shelters). The flowers are visited by honeybees and are a source of palmetto honey, as is the saw palmetto (*Serenoa repens*).

SAW PALMETTO
Serenoa repens (W. Bartram) Small
Palm family (Arecaceae)

Description: Branched palm with creeping or ascending trunks to 8' tall or more. The palmate leaves have sharp, recurved teeth on the petioles; the segmented leaf blades may be green or blue-gray. Creamy-white flowers are in large clusters, producing oblong, yellowish-orange, 1" fruits that ripen black.

Bloom Season: February to June

Habitat/Range: Pinelands, dunes, scrub, and woodlands of the southeastern United States

Comments: *Serenoa* honors American botanist Sereno Watson (1826–1892). The name *repens* means "creeping," alluding to the recumbent trunks. The fruits are processed into supplements to maintain prostate health, improve urinary tract function, regulate hormone levels, and prevent hair loss in men. The fruits are a favorite food of black bears; the leaves are larval food for the palmetto skipper and monk skipper. The flowers are a source of palmetto honey. The species is uncommon in the Florida Keys.

FLORIDA THATCH PALM
Thrinax radiata Lodd. Ex Schult. & Schult. f.
Palm family (Arecaceae)

Description: Solitary palm 10'–20' tall or more. Palmate leaves are green above and below, reaching 30"–40" across. Petioles are split basally. Flowers are creamy white, producing white, globose, ¼" fruits.

Bloom Season: All year

Habitat/Range: Pinelands, hammocks, and coastal strand of Collier, Miami-Dade, and Monroe (mainland and Keys) Counties, the Bahamas, Greater Antilles, and Mexico south into Central America

Comments: *Thrinax* is from New Latin meaning "three-pronged fork," alluding to the leaf shape. The name *radiata* refers to the radiating leaf segments. This state-listed endangered species is widely used in the South Florida landscape and can be seen as a street tree in the Florida Keys. Birds, including the endangered white-crowned pigeon, eat the fruits. It is the only member of the genus in Florida since the Key thatch palm (*Leucothrinax morrisii*) was separated from *Thrinax*.

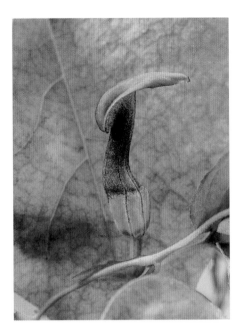

MARSH'S DUTCHMAN'S PIPE

Aristolochia pentandra Jacq.
Dutchman's Pipe family (Aristolochiaceae)

Description: Twining, herbaceous vine with 3-lobed, ovate to hastate, palmately veined, alternate leaves averaging 2"–3" long and 1½"–2½" wide. Ill-smelling flowers are solitary in the leaf axils on the new growth, measuring ¾"–1" tall. Mature capsules resemble upside-down parasols.

Bloom Season: All year

Habitat/Range: Coastal hammocks and lowlands of Broward, Miami-Dade, and Monroe County Keys, Texas, Mexico, Honduras, Cuba, Jamaica, and the Bahamas

Comments: *Aristolochia* is Greek for "best delivery," in reference to the plant's ancient herbal use to aid in childbirth. The name *pentandra* means "with five stamens." This state-listed endangered species is a larval host plant of the polydamas swallowtail and is currently known in Florida from a single population in Broward County and in the Upper Florida Keys within Biscayne National Park (Miami-Dade County). Early botanists reported the species from the Miami-Dade County mainland; it was later extirpated but reintroduced at the Deering Estate.

TWINING SOLDIERBUSH

Myriopus volubilis (L.) Small
(Also *Tournefortia volubilis* L.)
Borage family (Boraginaceae)

Description: Twining perennial vine with narrow stems reaching 8' long or more with alternate, lanceolate to elliptic leaves 1½"–3½" long and 1"–1½" wide. Star-shaped flowers have very narrow petals and are followed by small oval fruits that ripen white.

Bloom Season: All year

Habitat/Range: Hammock margins and edges of trails from Volusia and Hillsborough Counties south through the coastal counties to the Florida Keys, West Indies, and from Texas south into South America

Comments: *Myriopus* is obscure but may allude to the abundance of flowers on the type species. The name *volubilis* means "twining" and relates to the species' growth habit. Birds eat the small white fruits. In the American tropics the leaves are mashed and used to relieve the itching of chiggers in the same manner as the leaves of its relative, chiggery grapes (*Tournefortia hirsutissima*).

SPANISH MOSS
Tillandsia usneoides (L.) L.
Pineapple family (Bromeliaceae)

Description: Rootless, epiphytic bromeliad with each plant composed of 3 narrowly linear, densely scaled leaves. The strands hang in long clumps from trees, especially oaks, cypress, and buttonwood. The leaves are 1"–2" long and 1/16" wide. Inconspicuous fragrant flowers appear in the leaf axils.

Bloom Season: April to August

Habitat/Range: A wide range of habitats across the southeastern United States and the neotropics

Comments: *Tillandsia* honors Swedish-born physician and botanist Elias Tillandz (1640–1693), who wrote the first botanical work for Finland. The name *usneoides* alludes to the plant's resemblance to the lichen genus Usnea. It has the largest natural range of all bromeliads and is the larval host plant of the black-winged dahana moth; also provides preferred habitat for a species of jumping spider (*Pelegrina tillandsiae*). The flowers are intensely fragrant at night. The related ball moss (*Tillandsia recurvata*) has recurved leaves that form a ball.

GIANT AIRPLANT
Tillandsia utriculata
Pineapple family (Bromeliaceae)

Description: Solitary, epiphytic bromeliad with linear-triangular leaves that form an open rosette. The leaves are widest at the base, reaching 10"–16" long and 1"–2½" wide. The green flower spike is erect, branching near the top, with tubular white flowers surrounded by green bracts.

Bloom Season: All year

Habitat/Range: Epiphytic on rough-barked trees in hammocks, mangrove-buttonwood associations, and deciduous forests from Flagler, Putnam, and Citrus Counties south through peninsular Florida to the Florida Keys, West Indies, and tropical America

Comments: The name *utriculata* means "inflated," alluding to the swollen leaf sheaths. This large species is always solitary because it is incapable of producing suckers (offsets) at the base of the plant like most other members of the genus. Therefore, it only spreads from seed and then dies. It is endangered due to the presence of an introduced Mexican weevil with larvae that kills the plants.

GUMBO LIMBO
Bursera simaruba (L.) Sarg.
Gumbo Limbo family (Burseraceae)

Description: Large, deciduous tree with smooth, red, peeling bark and alternate, odd-pinnate, compound leaves with 3–9 leaflets divided inequilaterally by the midrib. The 3/16" flowers are in panicles followed by ovoid, 3-valved, 3/8" fruits ripening orangish red.

Bloom Season: All year

Habitat/Range: Hammocks and pinelands from Pinellas and Volusia Counties south along the coast and across all of South Florida to the Florida Keys, West Indies, and tropical America

Comments: *Bursera* honors botanist Joachim Burser (1583–1639). The name *simaruba* is for the plant's resemblance to a Simarouba. It is a larval host plant of the rare dingy purplewing butterfly. The sticky sap is used as birdlime to trap birds for food or trade. The common name gumbo limbo comes from enslaved Bantu in Florida; they called it *ngombo ulimbo*, meaning "slave's birdlime." Kingbirds are fond of the fruits.

MEDICINE VINE OR ARTHRITIS VINE
Hippocratea volubilis L.
Staff-tree family (Celastraceae)

Description: Woody, twining liana bearing elliptic to ovate or oblanceolate opposite leaves that may reach 5" long and 3" wide. The yellowish-green (or white), bisexual flowers have 5 oblong lobes and are in much-branched clusters.

Bloom Season: February to July

Habitat/Range: Hammocks and wooded swamps of South Florida, West Indies, and tropical America

Comments: *Hippocratea* honors Greek physician Hippocrates (460–377 BC), whose contributions to the understanding of diseases revolutionized the practice of medicine. For this, he is often called the Father of Medicine. The name *volubilis* means "twining." In Cuba, the species is called *bejuco de vieja*, or "old woman's vine," alluding to its use to treat arthritis. The main stem can reach 4" in diameter, climbing high into trees and across shrubs, forming impenetrable thickets. It was previously included in the Hippocrateaceae.

FLORIDA BOXWOOD
Schaefferia frutescens Jacq.
Staff-tree family (Celastraceae)

Description: Dioecious bushy shrub or small tree to 16' tall or more with alternate, elliptic to lanceolate leaves averaging 1"–2" long and ⅝"–⅞" wide. Flowers are produced along the stems and measure about ³⁄₁₆" across. Small, round fruits reach about ¼" wide, ripening orange to red.

Bloom Season: Mostly April to August

Habitat/Range: Coastal thickets and hammocks of Miami-Dade and the Monroe County Keys, West Indies, and Mexico south to Ecuador

Comments: *Schaefferia* honors German botanist, zoologist, theologian, and clergyman Jacob Christian Schaeffer (1718–1790). The name *frutescens* means "shrubby." This state-listed endangered species appears on plant lists for Dagny Johnson, Lignumvitae, Long Key, John Pennekamp, and Windley Key State Parks. It is sparingly cultivated by native-plant enthusiasts, mostly for its bird-attracting fruits. It is sometimes called yellow-wood due to its bright yellow heartwood, used by woodworkers.

GUTTA-PERCHA OR FLORIDA MAYTEN
Tricerma phyllanthoides (Benth.) Lundell
(Also *Maytenus phyllanthoides* Benth.)
Staff-tree family (Celastraceae)

Description: Woody shrub or small tree to 16' tall with thick, fleshy, obovate leaves, rounded at the tip, and measuring ⅝"–1¾" long and ½"–¾" wide. Green, 5-lobed flowers are about ³⁄₁₆" across. The small fruits ripen red.

Bloom Season: Mostly May to December

Habitat/Range: Coastal beaches and edges of mangroves from Levy County south along the Gulf coast to the Monroe and Miami-Dade County mainland into the Monroe County Keys, Texas, Mexico, Bahamas, and Cuba

Comments: *Tricerma* is Greek for "three" and "coin," somehow alluding to the fruits. The name *phyllanthoides* relates to the species' resemblance to the genus *Phyllanthus* (Euphorbiaceae). The leaves of this state-listed threatened species yield a gum used as gutta-percha, a rubberlike substance used in dentistry to fill root canals. This species often grows in coastal areas that flood at high tide.

SAWGRASS

Cladium jamaicense Crantz
Sedge family (Cyperaceae)

Description: Rhizomatous perennial sedge to 8' tall or more with long, narrow, channeled leaves armed with sawlike teeth along the margins. The much-branched inflorescence is erect, to 20" tall or more, with chestnut-brown spikelets.

Bloom Season: Mostly April to August

Habitat/Range: Moist or flooded soils of fresh-water wetlands, coastal brackish marshes, and fringes of mangroves throughout most of Florida north to Virginia, across to Texas, and through the neotropics

Comments: *Cladium* is Greek for "a branch," alluding to the numerous branches on the inflorescence. The name *jamaicense* means "of Jamaica." This is a dominant species in the Florida Everglades, forming vast stands that may stretch for miles. The leaf margins are wickedly sharp and can cause razor-like cuts. The species has scattered local populations in the Florida Keys but is most common on Big Pine Key, visible along roadsides.

BLODGETT'S SILVERBUSH

Argythamnia argothamnoides (Bertero ex Spreng.) J. W. Ingram
(Also *Argythamnia blodgettii* [Torr. ex Chapm.] Chapm.)
Spurge family (Euphorbiaceae)

Description: Herbaceous perennial 8"–12" tall with alternate, elliptic to ovate or obovate, hairy leaves that measure 1"–2" long and ½"–1" wide. Male and female flowers, produced on the same plant, measure about ¼" across.

Bloom Season: All year

Habitat/Range: Pine rocklands, hammock margins, and coastal strand of Miami-Dade County and the Monroe County Keys, South America, and adjacent islands

Comments: *Argythamnia* is Greek for "silvery bush," alluding to the silvery hairs on the type species. The name *argothamnoides* relates to "resembling an *Argythamnia*," from when the species was *Croton argothamnoides*. In the Florida Keys, this state-listed endangered and globally imperiled species is known from Lignumvitae Key, Long Key, and Windley Key State Parks and the National Key Deer Refuge on Big Pine Key.

WEDGE SANDMAT
Euphorbia deltoidea Engelm. ex Chapm. subsp.
serpyllum (Small) Y. Yang
(Also *Chamaesyce deltoidea* [Engelm. ex Chapm.]
Small subsp. *serpyllum* [Small] D. G. Burch)
Spurge family (Euphorbiaceae)

Description: Herbaceous perennial with prostrate stems bearing wedge-shaped (deltoid) leaves to about ¼" long and wide, forming mats to about 4" across. Greenish-white flowers are only about ¹⁄₁₆" wide.

Bloom Season: All year

Habitat/Range: Endemic to pine rockland habitat on Big Pine Key

Comments: *Euphorbia* honors Trojan War hero Euphorbus, physician to King Juba II of the ancient kingdom of Numidia in northwest Africa. The name *deltoidea* refers to the deltoid leaf shape; *serpyllum* alludes to the plant's resemblance to wild thyme (*Thymus serpyllum*). This critically imperiled state-listed endangered subspecies of *Euphorbia deltoidea* is only known from the National Key Deer Refuge and The Nature Conservancy's Terrestris Preserve on Big Pine Key.

FIDDLER'S SPURGE
Euphorbia heterophylla L.
(Also *Poinsettia heterophylla* [L.] Klotzsch & Garcke ex Klotzsch)
Spurge family (Euphorbiaceae)

Description: Herbaceous annual, often with lanceolate or broadly obovate leaves, then usually pandurate (fiddle-shaped) and typically white at the base (never red like *Euphorbia cyathophora*). The sap is white. Small, greenish-white, male and female flowers are in terminal clusters, followed by 3-parted fruits.

Bloom Season: All year

Habitat/Range: Mostly open disturbed sites across the southern United States through tropical America

Comments: The name *heterophylla* means "different leaves," alluding to the varying leaf shapes on the same plant. The nativity of this species in the United States is uncertain; it is considered native in the *Flora of Florida*, while the *Flora of North America* regards it as likely naturalized. It is quite weedy and can be found in disturbed soils in vacant lots, along roadsides, and residential landscapes throughout Florida.

MANCHINEEL

Hippomane mancinella L.
Spurge family (Euphorbiaceae)

Description: Deciduous tree, typically less than 14' tall, with a spreading crown. Broadly ovate-elliptic leaves average 2½"–3" long and 1½"–2" wide, with long, yellow petioles and crenate (scalloped) leaf margins. Flowers are on short, erect spikes; the round, 1½" fruits are green or blushed with pink on one side.

Bloom Season: Mostly January to June

Habitat/Range: Coastal hammocks of Miami-Dade and Monroe (mainland and Keys) Counties, West Indies, and from Central America into South America, including the Galapagos Islands

Comments: *Hippomane mancinella* combines to mean "little apple that makes horses mad," in reference to the toxic fruits. The sap of this tree can cause intense burning and temporary blindness if conveyed to the eyes and can cause severe skin blisters. If consumed, the fruits can cause mild to severe gastrointestinal problems, depending on the individual. There are reported fatalities from consuming the fruits, and although such reports are usually exaggerated, a Spanish name is *arbol de la muerte* (tree of the dead). The sap has been used as an arrow poison. It is claimed that the Calusa used manchineel sap on their arrows to kill Juan Ponce de Leon (1474–1521) on his second voyage to Florida, but this tree does not occur in the region where he encountered the Calusa.

FLORIDA KEYS NOSEBURN
Tragia saxicola Small
Spurge family (Euphorbiaceae)

Description: Herbaceous perennial 4"–8" tall with stinging hairs covering the stems and leaves. The coarsely toothed, ovate leaves range ½"–1¼" long and ⅜"–1" wide. The 3-parted fruits are covered with stinging hairs.

Bloom Season: March to October

Habitat/Range: Endemic to pine rocklands of Miami-Dade County and the Monroe County Keys (Big Pine Key)

Comments: *Tragia* honors physician and herbalist Jerome Bock (1498–1554), who latinized his name to Hieronymus Tragus. The name *saxicola* relates to "growing on rocks"—in this case, oolitic limestone. The hairs on this endemic, state-listed threatened species cause long-lasting intense burning when touched. In the West Indies, names for other members of the genus include *pingamoza* (child stinger), *picacula* (tail sticker), and *pois graté* (irritating pea). Whoever gave it the common name noseburn must have tried to smell the flowers.

WEST INDIAN MAHOGANY
Swietenia mahagoni (L.) Jacq.
Mahogany family (Meliaceae)

Description: Large tree to 60' or more with compound leaves and 2–5 pairs of leaflets averaging 1"–1½" long and about ¾" wide, with the midrib dividing the leaflets inequilaterally. Small flowers are in open panicles. Woody, oblong fruits split open in sections to release the seeds.

Bloom Season: March to August

Habitat/Range: Coastal hammocks from Broward and Lee Counties south along both coasts to the Upper and Middle Monroe County Keys through the West Indies

Comments: *Swietenia* honors Dutch botanist and physician Gerard van Swieten (1700–1772). The name *mahagoni* is a native name in the West Indies. This common landscape and street tree in southern Florida has been planted well outside of its natural range and sometimes invades natural habitats where it was not historically present. The national champion is along the Mahogany Hammock boardwalk in Everglades National Park.

WAX MYRTLE OR SOUTHERN BAYBERRY
Morella cerifera (L.) Small
(Also *Myrica cerifera* L.)
Bayberry family (Myricaceae)

Description: Shrub or small tree with coarsely toothed, linear-oblanceolate leaves that are aromatic when crushed. Male and female flowers are on separate plants, produced along the stems. Round, bluish-gray, waxy fruits are about ⅛" wide.

Bloom Season: December to May

Habitat/Range: Pinelands, sandhills, swamps, and hammock margins from Delaware to Texas, south through Florida, West Indies, Bermuda, and Mexico to Central America

Comments: *Morella* alludes to the fruits of some species resembling those of a *Morus* (mulberry). The name *cerifera* means "bearing wax," alluding to the waxy coating on the fruits. Birds are attracted to fruiting trees, especially tree swallows, which swarm into the trees to devour the fruits. The waxy fruits are the source of bayberry-scented candles; the Seminole used the fragrant leaves to flavor their tobacco and to make it last longer.

BLOLLY
Guapira discolor (Spreng.) Little
Four O'clock family (Nyctaginaceae)

Description: Evergreen, dioecious tree to 30' tall, but usually half that height, with glabrous or slightly pubescent broadly or narrowly elliptic, opposite leaves averaging 1"–1½" long and ½"–¾" wide. Small, green flowers are in open clusters with female trees producing scarlet, fleshy fruits to about ⁵⁄₁₆" long.

Bloom Season: May to August

Habitat/Range: Hammocks and pinelands from Central Florida south through the Florida Keys, the Bahamas, Greater Antilles, and the Cayman Islands

Comments: *Guapira* is an aboriginal name from Brazil that is usually applied to *Avicennia* species. The name *discolor* means "of two colors," alluding to the pale undersides of the leaves. Fruiting female trees are very ornamental, and the fruits attract a variety of birds, evidenced by the name pigeonberry in the Bahamas. Another species, *Guapira obtusata*, was discovered once on Stock Island in 1984 but has not been reported since.

COCKSPUR OR SMOOTH DEVIL'S CLAWS
Pisonia rotundata Griseb.
Four O'clock family (Nyctaginaceae)

Description: Thornless, dioecious tree to about 15' tall but kept shrubby by fire in pinelands. The coarse, ovate to oval leaves are leathery and average 1½"–2" long and wide. Flowers are in dense clusters emerging from the leaf axils. The small, club-shaped fruits are covered with adhesive glands that enable them to stick to hair, feathers, and clothes.

Bloom Season: April to July

Habitat/Range: Hammocks and pinelands of the Monroe County Keys (Big Pine Key) and the West Indies

Comments: *Pisonia* honors Dutch physician and naturalist Willem Piso (1611–1678), who was the physician on an expedition to Dutch Brazil from 1637–1644. He is also commemorated by the minor planet named 11240 Piso. The name *rotundata* relates to the rounded leaves. In Florida, this state-listed endangered species is only known from the National Key Deer Refuge on Big Pine Key.

FLORIDA PRIVET OR SWAMPPRIVET
Forestiera segregata (Jacq.) Krug & Urb.
Olive family (Oleaceae)

Description: Diffusely branched, dioecious shrub or small tree to 14' tall with opposite, elliptic leaves averaging ½"–1" long and ⅜"–½" wide. Flowers are clustered in the leaf axils and are followed by bluish-purple, oblong fruits to about ½" long and ¼" wide.

Bloom Season: May to November

Habitat/Range: Pinelands and hammock margins from Duval and Dixie Counties south along both coasts through the Florida Keys, Bermuda, and West Indies

Comments: *Forestiera* honors French botanist and physician Charles Le Forestier (1742–1820), who studied in Saint-Quentin and was the first botanical master of Jean Louis Marie Poiret (1755–1836). The name *segregata* means "kept apart." Although not widely cultivated, bees and butterflies visit the flowers, and birds savor the small, olive-like fruits. It is related to the olive of commerce (*Olea europaea*) native to Mediterranean Europe, Asia, and Africa.

BUTTERFLY ORCHID
Encyclia tampensis (Lindl.) Small
Orchid family (Orchidaceae)

Description: Epiphytic orchid with elliptic to ovoid pseudobulbs bearing 1–3 linear-lanceolate leaves 3"–12" long and ⅜"–¾" wide, resembling a bunch of scallions attached to the tree. Fragrant, ¾" flowers number from a few to a dozen or more on terminal, branching spikes. The sepals and petals range from green to brownish green, or pale with a pinkish tinge. The lip is typically white with a magenta blotch or lines in the center. Albino forms with a purely white lip are rare.

Bloom Season: May to July, but sporadically all year

Habitat/Range: Epiphytic on a variety of trees in hardwood forests, wooded swamps, and mangroves from Levy and Putnam Counties south through the Florida Keys and the northern Bahamas

Comments: *Encyclia* means "to encircle," alluding to the lateral lobes that encircle the column. The name *tampensis* refers to the Tampa Bay region, where it was first discovered in 1846. The common name is for the fanciful allusion that a spray of flowers resembles a swarm of butterflies. A state-listed commercially exploited species due to illegal collecting, it is still regarded as the most common epiphytic orchid in Florida.

CHINESE CROWN ORCHID
Eulophia graminea Lindl.
Orchid family (Orchidaceae)

Description: Terrestrial orchid with hard, ovoid pseudobulbs that can reach 3" across with erect, grasslike, linear-lanceolate leaves measuring 6"–12" long and ½" wide.

Bloom Season: April to October

Habitat/Range: Invasive in pinelands, hammocks, and mulched areas in landscapes and parking lot islands from north-central Florida south through the Florida Keys. Native to Asia.

Comments: *Eulophia* refers to the crest on the lip of the flower. The name *graminea* alludes to the grasslike leaves. It was first collected in 1833 Singapore, where its common name is *Mei Guan Lan*, translating to "beautiful crown orchid." The species was first discovered in Miami-Dade County in 2007 and has since spread south through the Florida Keys and at least as far north as Alachua County; it is expected to invade the Gulf states in time. Seeds were allegedly imported in red-dyed mulch shipped from China, which would explain its rapid spread.

CORKYSTEM PASSIONFLOWER
Passiflora suberosa L.
Passionflower family (Passifloraceae)

Description: Herbaceous vine climbing by tendrils and with corky outgrowths on mature stems. The alternate leaves are extremely variable in size and shape, averaging 1"–3" long and ranging from narrowly linear to lanceolate or variously 1–3 lobed to 2" wide.

Bloom Season: All year

Habitat/Range: Pinelands, hammocks, and coastal strand of peninsular Florida, the Florida Keys, and the neotropics

Comments: *Passiflora* is Latin for "passion flower" and relates to the crucifixion of Christ, or the Passion. The name *suberosa* means "corky" and relates to the mature stems. It is a preferred larval host plant of the zebra longwing, Julia heliconian, and gulf fritillary butterflies. The *Flora of North America* refers to this species as *Passiflora pallida*, with *P. suberosa* being a separate species native to the West Indies and Mexico south into South America.

BAHAMA MAIDENBUSH

Heterosavia bahamensis (Britton) Petra Hoffm.
(Also *Savia bahamensis* Britton)
Leafflower family (Phyllanthaceae)

Description: Dioecious shrub or small tree to 15' tall, typically with ascending branches lined with glossy, alternate, oblong-obovate to broadly elliptic leaves averaging 1"–2" long and ½"–1" wide. Male flowers are numerous along the stem; female flowers are solitary in the leaf axils. Male and female flowers are borne on separate plants.

Bloom Season: Mostly March to October

Habitat/Range: Hammocks and rocky thickets of the Florida Keys to the West Indies

Comments: *Heterosavia* combines the Greek hetero, meaning "other or different from," with the genus *Savia*, named for Italian physician and botanist Gaetano Savi (1769–1844). In other words, it is different from the genus Savia, in which it was once placed. It is a state-listed endangered species and in Florida is found only in the Florida Keys, although nurseries on the mainland cultivate it as a landscape plant.

MILKBARK OR WHITEWOOD

Drypetes diversifolia Krug & Urb.
Guiana Plum family (Putranjivaceae)

Description: Dioecious tree to 20' tall or more with alternate, ovoid to ellipsoid leaves averaging 2"–3½" long and ¾"–1½" wide. Seedling leaves have spiny margins, but mature leaves are entire. Flowers are clustered in the leaf axils; female trees bear obovoid to ellipsoid whitish fruits ½"–¾" long.

Bloom Season: All year

Habitat/Range: Hammocks of Miami-Dade and Monroe County Keys into the Bahamas

Comments: *Drypetes* is Greek for a drupe (a 1-seeded fruit). The name *diversifolia* relates to the differing forms of seedling and mature leaves. This state-listed endangered species has recently been separated from the Euphorbiaceae. The name milkbark alludes to the white bark on mature trees. In Florida, milkbark is only known from Elliott Key (Miami-Dade County) through the Monroe County Keys. Although attractive, it is surprisingly seldom seen in cultivation.

GUIANA PLUM

Drypetes lateriflora (Sw.) Krug & Urb
Guiana Plum family (Putranjivaceae)

Description: Dioecious tree to 30' tall with drooping branches lined with alternate, elliptic leaves to about 4" long and 2" wide with intricate venation. Fragrant flowers are in axillary clusters; female trees bear ⅜" ovoid to subglobose fruits that ripen dark brown to orange-red.

Bloom Season: Mostly March to August

Habitat/Range: Hammocks of Brevard, Martin, and Collier Counties south through the Florida Keys, West Indies, and Mexico south into Central America

Comments: The name *lateriflora* alludes to the flowers being produced laterally in the leaf axils. This state-listed threatened species was first described as *Schaefferia lateriflora* in 1788 by Swedish botanist Olof Peter Swartz (1760–1818) from trees he found in the Dominican Republic, but it was transferred to the genus *Drypetes* in 1892. Its wood is valued as lumber within its range outside of Florida.

GREENHEART

Colubrina arborescens (Mill.) Sarg.
Buckthorn family (Rhamnaceae)

Description: Tree to 18' tall or more with branches covered in dense, reddish-brown pubescence. Alternate, ovate to elliptic leaves average 3"–5" long to 2"–3" wide and are covered with reddish-brown pubescence. Green flowers measure ¼" wide and are in axillary clusters.

Bloom Season: All year

Habitat/Range: Hammock margins, canopy gaps, and pinelands of Miami-Dade and Monroe Counties (both mainland and Keys), West Indies, Mexico, and Central America

Comments: *Colubrina* means "snakelike," alluding to either the serpentine furrows in the bark or the shedding bark of some species. The name *arborescens* means "becoming treelike." This is a very fast-growing tree with horizontal branches that break off as the tree grows. The aroma of the flowers has been described as resembling horse urine. Buntings, cardinals, and sparrows eat the small, shiny black seeds. It is a state-listed endangered species.

LATHERLEAF
Colubrina asiatica (L.) Brongn.
Buckthorn family (Rhamnaceae)

Description: Vine-like shrub with alternate, glossy, ovate leaves 2"–3" long and 1"–1½" wide with serrate to crenate margins. Green, star-shaped flowers are about ³⁄₁₆" across. Small seeds are dark gray.

Bloom Season: May to November

Habitat/Range: Invasive along hammock margins, mangroves, coastal strand, roadsides, and trail margins of east-central and southern Florida. Native to Asia, Africa, India, Australia, and Pacific islands.

Comments: The name *asiatica* means "of Asia." This is a Category I invasive species introduced by the Florida nursery trade and can adversely alter natural habitats by forming dense monocultures. It is often seen lining roadsides adjacent to natural areas in the Florida Keys. The seeds float in seawater, enabling them to travel long distances in ocean currents. The leaves lather in water and are used as soap within its native range.

SOLDIERWOOD
Colubrina elliptica (Sw.) Brizicky & W. L. Stern
Buckthorn family (Rhamnaceae)

Description: Tree to about 20' tall with alternate, elliptic leaves that average 2½"–3½" long and 1½"–2" wide. Green, star-shaped, ¼" flowers are congested in the leaf axils. The fruits are orange-red with tiny, glossy black seeds.

Bloom Season: All year

Habitat/Range: Hammocks of the Florida Keys (Miami-Dade and Monroe Counties), West Indies, and tropical America

Comments: The name *elliptica* alludes to the elliptic leaves. The bark of this state-listed endangered tree peels off in strips, which are used by federal-endangered Key Largo woodrats in the construction of their aboveground nests in the hammocks of the Florida Keys. A Florida Audubon Society migratory bird survey conducted in the 1990s found that more migratory birds were attracted to soldierwood trees than any other species. Warblers, vireos, gnatcatchers, and flycatchers were all seen eating soldierwood flowers and the associated insects.

BLACK IRONWOOD

Krugiodendron ferreum (Vahl) Urb.
Buckthorn family (Rhamnaceae)

Description: Tree to 30' tall with glossy, opposite, ovate or broadly elliptic leaves averaging 1"–1¼" long and notched at the tip. Green to yellow-green, star-shaped flowers are about ³⁄₁₆" wide with a fragrance of almonds. Small, globose fruits are black.

Bloom Season: All year

Habitat/Range: Hammocks from Brevard County south along the coastal counties to Miami-Dade and Monroe Counties (mainland and Keys), through the West Indies, and from southern Mexico into Central America

Comments: *Krugiodendron* honors German naturalist Carl Wilhelm Leopold Krug (1833–1898), who moved to Puerto Rico and studied the West Indian flora. The name *ferreum* relates to iron, for the species' dense wood. This tree produces one of the densest woods in the world, weighing 89½ pounds per cubic foot. It is an exceptionally handsome tree and deserves wider use in the southern Florida landscape and as a street tree.

DARLING PLUM

Reynosia septentrionalis Urb.
Buckthorn family (Rhamnaceae)

Description: Small tree to 15' tall with opposite, elliptic to oval leaves, usually notched at the tip, measuring ¾"–1¼" long and ½"–¾" wide. Green to greenish-yellow, ¼" flowers are borne in the leaf axils. Round, dark purple fruits reach about ½" long.

Bloom Season: All year

Habitat/Range: Hammocks and rocky coastal flats of Miami-Dade and the Monroe County Keys, the Bahamas, Cuba, and Guatemala

Comments: *Reynosia* honors Cuban chemist and agriculturist Alvaro Reynoso (1829–1888), who revolutionized the sugar industry. The name *septentrionalis* means "northernmost," pertaining to the species' range. This state-listed threatened species has very hard wood and is sometimes called red ironwood. The fruits are edible and have been used to make wine. The species was first described in 1899 by German botanist Ignatz Urban (1848–1931), who is best known for his work on the flora of the Caribbean and Brazil.

SATINLEAF

Chrysophyllum oliviforme L.
Sapodilla family (Sapotaceae)

Description: Tree to 30' tall or more with alternate, ovate to elliptic leaves that are dark green above and coppery pubescent below, measuring 2"–3½" long and 1½"–2" wide. Fragrant, 5-lobed, ¼" flowers are in axillary clusters. Dark purple, oblong fruits reach ¾" long and ½" wide.

Bloom Season: Mostly July to March

Habitat/Range: Hammocks and pinelands from Brevard, Hendry, and Collier Counties south through the Florida Keys, the Bahamas, Greater Antilles, and British Honduras

Comments: *Chrysophyllum* describes the coppery pubescence on the underside of the leaves. The name *oliviforme* means "olive shaped," alluding to the fruits. This state-listed threatened species is prized in the southern Florida native-plant landscape trade. The fruits are edible, but the sap is sticky and astringent if unripe. The Seminole placed a decoction of wood ashes from the tree on the tongue of newlyweds to "strengthen the marriage."

WILD DILLY

Manilkara jaimiqui (C. Wright ex Griseb.) Dubard subsp. *emarginata* (L.) Cronquist
(Also *Manilkara bahamensis* [Baker] H. J. Lam & B. Meeuse)
Sapodilla family (Sapotaceae)

Description: Tree to 18' or more but often shorter. Oblong-elliptic leaves are notched at the tip and measure 1½"–4" long and ¾"–1½" wide. Axillary, greenish-yellow, ⅜" flowers have 6 hairy sepals and 6 lobes. Brown, oval fruits reach 1¼" wide.

Bloom Season: Periodically all year

Habitat/Range: Rocky flats and coastal berms of southern Florida to the Bahamas and Greater Antilles

Comments: *Manilkara* is from *manyl-kara*, a name for a related tree in India. The name *jaimiqui* is from *jai-mi-ki*, meaning "water crab spirit" in the language of the Taino, and the name *emarginata* refers to the notched leaf tip. The fruits are edible, and the white sap of the related sapodilla (*Manilkara zapota*) was once the source of chicle, the natural base of chewing gum.

WHITE FLOWERS

Moonflower (*Ipomoea alba*)

BLACK MANGROVE
Avicennia germinans (L.) L.
Acanthus family (Acanthaceae)

Description: Tree to 30' tall with opposite, lanceolate leaves averaging 2"–4" long and ¾"–1½" wide, green above and grayish pubescent below. Fragrant 4-lobed flowers are in branched, axillary clusters. Aerial root extensions, called pneumatophores, stand 6"–8" tall and surround the tree beneath the canopy.

Bloom Season: All year

Habitat/Range: Coastal shorelines and brackish estuaries from Franklin and St. Johns Counties south along both coasts of Florida, through the Monroe County Keys west to Texas and through coastal tropical America, Bermuda, and West Indies

Comments: *Avicennia* honors Iranian physician and philosopher Avicenna (980–1037). The name *germinans* refers to the seeds germinating on the tree. Black mangrove exudes salt out of leaf glands that crystalizes and makes the leaves glisten in sunlight and taste salty when licked. It is a larval host plant of the mangrove buckeye butterfly.

SPANISH BAYONET
Yucca aloifolia L.
Agave family (Agavaceae)

Description: Perennial species 8'–10' tall with stiff, linear-lanceolate leaves armed with a sharp tip at the apex. Terminal panicles of leathery flowers reach 3' tall.

Bloom Season: January to August

Habitat/Range: Dunes, open sandy habitats, and coastal thickets throughout much of Florida and in tropical and subtropical regions of both hemispheres

Comments: *Yucca* is a native Haitian name. The name *aloifolia* means "leaves resembling an *Aloe*" (Asphodelaceae). The sharp-tipped leaves can cause serious eye damage to people and pets. The roots of this and other species were used by the Seminole to create a lathery substance to wash hair, "which leaves the hair smooth and glossy," as reported by Army officer Oliver Otis Howard (1830–1909) in his 1907 autobiography, *My Life and Experiences with the Hostile Indians*. It is a larval host plant of the yucca giant skipper and the cofaqui giant-skipper.

SLENDER SEAPURSLANE

Sesuvium maritimum (Walt.) B.S.P.
Carpetweed family (Aizoaceae)

Description: Herbaceous annual with prostrate, spreading stems and succulent, opposite, oblong to elliptic leaves averaging ¼"–½" long and about ¼"–⅜" wide. The tiny axillary, star-shaped flowers are mostly white and measure about ³⁄₁₆" across.

Bloom Season: All year

Habitat/Range: Sandy and rocky coastlines of the eastern and southern United States through the West Indies

Comments: *Sesuvium* is for the *Sesuvii*, a Gallic tribe mentioned by Julius Caesar (100–44 BC). The name *maritimum* alludes to its coastal, or maritime, habitat. This species resembles a miniature version of shoreline seapurslane (*Sesuvium portulacastrum*) in the "Pink Flowers" section of this guide. The leaves of both species are eaten as famine food in the West Indies, and hot poultices are made from the leaves to relieve chest congestion. *Sesuvium* species are one of the richest sources of ecdysterone, a naturally occurring steroid hormone claimed to enhance physical performance.

LANCELEAF ARROWHEAD

Sagittaria lancifolia L.
Water Plantain family (Alismataceae)

Description: Succulent, herbaceous perennial with leaves that spread fanlike from the base. Lance-shaped leaf blades measure up to 16" long and 4" wide. Flowers are on an erect stalk in whorls of 3, with female flowers toward the bottom of the stalk, males above.

Bloom Season: February to October

Habitat/Range: Freshwater wetlands and roadside ditches from Delaware and Maryland to Oklahoma, Texas, and Florida into the neotropics

Comments: *Sagittaria* is Latin for "an arrow," alluding to the leaf shape of some species. The name *lancifolia* refers to the lance-shaped leaves. It is also called duck potato, derived from ducks feeding on the corms on the rhizome tips. This species is common on the Florida mainland but rare in the Keys because of the lack of freshwater habitats. It is known from Big Pine Key in and around the Blue Hole in the National Key Deer Refuge.

YELLOW JOYWEED

Alternanthera flavescens Kunth
Amaranth family (Amaranthaceae)

Description: Herbaceous perennial with long, spreading stems and opposite, lanceolate or elliptic, somewhat succulent leaves measuring 1"–2½" long and ½"–¾" wide. Flowers are clustered in silvery or yellowish subglobose cone-like heads on long axillary stems.

Bloom Season: All year

Habitat/Range: Coastal strand from Manatee and Brevard Counties south through the Monroe County Keys, West Indies, and tropical America

Comments: *Alternanthera* means "alternating anthers"; *flavescens* relates to "yellowish," alluding to the sometimes-yellowish heads. This species is regarded as native in the *Atlas of Florida Plants* but is oddly considered introduced in the treatment for the *Flora of North America*. It is a common inhabitant of coastal habitats in the Florida Keys. The native seaside joyweed (*Alternanthera maritima*) and the non-native smooth joyweed (*Alternanthera philoxeriodes*) also occur in the Florida Keys.

SAMPHIRE OR SILVERHEAD

Blutaparon vermiculare (L.) Mears
(Also *Philoxerus vermicularis* [L.] Beauv.)
Amaranth family (Amaranthaceae)

Description: Herbaceous perennial with prostrate or ascending stems bearing thick, fleshy, opposite, linear-oblong leaves averaging 1"–1½" long and ¼"–⅜" wide. Round to subglobose heads of white bracts surround many small, yellow flowers.

Bloom Season: All year

Habitat/Range: Saline soils of shoreline habitats from Florida through the West Indies, west to Texas, and south from Mexico to Brazil

Comments: *Blutaparon* is abridged from an ancient Latin name, Bulutaparon. The name *vermiculare* means "resembling worms," for its non-twining stems. It is called saltweed in the Bahamas for the salty taste of the leaves and is cooked as a pre-salted potherb. The name silverhead relates to the flower heads turning silvery when dried. This plant is the namesake of Samphire Key in Florida Bay within Everglades National Park.

WEST INDIAN COCK'S COMB
Celosia nítida Vahl
Amaranth family (Amaranthaceae)

Description: Herbaceous perennial with spreading or erect green or burgundy stems, branching from the rootstock, and averaging 12"–36" tall. Leaves are typically rhombic or triangular-lanceolate, measuring 1"–3" long and ½"–1½" wide. Star-shaped, ⅜" flowers are greenish white or pinkish white.

Bloom Season: August to February

Habitat/Range: Coastal dunes, rock barrens, middens, and hammock margins from Lee County south along the Gulf coast to Miami-Dade County and the Monroe County Keys; disjunct in Lake, Manatee, and St. Lucie Counties. Also Texas, Mexico, West Indies, and South America.

Comments: *Celosia* is from the Greek *ke⁻los*, meaning "burnt or dry," for the appearance of the flowers of some species. The name *nitida* is Latin for "shining," for the glossy seeds. This state-listed endangered species is the only native member of the genus in Florida and is more common in the Florida Keys than on the mainland.

JUBA BUSH
Iresine diffusa Humb. & Bonpl. ex Willd.
Amaranth family (Amaranthaceae)

Description: Much-branched herbaceous perennial with opposite, ovate to lanceolate leaves measuring ⅝"–4½" long and ⅜"–2" wide. The stems and leaves are sometimes red. Tiny flowers are in an airy, diffusely branched panicle.

Bloom Season: All year

Habitat/Range: Dry disturbed sites and coastal strand across the southern United States through the West Indies and tropical America

Comments: *Iresine* is Greek for "wool," for the long cottony hairs encircling the calyx. The name *diffusa* alludes to the species' diffuse branching habit. Juba is a mesmerizing dance step practiced by enslaved Afro-Caribbean people and a name given to this plant in the West Indies because the inflorescence dances in the wind. Another name is bloodleaf. The plant is sold in tropical American markets for medicinal use in treating coughs, colds, and colic. It is a larval host plant of Hayhurst's scallopwing butterfly.

BEACH SPIDER-LILY

Hymenocallis latifolia (Mill.) M. Roem.
Amaryllis family (Amaryllidaceae)

Description: Herbaceous perennial with long strap-shaped leaves that reach 30"–36" long and 2½"–4" wide. The fragrant flowers are in terminal clusters atop a fleshy stalk to 48" tall or more, with 7–15 flowers per inflorescence. The sepals and petals (tepals) are lax and spread beneath a thin, cuplike membrane connecting the stamen filaments. The orange pollen is a key identifying character among Florida species.

Bloom Season: March to October

Habitat/Range: Beach dunes, rocky shorelines, and mangrove forests from Central Florida (disjunct in Franklin County) south through the Florida Keys and the West Indies

Comments: *Hymenocallis* means "beautiful membrane" for the hymen-like membrane between the stamens. The name *latifolia* means "wide leaves." Of the thirteen members of the genus in Florida, this is the only species found in the Florida Keys. It is cultivated throughout its Florida range, especially in coastal landscapes where salt tolerance is a requirement. The flowers are pollinated by sphinx moths that transfer pollen on their wings as they sip nectar. It is also called mangrove spider-lily and perfumed spider-lily. Flightless lubber grasshoppers sometimes eat the leaves down to the ground.

DEVIL'S POTATO
Echites umbellatus Jacq.
Dogbane family (Apocynaceae)

Description: Herbaceous twining vine with opposite, broadly ovate to oblong elliptic leaves averaging 2"–3½" long and 1½–2" wide with clear, sticky sap. The flowers measure about 2" wide with 5 curved lobes. Cylindrical pods are 6"–8" long, extending outward from each other. Seeds are wind-dispersed.

Bloom Season: All year

Habitat/Range: Pinelands from Brevard County south through the coastal counties to Miami-Dade and Monroe (mainland and Keys) Counties and from the West Indies to northern South America

Comments: *Echites* is Greek for "viper," alluding to the vine's twining stems and perhaps its toxicity. The name *umbellatus* is for the umbels of flowers. The common name is fair warning to not eat the poisonous, tuberous root. This is a larval host plant of the red, white, and blue day-flying faithful beauty moth. The larvae are bright scarlet with iridescent blue spots designed to warn birds of their toxicity. Conveying the sap to an open wound has reportedly caused vomiting. In the Keys the species is most common in the National Key Deer Refuge on Big Pine Key but also occurs in Dagny Johnson, John Pennekamp, and Curry Hammock State Parks.

WHITE TWINEVINE
Funastrum clausum (Jacq.) Schltr.
(Also *Sarcostemma clausum* [Jacq.] Schult.)
Dogbane family (Apocynaceae)

Description: Herbaceous perennial vine with glabrous stems and opposite, elliptic-lanceolate leaves typically 2"–3" long and ½"–¾" wide. The stems and leaves exude white, sticky sap if broken. The 5-lobed, starlike flowers are in rounded clusters, each flower measuring ⅜"–½" wide. The base of each lobe is purple, forming a ring.

Bloom Season: June to January

Habitat/Range: Moist soils of coastal strand, cypress swamps, and mangroves of central and southern Florida through the neotropics

Comments: *Funastrum* is from Greek words meaning "star rope," alluding to the ropelike stems and starlike flowers. The name *clausum* means "closed," or "shut," with unknown reference to this plant. It is a larval host plant of the queen, monarch, and soldier butterflies. Toxins in the plant make their larvae distasteful to birds and other predators.

BLODGETT'S SWALLOWWORT
Metastelma blodgettii A. Gray
(Also *Cynanchum blodgettii* [A. Gray] Shinners)
Dogbane family (Apocynaceae)

Description: Herbaceous twining vine with narrow stems to about 36" long, sometimes twining into bundles of stems. Opposite, linear to linear-lanceolate leaves reach about 1" long and ⅛" wide. Flowers are ¼" long in axillary clusters spaced apart along the stems.

Bloom Season: All year

Habitat/Range: Pinelands and coastal habitats of Collier, Miami-Dade, and the Monroe County Keys to the Bahamas

Comments: *Metastelma* is from Greek words meaning "instead," and "a crown," alluding to the absence of a corona. The name *blodgettii* honors botanist John Loomis Blodgett (1809–1853), who was an important figure in the early botanical history of southern Florida. This state-listed threatened species is a larval host of the soldier butterfly and was formerly placed in the Asclepiadaceae, or Milkweed family. The stems and leaves exude sticky white sap when broken.

FRAGRANT SWALLOWWORT

Metastelma northropiae Schltr.
(Also *Cynanchum northropiae* [Schltr.] Alain)
Dogbane family (Apocynaceae)

Description: Herbaceous twining vine up to 6' long with opposite, ovate to oblong-lanceolate leaves to 1" long, exuding sticky, milky sap when broken. Fragrant star-shaped flowers are produced in few-flowered cymes. Seeds are in a linear follicle and are dispersed by wind.

Bloom Season: June to November

Habitat/Range: Coastal habitats of Brevard, Miami-Dade, and the Monroe County Keys, the Bahamas, and Cuba

Comments: The name *northropiae* honors American botanist Alice Belle Northrop (1864–1922), who is best known for promoting access to nature for New York's schoolchildren and the author of *Flora of New Providence and Andros*, published in 1902. Look for this species twining on stems of coastal shrubs and small trees along nature trails in Florida Keys state parks. It is sometimes used by queen and soldier butterflies as a larval host plant.

GULF COAST SWALLOWWORT

Pattalias palustre (Pursh) Fishbein
(Also *Cynanchum angustifolium* Pers.)
Dogbane family (Apocynaceae)

Description: Herbaceous twining vine with slender stems that exude white, sticky sap when broken. Opposite, narrowly linear leaves 1"–1½" long to about ⅛" wide. Flowers reach ¼" wide in axillary clusters along the stem.

Bloom Season: All year

Habitat/Range: Salt marshes and other coastal habitats from South Carolina to Texas, south through Florida, the Bahamas and Cuba

Comments: *Pattalias* is Greek for "two-year-old stag," alluding to the fanciful resemblance of the petals to the short, unbranched antlers of the Asian muntjac deer. The name *palustre* means "marsh" and relates to the species' habitat. Despite the common name, it occurs along both Florida coasts. It is a larval host plant for queen and soldier butterflies. A related species, leafless swallowwort (*Orthosia scoparia*) has similar flowers and is uncommon in the Florida Keys.

MANGROVE RUBBERVINE

Rhabdadenia biflora (Jacq.) Müll. Arg

Dogbane family (Apocynaceae)

Description: Twining vine with long, flexible stems bearing opposite, oblong or obovate-oblong leaves averaging 2"–3" long and 1"–1½" wide. The stems and leaves exude white, sticky sap if broken. White, or pink-tinged, funnel-shaped flowers have a yellow throat and measure about 2½" across. The linear fruits reach about 5" long.

Bloom Season: All year

Habitat/Range: Mangroves and coastal hammocks of the central and southern Florida peninsula through the Florida Keys, West Indies, and Mexico south into South America

Comments: *Rhabdadenia* means "wand gland" and alludes to the slender pods. The name *biflora* relates to the flowers, which are frequently produced in pairs. In the Florida Keys, look for this attractive, high-climbing vine in mangroves or along the edges of coastal hammocks bordering mangroves. The sticky, milky sap can produce skin blisters and is both purgative and toxic if taken internally, inflaming the mouth, throat, stomach, and intestines. It has been used in the tropical Americas to poison vermin. In the Keys it is known from Elliott Key within Biscayne National Park, the National Key Deer Refuge on Big Pine Key, and in Dagny Johnson, John Pennekamp, and Long Key State Parks.

PEARLBERRY
Vallesia antillana Woodson
Dogbane family (Apocynaceae)

Description: Shrub or small tree with somewhat drooping branches lined with alternate, elliptic-lanceolate leaves to 2"–3" long and ½"–1" wide. Flowers are about ⅜" wide, followed by oval-oblong opalescent fruits to about ½" long and ¼" wide.

Bloom Season: All year

Habitat/Range: Coastal habitats of the Miami-Dade and Monroe County mainland and Keys, the Bahamas, Cuba, Jamaica, and Hispaniola

Comments: *Vallesia* was named in 1794 by botanists Hipolito Ruiz (1754–1816) and José Antonio Pavón (1754–1840) to honor Spanish pharmacist and physician Francisco Vallés (1524–1592), who was the chief physician to King Phillip II. The name *antillana* alludes to the Antilles chain of Caribbean islands. Another common name for this state-listed endangered species is tearshrub, for the fruits that resemble tears. The name pearlberry also refers to the fruits. This tree was only recently discovered in Everglades National Park on the Florida mainland.

COASTAL RAGWEED
Ambrosia hispida *Pursh*
Aster family (Asteraceae)

Description: Rhizomatous perennial averaging 6"–10" tall, forming spreading colonies. The pinnately lobed leaves are mostly opposite, ovate or elliptic in outline. Flowers are unisexual, with the female (pistillate) heads close to the male (staminate) heads on erect stems 4"–6" tall.

Bloom Season: Mostly March to June

Habitat/Range: Sandy beaches of Brevard, Lee, Collier, Miami-Dade, and the Monroe County Keys, West Indies, and Central America

Comments: *Ambrosia* is Greek for "delicious," "divine," or "immortal"—and the food and drink of the gods in Greek mythology. The name *hispida* alludes to the stiff (hispid) hairs on the plant. Ragweeds are best known for their airborne pollen that causes severe allergies in many people, especially common ragweed (*Ambrosia artemisiifolia*). Ragweeds are larval hosts of the green cloverworm, common tan wave, olive-shaded bird-dropping, and ragweed flower moths in Florida.

SALTWATER FALSE WILLOW
Baccharis angustifolia Michx.
Aster family (Asteraceae)

Description: Woody, dioecious shrub with narrowly linear, 1-nerved leaves 1"–1½" long and ¼" wide or less, making it easy to separate from other native Baccharis species. Both male (staminate) and female (pistillate) flowers are white. Seeds are wind-dispersed.

Bloom Season: August to November

Habitat/Range: Brackish marshes, beaches, and other coastal habitats from North Carolina to Louisiana, south through coastal counties of Florida and into the Florida Keys

Comments: *Baccharis* honors Bacchus, the Roman god of agriculture, wine, and fertility; *angustifolius* means "narrow leaves." The species was first described by French botanist André Michaux (1746–1802) and published in 1803, the year after he died in Madagascar of a tropical fever. In the Florida Keys, this species can be locally common along roadsides and trails that bisect mangroves, salt marsh habitat, and coastal hammocks.

SALTBUSH OR SEA MYRTLE
Baccharis halimifolia L.
Aster family (Asteraceae)

Description: Bushy shrub or small tree with alternate, elliptic to broadly obovate or rhombic leaves averaging about 1" long and ½"–⅝" wide, usually with coarse teeth across the broad tip. Male and female flowers are on separate plants, and the seeds can cover the entire canopy. Flower heads are stalked (pedunculate).

Bloom Season: August to November

Habitat/Range: Open sandy habitats across much of the eastern and midwestern United States to Mexico and West Indies

Comments: The name *halimifolia* alludes to the resemblance of the leaves to those of a *Halimium* (Cistaceae). The leaves contain cardiac glycosides and have caused death in humans and grazing sheep. Other common names are consumption weed, high tide bush, groundsel tree, and silverling. A very similar species, *Baccharis glomeruliflora*, also occurs in the Florida Keys and differs by having sessile flower heads.

SPANISH NEEDLES
Bidens alba (L.) DC.
Aster family (Asteraceae)

Description: Herbaceous perennial averaging 12"–24" tall with leaves to about 2" long, divided into 3 or 5 segments. The segments are ovate to lanceolate, with toothed margins. The lowermost leaves are frequently undivided. Flowers measure about 1" across, with white rays and yellow disks. The ½" dry seeds (achenes) have a pair of barbs (awns) on one end.

Bloom Season: All year

Habitat/Range: Open, sunny habitats, including roadsides, vacant lots, fallow fields, and urban landscapes in tropical, subtropical, and warm temperate regions worldwide

Comments: *Bidens* means "two-toothed," for the 2 awns on the achene. The name *alba* means "white," for the ray florets. This well-known plant is either beloved as a major attractor of butterflies, bees, and other pollinators or despised as a persistent and troublesome weed in gardens, with seeds that stick to clothes, feathers, and fur. This is a simple way for the plant to disperse its seeds. Besides the flowers being constantly visited by butterflies, the plant is also a larval host of the dainty sulphur butterfly, so it is a weed worth tolerating, if not encouraging. The tender new leaves are edible and are higher in iron than spinach; soaking the leaves in cold water overnight removes some of the resinous taste. Other names are sticktights, beggarticks, devil's pitchfork, and old ladies' clothespins.

WHITE SUNBONNETS
Chaptalia albicans (Sw.) Vent. ex B. D. Jacks.
Aster family (Asteraceae)

Description: Herbaceous perennial with wavy, obovate-elliptic leaves that form a basal rosette. The leaves are green above, covered with white pubescence below, 1"–5½" long and ½"–1½" wide. Flower heads are on erect spikes to about 6" tall.

Bloom Season: March to November

Habitat/Range: Pinelands and grassy areas of Miami-Dade County and the Monroe County Keys, West Indies, Mexico, and Central America

Comments: *Chaptalia* honors noted French chemist and statesman Jean-Antoine-Claude Chaptal (1756–1831), who developed the process of adding cane sugar to pressed grape juice to raise the alcohol content of wine. The name *albicans* means "off white," alluding to the ray flowers. This state-listed threatened species has not been vouchered in the Florida Keys, but it occurs in the National Key Deer Refuge on Big Pine Key.

FALSE DAISY
Eclipta prostrata (L.) L.
(Also *Eclipta alba* [L.] Hassk.)
Aster family (Asteraceae)

Description: Annual or short-lived perennial with erect or prostrate stems that sometimes root at the nodes. Opposite, linear-lanceolate to narrowly elliptic leaves measure 2"–4" long and ¼"–½" wide, either clasping, sessile, or with very short petioles. Solitary flower heads are about ¼" across on axillary stems.

Bloom Season: All year

Habitat/Range: Moist, open habitats, including gardens, throughout Florida and tropical, subtropical, and temperate regions of the New World

Comments: *Eclipta* is Greek for "to be without" or "a failing," alluding to the lack of a crown of bristles (pappus) at the tip of the achene. The name *prostrata* relates to the plant's prostrate branches. It has a low toxicity to humans, horses, dogs, and cats. Other common names are mayweed, stinking chamomile, and poison daisy. The species has a traditional medicinal use as a liver tonic and shows beneficial effects against diabetes.

OAKLEAF FLEABANE
Erigeron quercifolius Lam.
Aster family (Asteraceae)

Description: Herbaceous perennial with lobed, hairy leaves 2"–7" long and ⅝"–1½" wide, forming a rosette with smaller leaves up the flowering stem. The ⅜"–½" flower heads are in open clusters on top of branching stems. The narrow ray flowers can be white, pinkish, or blue with yellow disk flowers.

Bloom Season: All year

Habitat/Range: Pinelands, prairies, and disturbed sites across the southeastern United States into the Bahamas

Comments: *Erigeron* means "woolly" and "old man," alluding to the woolly hairs on some species. The name *quercifolius* relates to the leaves resembling those of species of oaks in the genus Quercus. The common name fleabane relates to plants used as a flea repellent by placing their leaves in bedding. The leaves of this species are fragrant when crushed. This species is recorded for Big Pine Key in the Lower Florida Keys.

PINELAND SQUARESTEM
Melanthera parvifolia Small
Aster family (Asteraceae)

Description: Herbaceous perennial with sprawling or weakly ascending square stems bearing scabrous, coarsely toothed, ovate or 3-lobed leaves ¾"–1½" long and ½"–¾" wide. Flower clusters are on long stems and measure about 1" across. The anthers are black.

Habitat/Range: Endemic to pine rocklands of the southern Florida mainland and Big Pine Key in the Lower Florida Keys

Bloom Season: All year

Comments: *Melanthera* means "black anthers." The name *parvifolia* means "small leaves." This state-listed threatened species was first described in 1903 by American botanist John Kunkel Small (1869–1938). A more common species with identical flowers, snow squarestem (*Melanthera nivea*), occurs locally throughout the Florida Keys and differs by having longer leaves (up to 4¾") and becoming bushy. Members of this genus have been used medicinally to treat headache and also as cattle fodder. Small butterflies visit the flowers.

149

CLIMBING HEMPVINE
Mikania scandens (L.) Willd.
Aster family (Asteraceae)

Description: Twining vine with opposite, elongate-deltoid, shallowly lobed leaves to about 2" long. Sweet-scented white flowers are in flat-topped arrangements along the stems. Seeds are wind-dispersed.

Bloom Season: All year

Habitat/Range: Pinelands, hammock margins, sandhills, and marshes from southern Canada and the eastern half of the United States through the West Indies and from Mexico south into South America

Comments: *Mikania* honors Austrian-Czech botanist and professor Joseph Gottfried Mikan (1743–1814). The name *scandens* means "climbing," for the vine's growth habit. A bonanza of insects, including butterflies, can be found around flowering plants of this species, and it is a larval host plant of the little metalmark butterfly and the scarlet-bodied wasp moth. It has been used medicinally by the Seminole in Florida to treat "snake sickness," and is also used throughout the Caribbean to treat venomous snakebite, diarrhea, rheumatism, and stomach problems.

CURE-FOR-ALL
Pluchea carolinensis (Jacq.) G. Don
Aster family (Asteraceae)

Description: Perennial shrub to 6' tall with alternate, pubescent, elliptic to ovate leaves 4"–6" long and 2"–3" wide. Pale pink to white flower heads are in branched clusters, with each head about ¼" wide.

Bloom Season: February to August

Habitat/Range: Invasive along forest margins and disturbed sites from Central Florida south through the Florida Keys. Native to the West Indies and tropical America.

Comments: *Pluchea* honors French clergyman, naturalist, and professor Noël-Antoine Pluche (1688–1761). The name *carolinensis* means "of Carolina." When this species was named in 1789, it was believed to be native to the Carolinas, but it has since been determined to be an invasive exotic. The strongly aromatic leaves are used medicinally to treat asthma, bronchitis, cholera, toothache, night sweats, twitching muscles, neuralgia, stomach disorders, wheezing, hypertension, fever, menstrual difficulties, and more, hence the common name cure-for-all.

BLACKROOT

Pterocaulon pycnostachyum (Michx.) Elliott
Aster family (Asteraceae)

Description: Herbaceous perennial with conspicuously winged stems that reach 8"–24" tall. Alternate, often shallowly toothed lanceolate leaves reach up to 4" long and about ½" wide, green above, woolly white below, with a white midrib. Flowers are creamy white and packed in cone-shaped clusters, opening from the bottom upward.

Bloom Season: All year

Habitat/Range: Flatwoods, pinelands, and disturbed sites from North Carolina to Mississippi, south through Florida

Comments: *Pterocaulon* means "winged stem"; *pycnostachyum* is descriptive of the tightly packed flowers. The black, tuberous roots are poisonous to eat. Another common name in Florida is rabbit tobacco, which means "wild tobacco" and has nothing to do with a bunny. The plant contains a chemical called *coumarin* used in pipe tobacco as an aroma enhancer and added to rat poison as an anticoagulant.

BAHAMA SACHSIA

Sachsia polycephala Griseb.
(Also *Sachsia bahamensis* Urb.)
Aster family (Asteraceae)

Description: Herbaceous perennial with toothed spatulate leaves that form a ground-hugging rosette. The leaves average 1"–2½" long and ½"–¾" wide. Flowering stems may reach 20" tall, branching near the top with heads of rayless flowers to about ⅜" long and ⅛" wide.

Bloom Season: All year

Habitat/Range: Rocky pinelands of Miami-Dade County and the Monroe County Keys, the Bahamas, and Greater Antilles

Comments: *Sachsia* honors German plant physiologist Julius von Sachs (1832–1897). The name *polycephala* refers to the many heads of flowers. This state-listed threatened species was first described in 1866 by German botanist August Heinrich Rudolf Grisebach (1814–1879) from plants collected in Cuba. In the Florida Keys it is only known from the pine rocklands of Big Pine Key. There are only two other species in the genus, and both are endemic to Cuba.

BAHAMAN ASTER

Symphyotrichum bahamense (Britton) G. L. Nesom
(Also *Symphyotrichum subulatum* [Michx.] G. L.
Nesom var. *elongatum* [Bosserdet ex A. G. Jones &
Lowry] S. D. Sundberg)
Aster family (Asteraceae)

Description: Herbaceous annual with thin, narrowly lanceolate basal leaves but mostly leafless when flowering. Flower heads are about ⁵⁄₁₆" across and appear in open, diffuse arrays. Rays may be white, pink, or lavender with yellow disk florets.

Bloom Season: All year

Habitat/Range: Disturbed roadsides, freshwater marshes, and coastal salt marshes of the eastern Florida Panhandle throughout much of the peninsula to the Florida Keys, the Bahamas, and Cuba

Comments: *Symphyotrichum* is Greek for "hair junction" and is believed to allude to the basal bristles of a cultivar in Europe used by botanist Christian Gottfried Daniel Nees von Esenbeck (1776–1858) to describe the genus. The name *bahamense* means "of the Bahamas," where it was first collected and described in 1914 by botanist Nathaniel Lord Britton (1859–1934) as *Aster bahamensis*.

RICE BUTTON ASTER

Symphyotrichum dumosum (L.) G. L. Nesom
Aster family (Asteraceae)

Description: Rhizomatous perennial with slender, much-branched stems averaging 12"–24" tall. The recurved, scabrous leaves may be entire or with slightly crenate margins, and both the basal and lower stem leaves wither by flowering. Flower heads are in panicles with rays that may be white, pink, or lavender.

Bloom Season: July to November

Habitat/Range: Pinelands, wetlands, and other open habitats across the eastern United States into Canada

Comments: The name dumosum means "bushy," for the species' growth habit. In the Florida Keys, this species only appears on plant lists for Big Pine Key. It is a larval host plant of the pearl crescent butterfly.

SOUTHWESTERN ANNUAL SALTMARSH ASTER

Symphyotrichum expansum (Poepp. ex Spreng.) G. L. Nesom

(Also *Symphyotrichum subulatum* [Michx.] G. L. Nesom var. *parviflorum* [Nees] S. D. Sundberg) Aster family (Asteraceae)

Description: Herbaceous annual 36"–48" tall, often with short, leafy branches and with basal leaves that wither before flowering. Basal leaves are ovate to oblanceolate; the upper leaves are mostly narrowly lanceolate. The ray florets are typically white but may be pink or lavender. Flower heads are about ⁵⁄₁₆" wide.

Bloom Season: July to November

Habitat/Range: Roadsides, trail margins, and marshy habitats from Florida across the southern and midwestern states to California, south through Mexico, Central America, and northern South America across the West Indies

Comments: The name *expansum* relates to the species' extensive natural range. It was first described as *Erigeron expansus* in 1826 by German physician and botanist Eduard Friedrich Poeppig (1798–1868) from plants collected in Cuba. It was photographed on North Key Largo.

PERENNIAL SALTMARSH ASTER

Symphyotrichum tenuifolium (L.) G. L. Nesom Aster family (Asteraceae)

Description: Herbaceous, rhizomatous perennial with erect or ascending stems to 30" tall. Lower leaves are petiolate; upper leaves are sessile. The narrowly ovate or oblanceolate leaves reach 5"–10" long, withering before flowering. Flower heads are in an open, airy array with white or pinkish ray florets and yellow disks that turn purplish with age.

Bloom Season: All year

Habitat/Range: Salt and brackish marshes throughout coastal Florida west along the Gulf coast to Texas and up the Atlantic coastline to Maine

Comments: The name *tenuifolium* means "slender-leaved." This species was first described in 1753 as *Aster tenuifolius* by Swedish botanist Carolus Linnaeus (1707–1778) and moved to the genus *Symphyotrichum* in 1995 by American botanist Guy L. Nesom (1945–). This species is locally common along roadsides in the Florida Keys that bisect its habitat.

COATBUTTONS
Tridax procumbens L.
Aster family (Asteraceae)

Description: Herbaceous annual or perennial with recumbent stems and hairy, opposite, ovate to ovate-lanceolate leaves ¾"–1½" long and ½"–¾" wide that are coarsely toothed along the margins. Flower heads are on terminal spikes. Seeds are wind-dispersed.

Bloom Season: All year

Habitat/Range: Invasive mostly in disturbed sites of north-central Florida south through the Florida Keys. Native to the neotropics.

Comments: *Tridax* alludes to the 3 teeth on the ray flowers. The name *procumbens* refers to the stems that lie flat on the ground. This species is commonly found in lawns, along roadsides and trail margins, and even in cracks in sidewalks. It is not a listed invasive species because it does not negatively alter the function of natural habitats, but it is a ubiquitous weed. The common name is a fanciful allusion to the resemblance of the flowers to coat buttons.

SALTWORT
Batis maritima L.
Saltwort family (Bataceae)

Description: Herbaceous perennial with numerous spreading branches that root at the tip, forming extensive colonies. The succulent, linear leaves are opposite and average 1"–2" long. Ovoid-cylindric, axillary spikes bear tiny male and female flowers.

Bloom Season: All year

Habitat/Range: Salt marshes, mangroves, and coastal strand across the American tropics. In Florida it occurs in coastal counties along both coasts through the Florida Keys.

Comments: *Batis* is Greek for the imaginative resemblance of the fruits to a blackberry. The name *maritima* relates to its coastal, or maritime, habitat. This is the dominant species in salt marsh prairies, with intertwined branches that make travel through this habitat slow and arduous. Great southern white and eastern pygmy blue butterflies use it as a larval host plant. The salty leaves are eaten as a potherb or a pre-salted salad, used medicinally to treat syphilis, or burned and mixed with animal fat to make soap.

SMOOTH STRONGBACK
Bourreria cassinifolia (A. Rich.) Griseb.
Borage family (Boraginaceae)

Description: Evergreen shrub or small tree 6'–10' tall with oblanceolate to narrowly obovate leaves that average about ¾" long and ½" wide. Round, orange fruits are about ⅜" wide.

Bloom Season: All year

Habitat/Range: Rocky pinelands of Miami-Dade County, the Monroe County Keys, and Cuba

Comments: *Bourreria* honors German apothecary Johann Ambrosius Beurer (1716–1754), who studied medicine and botany in Nuremberg. The name *cassinifolia* relates to the leaves resembling those of a species of *Cassine* (Celastraceae). It is often called "strongbark," but that name is a corruption of "strongback," which relates to a tea brewed from the leaves "to give men a strong back," with sexual implications. The flowers of this state-listed endangered species attract butterflies, sphinx moths, bees, wasps, and hummingbirds; the fruits attract a wide variety of birds. This and the following species are larval host plants of the tersa sphinx moth.

BAHAMA STRONGBACK
Bourreria succulenta Jacq.
Borage family (Boraginaceae)

Description: Tree to 20' tall or more with weeping branches bearing alternate, ovate to suborbicular leaves averaging 2"–3" long and 1"–2" wide. The 5-lobed, ½" flowers are in open clusters (cymes) and produce orange fruits to about ⅜" wide.

Bloom Season: All year

Habitat/Range: Hammocks of Lee, Miami-Dade, and the Monroe County Keys, West Indies, and tropical America

Comments: The name *succulenta* relates to the fleshy leaves. The flowers of this state-listed endangered species are visited by hummingbirds, butterflies, bees, wasps, and a variety of moths; birds feast on the fruits. For this reason it is becoming more popular among gardeners in southern Florida, and it is far more common in hammocks of the Florida Keys than on the mainland. Rough strongback (*Bourreria radula*) was historically present in the Florida Keys but has been extirpated from Florida as a wild plant.

SCORPIONTAIL

Heliotropium angiospermum Murray
Borage family (Boraginaceae)

Description: Shrubby herbaceous perennial to 5' tall with elliptic to broadly lanceolate leaves 2"–3" long and ¾"–1¼" wide. Flowers are in 2 ranks on scorpioid cymes that unfurl as new flowers form.

Bloom Season: All year

Habitat/Range: Hammock margins, shell middens, edges of mangroves, and disturbed sites of the central and southern peninsula through the Florida Keys, West Indies, and Texas south to South America

Comments: *Heliotropium* relates to turning toward the sun, in the mistaken belief that the flowers face the sun. The name *angiospermum* means "with covered seeds," alluding to the conspicuous scales surrounding the seeds. Male monarch and queen butterflies are strongly attracted to the flowers to obtain pheromones used to stimulate females into mating. This species readily spreads from seed in home landscapes but is worth cultivating for its continuous flowering and butterfly-attracting attributes.

SEASIDE HELIOTROPE

Heliotropium curassavicum L.
Borage family (Boraginaceae)

Description: Herbaceous perennial with prostrate or ascending stems spreading outward from the base with grayish-green succulent leaves ½"–1½" long and ¼"–⅜" wide. Inflorescences consist of coiled double rows of ³⁄₁₆" yellow- or purple-centered white flowers.

Bloom Season: All year

Habitat/Range: Beach strand, tidal marshes, and coastal disturbed sites of the southern United States, West Indies, and tropical America

Comments: The name *curassavicum* means "of Curaçao," a Dutch island nation in the West Indies. The plant is eaten in salads or cooked as a potherb, dried as a tea substitute, and the ashes used as a salt substitute. Long-term consumption may have a negative cumulative effect on body organs, but an extract from the plant is widely used to treat gout, rheumatism, arteriosclerosis disorders, muscular pain, and inflammation of veins (phlebitis).

SEA LAVENDER

Heliotropium gnaphalodes L.
(Also *Argusia gnaphalodes* [L.] Heine; *Mallotonia gnaphalodes* [L.] Britton; *Tournefortia gnaphalodes* [L.] R. Brown ex Roem. & Schult.)
Borage family (Boraginaceae

Description: Much-branched woody shrub to 6' tall, forming mounds of stems covered with silvery-pubescent gray-green, linear to linear-spatulate leaves averaging 1½"–2½" long and ¼"–⅜" wide. Fragrant white flowers become pink with age and are in 2 rows on coiled spikes equal to the length of the leaves.

Bloom Season: All year

Habitat/Range: Sandy beaches and rocky ocean shores from east-central Florida to Cape Sable and the Florida Keys, West Indies, Bermuda, and tropical America

Comments: The name *gnaphalodes* alludes to the similarity of the leaves to members of the genus *Gnaphalium* (Asteraceae). This state-listed endangered species is local in the Florida Keys and occasionally visible along the oceanside of the Overseas Highway. It is very ornamental and sometimes cultivated by gardeners but is not widely available. Good places to view wild plants are Long Key and Bahia Honda State Parks.

CURACAO BUSH OR BUTTERFLY BUSH

Varronia globosa Jacq.
(Also *Cordia globosa* [Jacq.] Kunth)
Borage family (Boraginaceae)

Description: Woody shrub averaging 3'–5' tall and bearing alternate, rhombic-ovate to ovate-lanceolate toothed leaves with appressed hairs on the upper and lower surfaces. The leaves average 1"–2" long and ¾"–1" wide. The ¼" flowers are arranged in globose heads, followed by round ¼" fruits that ripen red.

Bloom Season: All year

Habitat/Range: Pinelands, hammock margins, and disturbed sites of the South Florida mainland and the Monroe County Keys through the neotropics

Comments: *Varronia* honors Roman scholar and writer Marcus Terentius Varro (116–27 BC).. The name *globosa* alludes to the nearly spherical heads of flowers. This state-listed endangered species is cherished by gardeners because butterflies are a constant sight around the flowers and birds feast on the red fruits.

COASTAL SEAROCKET

Cakile lanceolata (Willd.) O. E. Schulz
Mustard family (Brassicaceae)

Description: Herbaceous, much-branched annual with toothed or deeply lobed, oblong-elliptic to linear-oblanceolate leaves averaging 2"–3" long and ½"–1" wide. The 4-petaled, ½" flowers are in lax racemes and produce narrowly linear pods that are explosively dehiscent.

Bloom Season: All year

Habitat/Range: Coastal beaches of Florida, the Bahamas, and Mexico south to South America

Comments: *Cakile* is an Arabic name originally applied to cardamon (*Elettaria cardamomum*). The name *lanceolata* is descriptive of the lance-shaped leaves, which are commonly cooked and eaten in parts of its range. Another common name is ocean arugula, and the name searocket originated from roquette, a French name given to arugula (*Eruca vesicaria*). In the Caribbean it is often cooked with pork and is commonly called pork bush. It is the namesake for the Florida Native Plant Society's Sea Rocket Chapter in Brevard County.

LIMBER CAPER OR BAYLEAF CAPERTREE

Cynophalla flexuosa (L.) J. Presl
(Also *Capparis flexuosa* [L.] L.)
Mustard family (Brassicaceae)

Description: Shrub or small tree to about 12' tall with long, flexible branches lined with oblong to obovate alternate leaves averaging 1"–2½" long and ¾"–1½" wide. Showy, fragrant, short-lived flowers consist mostly of numerous stamens. Linear pods split open to reveal white seeds embedded in red pulp.

Bloom Season: February to October

Habitat/Range: Hammocks and coastal scrub from Volusia and Collier Counties south along the coasts to the Florida Keys, West Indies, and tropical America

Comments: *Cynophalla* translates to "dog penis," for the shape of the fruits, proving that Bohemian botanist Jan Svatopluk Presl (1791–1849) had a sense of humor when he created the genus in 1825. The name *flexuosa* refers to the bends in the branches. Native-plant enthusiasts cultivate the shrub for its attractive flowers and as a larval host plant of the Florida white butterfly.

JAMAICAN CAPERTREE

Quadrella jamaicensis (Jacq.) J. Presl
(Also *Capparis cynophallophora* L., misapplied)
Mustard family (Brassicaceae)

Description: Small tree to about 14' tall with a dense crown of alternate, elliptic-oblong leaves. The flowers are nocturnal, opening white and later turning light pink then fading to dark pink. Linear-cylindric pods.

Bloom Season: March to July

Habitat/Range: Coastal habitats from Brevard and Pinellas Counties south through the Florida Keys, Cuba, Jamaica, and Central America

Comments: *Quadrella* alludes to the square perianth. The name *jamaicensis* means "of Jamaica," where it was first collected and later described in 1760 by Austrian botanist Nikolaus Joseph von Jacquin (1727–1817). It is also called black willow, dog caper, and zebrawood in the West Indies. The flowers are pollinated by sphinx moths that transfer pollen on their wings. The pickled flower buds of the related Mediterranean capertree (*Capparis spinosa*) are the capers of commerce used in salads and cooking.

BARBWIRE CACTUS
Acanthocereus tetragonus (L.) Hummelinck
Cactus family (Cactaceae)

Description: Vine-like cactus with 3- or 4-angled stems armed with regularly spaced clusters of 3–5 sharp spines. Stems measure 2"–3" wide and may reach 12' or more in length. The heavily perfumed nocturnal flowers are about 4" wide and produce red, ovoid, edible fruits to about 2" wide.

Bloom Season: May to August

Habitat/Range: Dry coastal hammocks from Lee and St. Lucie Counties south along both coasts to the Florida Keys, West Indies, Texas, and Mexico south to northern South America

Comments: *Acanthocereus* combines "thorn" with *Cereus*, a cactus genus. The name *tetragonus* relates to the 4-angled stems, which may also be 3-angled. The species is also called triangle cactus and dildo cactus. This state-listed threatened species can form impenetrable thickets of stems in coastal hammocks, sometimes reaching into the lower canopy of trees. In the Upper Florida Keys, the critically imperiled Key Largo woodrat may chew the fleshy portions of the stems down to the central core. Unfortunately, the flowers are seldom seen because they open late at night in the presence of dense, intolerable swarms of salt marsh mosquitoes.

INDIAN RIVER PRICKLY-APPLE
Harrisia fragrans Small ex Britton & Rose
Cactus family (Cactaceae)

Description: Columnar or clambering cactus with ribbed, stems 6'–16' long, lined with clusters of sharp, ½"–¾" spines. Fragrant, nocturnal flowers measure 4" across and produce 2", red to orange-red, globose fruits.

Bloom Season: May to October

Habitat/Range: Endemic to coastal habitats from Volusia County south along Florida's east coast to the Florida Keys

Comments: *Harrisia* honors British botanist William Harris (1860–1920), director of Public Gardens and Plantations of Jamaica. The name *fragrans* alludes to the fragrant flowers. This is both a federal- and state-listed endangered species. Botanist John Kunkel Small (1869–1938) wrote in 1932 that birds are "ravenously fond of the seeds." *Harrisia simpsonii* was once separated as a distinct species based mostly on the prominently ridged, as opposed to smooth, floral tube but has been sunk under synonymy with this species. The federal- and state-listed endangered *Harrisia aboriginum* is endemic to Manatee, Sarasota, and Lee Counties on Florida's southwest coast and differs from this species principally by its yellow fruits.

OLD MAN CACTUS OR WILD FIG
Pilosocereus millspaughii (Britton) Byles & G. D. Rowley
(Also *Cephalocereus millspaughii* Britton)
Cactus family (Cactaceae)

Description: Columnar cactus to 12' tall or more with ribbed stems lined with clusters of sharp spines and dense tufts of white, shaggy hairs (aging gray) on the flowering areoles. The 2"-wide flowers have a subtle odor of garlic. The ovoid fruits are bluish in color.

Bloom Season: June to August

Habitat/Range: Mixed mangrove-buttonwood and hardwood forests of Key Largo in the Upper Florida Keys, the Bahamas, and Cuba

Comments: *Pilosocereus* translates to "shaggy wax candle," for the long, shaggy, silken hairs on the areoles and the waxy, upright stems. The name *millspaughii* honors botanist Charles Frederick Millspaugh (1854–1923). This critically imperiled species was first discovered on Key Largo in 1992 by botanist Joe O'Brien (1964–) and identified as *Pilosocereus bahamensis*, but that name was later placed under synonym with the widespread *Pilosocereus polygonus*. Florida International University taxonomist Alan Franck (1980–) believes it is *Pilosocereus millspaughii*, which it most closely resembles. The flowers open at night and close the following morning.

KEY TREE CACTUS

Pilosocereus robinii (Lem.) Byles & G. D. Rowley)
Cactus family (Cactaceae)

Description: Columnar cactus with green to grayish-green stems to 12' tall or more with stout, usually 10-ribbed stems ranging 3"–4" in diameter and lined with vertical rows of clustered, sharp spines. Flowers are about 2" across, opening at night and closing by midmorning.

Bloom Season: April to October

Habitat/Range: Coastal hammocks of the Florida Keys, Cuba, and Hispaniola

Comments: French botanist Charles Antoine Lemaire (1800–1871) described this species in 1864 to honor Frenchman Charles Philippe Robin (1821–1885), who first discovered it in Cuba. It is both federal- and state-listed endangered due to its restricted range and rarity in Florida. The flowers smell strongly of garlic and attract beetles as pollinators. Fairchild Tropical Botanic Garden is assisting in reintroducing this species in the Florida Keys, and there are successful outplantings on Key Largo and Windley Key.

FLORIDA TREMA

Trema floridanum Britton ex Small
Hemp family (Cannabaceae)

Description: Tree to 18' tall with horizontal branches and inequilateral, broadly ovate to elliptic-ovate, rough leaves with toothed margins, each averaging 2"–3" long 1½"–2" wide. Clusters of axillary, ⅛" flowers are followed by orange ⅛" fruits.

Bloom Season: All year

Habitat/Range: Pinelands, hammock margins, roadsides, and disturbed sites from Sarasota, Lee, and Hendry Counties south through the Florida Keys, Mexico, and Central America

Comments: *Trema* is Latin for "to quiver," alluding to the leaves of some species that quiver in the wind. The name *floridanum* means "of Florida," where it was first collected and later described in 1903 by American botanist Nathaniel Lord Britton (1859–1934). It had been referred to as *Trema micranthum*, but that is a non-native introduced species found around Lake Okeechobee. The genus *Trema* has been previously placed in the Ulmaceae (Elm family) and the Celtidaceae (Hackberry family).

WEST INDIAN TREMA
Trema lamarckianum (Schult.) Bloom
Hemp family (Cannabaceae)

Description: Shrub or small tree to 12' tall with roughly pubescent, ovate leaves that are mostly 1"–1¾" long and ½"–¾" wide. Clusters of ⅛" flowers are followed by round, ⅛" pink fruits.

Bloom Season: All year

Habitat/Range: Pinelands, hammock margins, roadsides, and disturbed sites of Collier, Miami-Dade, and Monroe (mainland and Keys) Counties to the West Indies

Comments: The name *lamarckianum* honors noted French botanist Jean-Baptiste Lamarck (1744–1829). This is a state-listed endangered species that colonizes disturbed sites, especially roadsides and canal banks. In the Bahamas it is called pain-in-the-back, in reference to medicinal uses for back pain. A decoction from the bark is also used medicinally in the Bahamas to increase female fertility and to relieve colds and asthma. Birds are fond of the fruits of both *Trema* species. This species is far less common in Florida than Florida trema.

WEST INDIAN FALSE BOXWOOD
Gyminda latifolia (Sw.) Urb.
Staff-tree family (Celastraceae)

Description: Dioecious, much-branched tree with 4-angled branches and bright green, ovate to elliptic-obovate leaves ¾"–1½" long and ½"–1" wide. The 4-lobed white flowers are in axillary clusters and measure about ¼" across.

Bloom Season: Mostly March to October

Habitat/Range: Coastal hammocks of Miami-Dade County and the Monroe County Keys, West Indies, and southern Mexico

Comments: *Gyminda* is an anagram of the genus *Myginda*, created in 1788 by botanist Olof Peter Swartz (1760–1818) to honor eighteenth-century German nobleman and botanist Francis von Mygind. It was named *Gyminda grisebachii* in 1891 by botanist Charles Sprague Sargent (1841–1927). The name *latifolia* means "broad leaved." This state-listed endangered species is quite uncommon in Florida, with sporadic populations in the Florida Keys.

COCO PLUM
Chrysobalanus icaco L.
Coco Plum family (Chrysobalanaceae)

Description: Spreading shrub or tree with broadly elliptic alternate leaves 1"–2" long and wide. The 5-lobed flowers are about ¼" wide with purple, pink, or white oval fruits averaging ¾"–1" wide.

Bloom Season: All year

Habitat/Range: Hammocks, wooded swamps, pinelands, and beaches from coastal Central Florida across southern Florida into the Florida Keys, West Indies, and Mexico south to eastern South America

Comments: *Chrysobalanus* means "golden acorn," alluding to the yellow fruits of the type species. The name *icaco* comes from *hicaco*, the indigenous Taino name for the plant in Hispaniola. The fruits are edible and have been described as tasting like marshmallows; the seed kernel tastes like almonds. The dried, oily seeds can be strung on sticks and burned like candles. Plants with purple fruits produce red new growth; those with white fruits have pale green new growth.

GOPHER APPLE
Geobalanus oblongifolius Michx.
(Also *Licania michauxii* Prance)
Coco Plum family (Chrysobalanaceae)

Description: Rhizomatous perennial typically only 6"–8" tall with new stems arising from the rhizome tips, sometimes forming large colonies. Oblanceolate to narrowly oblong leaves reach 2"–3" long and ½"–1" wide. Flowers measure ⅜" wide and are in terminal clusters. The oval, 1" fruits ripen white, sometimes blushed with pink.

Bloom Season: March to August

Habitat/Range: Sandhills, scrubby flatwoods, and pinelands from South Carolina to Louisiana south throughout mainland Florida and on Big Pine Key in the Lower Florida Keys

Comments: *Geobalanus* means "earth acorn," relating to the fruits being developed near the ground. The name *oblongifolius* alludes to the oblong leaves. The common name relates to the edible fruits being produced at eye level to a hungry gopher tortoise. Florida Atlantic University professor Daniel F. Austin (1944–2015) described the fruits as tasting "like a new plastic shower curtain smells."

BUTTONWOOD
Conocarpus erectus L.
Combretum family (Combretaceae)

Description: Rough-barked tree to about 40' tall with alternate, lanceolate leaves 1½"–4" long and ½"–1" wide, either green or covered with silvery pubescence. Tiny flowers are clustered in ⅜" globose heads on branched racemes.

Bloom Season: All year

Habitat/Range: Coastal hammocks, mangroves, and pinelands of Central and South Florida, the Bahamas, tropical America, and Africa

Comments: *Conocarpus* is Greek and refers to the cone-like heads of fruits. The name *erectus* means "upright." A booming charcoal industry was centered on buttonwood trees in southern Florida back in the early 1900s, and it was a favored wood for smoking fish and meats. Native orchids, ferns, and bromeliads are often found growing on the trunks and limbs of this tree. A form with dense, silvery pubescence on the leaves is called "silver buttonwood" but has no botanical standing. Both forms are sold as landscape trees.

WHITE MANGROVE
Laguncularia racemosa (L.) C. F. Gaertn.
Combretum family (Combretaceae)

Description: Tree to 40' tall with opposite, leathery, oblong to obovate leaves 1¼"–2" long and ¾"–1¼" wide with 2 glands on the petiole. Tiny glands are visible on the lower leaf surface. White to yellowish flowers are about ⅜" long.

Bloom Season: All year

Habitat/Range: Mangrove forests and coastal hammocks from Levy and St. Johns Counties south along both coasts of Florida through the Florida Keys, West Indies, tropical America, and tropical West Africa

Comments: *Laguncularia* is a fanciful allusion to the fruits being shaped like a flask. The name *racemosa* relates to the racemes of flowers. Bark extracts have shown to slow the progression of certain tumors. The dense wood is used for pilings and to smoke fish and meats. A leaf tea is brewed in the Caribbean as a tonic and to treat skin diseases.

OYSTER PLANT
Tradescantia spathacea Sw.
Spiderwort family (Commelinaceae)

Description: Herbaceous perennial easily identifiable by its rosette of lanceolate leaves that are green above and bright purple below. The fleshy leaves average 8"–12" long and 1½"–2" wide. Small white, axillary flowers are surrounded by a pair of purple bracts.

Bloom Season: All year

Habitat/Range: Invasive along hammock margins, disturbed sites, and residential areas of central and southern Florida. Native to tropical America.

Comments: *Tradescantia* honors famed British gardeners and plant explorers John Tradescant (1577–1638) and his son (1608–1662) of the same name. The name *spathacea* refers to the broad, sheathing, spathe-like bracts surrounding the flowers. This is a Category I invasive species, often invading natural habitats from discarded landscape plants. Along with being weedy in landscapes, it can sometimes be found growing on trees, on rock walls, and in rain gutters. Another common name is Moses-in-the-cradle.

BOLDINGH'S DODDER
Cuscuta boldinghii Urb.
Morning-Glory family (Convolvulaceae)

Description: Herbaceous, parasitic, leafless vine with very thin, orange to orangish-yellow stems that attach to leaves of grasses and other plants. Clustered, 5-lobed flowers measure about ³⁄₁₆" wide.

Bloom Season: February to September

Habitat/Range: Parasitic on herbs and low shrubs of the Florida Keys, Greater Antilles, and Mexico south through Central America

Comments: *Cuscuta* was taken from an Arabic word, *kusuta*, meaning "a tangled wisp of hair," alluding to the stems. The name *boldinghii* honors Netherlands botanist Isaäc Boldingh (1879–1938), who published *The Flora of the Dutch West Indies Islands* in 1909. This critically imperiled species is known from Upper Matecumbe Key and Big Pine Key but may occur elsewhere. It most commonly parasitizes *Sida* species growing along mowed roadsides and resembling patches of orange angel hair pasta. The stems of this species are thinner than the unrelated and more common lovevine (*Cassytha filiformis*).

FIVEANGLED DODDER
Cuscuta pentagona Engelm.
Morning-Glory family (Convolvulaceae)

Description: Herbaceous, parasitic, leafless vine with slender, loosely matted orange stems that attach to leaves of grasses and other plants. The tips on the 5 triangular corolla lobes are acute.

Bloom Season: All year

Habitat/Range: Parasitic on herbs and low shrubs from Massachusetts to Washington south through Florida, West Indies, and Mexico

Comments: The name *pentagona* relates to the 5-angled flowers. Native tribes in the American West used the stems of dodders to predict whether their suitors were sincere. Other tribes likened the parasitic vines to "women without children" and ate the plant as a contraceptive. In the neotropics, dodders are used medicinally to treat jaundice, dysentery, severe diarrhea, tuberculosis, and as a bath for malnourishment. Most all of the orange, leafless vines you see while traveling through the Florida Keys will be the unrelated lovevine (*Cassytha filiformis*).

FLATGLOBE DODDER
Cuscuta umbellata Kunth
Morning-Glory family (Convolvulaceae)

Description: Herbaceous, parasitic, leafless vine with slender orangish stems attached to its host plant. Flowers are in umbels, 3–7 in number, with the corolla lobes at least as long as the tube. The flowers measure about ¼" wide with narrow, acute-tipped corolla lobes.

Bloom Season: All year

Habitat/Range: Mostly coastal habitats across the southern United States, West Indies, and tropical America

Comments: The name *umbellata* alludes to the umbels of flowers. This species parasitizes *Portulaca, Atriplex,* and *Sesuvium,* which are all included in this guide. The plant photographed was parasitizing *Portulaca rubricaulis* on Lower Matecumbe Key. A fourth species, *Cuscuta americana,* also occurs in the Florida Keys, and there are ten species native to Florida. In Cuba this species is called *bejuco fideo,* or noodle vine, and in Venezuela it is known as *enreda cotorra,* or parrot catcher, because these birds are easy to catch when entangled in the stems.

GRISEBACH'S DWARF MORNING-GLORY

Evolvulus grisebachii Peter
Morning-Glory family (Convolvulaceae)

Description: Herbaceous perennial with hairy, ground-hugging stems lined with ovate leaves covered with long, white, shaggy hairs. The leaves average ⅜"–½" long and ¼"–⅜" wide. Flowers are about ½" wide.

Bloom Season: All year

Habitat/Range: Pine rocklands of Big Pine Key in the Lower Florida Keys and in Cuba

Comments: *Evolvulus* means "to unroll," alluding to the non-twining growth habit. The name *grisebachii* honors German botanist and professor August Heinrich Rudolf Grisebach (1814–1879), who authored his *Flora of the British West Indies Islands* in 1864. This species was described in 1891 by botanist Albert Peter (1853–1937). The best place to see this critically imperiled, state-listed endangered species is along rocky road swales that bisect pine rockland habitat in the National Key Deer Refuge on Big Pine Key. The lilliputian Key deer are a bonus.

SILVER DWARF MORNING-GLORY

Evolvulus sericeus Sw.
Morning-Glory family (Convolvulaceae)

Description: Herbaceous perennial with thin, ascending or decumbent stems to 12" long. Leaves are linear to narrowly elliptic, ½"–1" long and ¼"–⅜" wide, covered with fine, silky hairs. Flowers are about ⅜" wide.

Bloom Season: April to October

Habitat/Range: Pinelands, wet flatwoods, and roadsides across the southern United States, West Indies, and tropical America

Comments: The name *sericeus* means "silky," alluding to the silky pubescence covering the stems and leaves. Botanist Olof Peter Swartz (1760–1818) first described this species in 1788 from plants collected in Jamaica. This species is used in Mexico to treat burns and was called *havay ak*, or "leprosy vine," by the Mayans. On Big Pine Key it is often found growing in association with Grisebach's dwarf morning-glory (*Evolvulus grisebachii*), but they are decidedly different in growth habit. Some members of this genus are popular garden subjects.

MOONFLOWER OR MOONVINE
Ipomoea alba L.
Morning-Glory family (Convolvulaceae)

Description: Aggressive, twining vine with alternate, somewhat heart-shaped leaves that may be 3- 5-lobed and average 3"–5" long with an equal width. The flowers reach about 4" wide and are either single or sometimes with several flowers in cymes.

Bloom Season: All year

Habitat/Range: Commonly seen blanketing shrubs and trees along forest margins from northern peninsular Florida south to the Florida Keys. Pantropical.

Comments: *Ipomoea* is Greek for "wormlike" and relates to the twining stems of most species. The name *alba* refers to the white flowers. The flowers emit a pungent nocturnal fragrance and are visited by sphinx moths before the flowers close shortly after sunrise. This and other morning-glories in Florida are larval host plants of the pink-spotted hawk moth. Bats visit the flowers for nectar in parts of its range, but all species of Florida bats are insect eaters.

BEACH MORNING-GLORY
Ipomoea imperati (Vahl) Griseb.
Morning-Glory family (Convolvulaceae)

Description: Trailing perennial vine, rooting at the nodes, with fleshy, oblong or ovate leaves averaging 2"–3" long and 1½"–2" wide (entire or with 3–5 lobes). Axillary, solitary flowers are about 2½" across.

Bloom Season: All year

Habitat/Range: Beaches and rocky coastal habitats along both coasts of Florida; tropical, subtropical, and warm temperate coastlines worldwide

Comments: The name *imperati* is believed to be from the Latin *imperatus*, for "ruler," or "emperor." In the Caribbean an extract from the roots is used to treat venereal disease and dysentery. The plant is called *liane manger cochon* (hog-food vine) in Haiti and *puerco de costa* (coastal pig vine) in Puerto Rico. It shares coastlines in Florida with railroad vine (*Ipomoea pes-caprae*), and both species rely on ocean currents to disperse their seeds. The type specimen was collected near Naples, Italy, in 1692.

HAVANA CLUSTERVINE
Jacquemontia havanensis (Jacq.) Urb.
Morning-Glory family (Convolvulaceae)

Description: Herbaceous, twining vine (woody near the base) with alternate, elliptic or ovate to linear leaves, averaging ¾"–1½" long and ¼"–½" wide. The 5-lobed flowers are about ¾" wide.

Bloom Season: All year

Habitat/Range: Coastal hammock margins of the Florida Keys, the Bahamas, and Greater Antilles.

Comments: *Jacquemontia* honors French botanist Victor Jacquemont (1801–1832), who undertook a scientific expedition to India in 1828 to collect plants for the Museum National d'Histoire Naturelle but succumbed to a tropical disease. The name *havanensis* means "of Havana," near where it was first collected in 1767 by Austrian botanist Nikolaus Joseph von Jacquin (1727–1817) and described as *Convolvulus havanensis*. In Florida this critically imperiled, state-listed endangered species is known from just a few isolated populations on Key Largo and Bahia Honda. Two other very similar white-flowered native species, *Jacquemontia curtissii* and *J. reclinata*, occur on the southern Florida mainland.

BASTARD COPPERLEAF
Acalypha chamaedrifolia (Lam.) Müll. Arg.
Spurge family (Euphorbiaceae)

Description: Prostrate herbaceous perennial with many branches from a woody taproot. Ovate to lanceolate leaves are alternate with crenate-dentate margins, reaching 1" long and ½" wide. Tiny, white flowers are borne along a thickened, erect spike.

Bloom Season: March to October

Habitat/Range: Pinelands of Hillsborough, Martin, Miami-Dade, and Monroe (mainland and Keys) Counties and West Indies

Comments: *Acalypha* is the Greek name for a nettle, which some species resemble. The name *chamaedrifolia* refers to "leaves resting on the ground." In the Monroe County Keys this species is only known from Big Pine Key within the National Key Deer Refuge, but it is also recorded from Elliott Key (Miami-Dade County) within Biscayne National Park. It was first described as *Croton chamaedrifolius* by French naturalist Jean-Baptiste Antoine Pierre de Monnet de Lamarck (1744–1829), who was an early proponent of biological evolution.

TREAD SOFTLY OR STINGING NETTLE
Cnidoscolus stimulosus (Michx.) Engelm. & A. Gray
Spurge family (Euphorbiaceae)

Description: Herbaceous perennial with leaves and stems covered with stinging hairs. The leaves typically have 3–5 irregular lobes and average 3"–4" long and wide. The flowers are about ½" wide.

Bloom Season: All year

Habitat/Range: Pinelands, beaches, sandhills, and scrub of the southeastern United States

Comments: *Cnidoscolus* is Greek for "nettle" and "prickle." The name *stimulosus* means "stimulating," with obvious reference to the stinging hairs. Contact with the hairs will cause intense burning pain followed by a red rash, but contact can also cause difficulty breathing, tightness in the chest, and swelling of the mouth. Use sticky tape to remove any remaining hairs, then wash with soap and water. The leaves and roots can be boiled and eaten, and an herbal leaf tea was brewed by early settlers in Florida "to give a man courage," with sexual implications. The powdered root is available in capsule form for prostate and urinary health. The sap was also mixed with the ground roots of *Smilax* and whiskey or gin to increase sexual potency in men. It is one of many larval host plants of the echo moth.

SAND CROTON

Croton arenicola Small
(Also *Croton glandulosus* L. var. *septentrionalis*
Müll. Arg.)
Spurge family (Euphorbiaceae)

Description: Herbaceous annual, 6"–18" tall, with ovate to elliptic-ovate, ½"–1" toothed leaves covered with white, stellate hairs. Female flowers are arranged below the male flowers.

Bloom Season: April to December

Habitat/Range: Endemic to pinelands and dunes of southern Florida

Comments: *Croton* is a Greek word for a tick, alluding to the similarity of the seeds to one of the bloodsucking parasites. The name *arenicola* is Latin for "sand dweller," relating to species' sandy habitats. This species was first described by botanist Carolus Linnaeus (1707–1778) in 1753 as *Croton glandulosus* but was changed to *Croton arenicola* in 1905 by botanist John Kunkel Small (1869–1938). That name has recently been resurrected from synonymy with *Croton glandulosus* var. *septentrionalis*, which ranges across the midwestern and eastern United States.

PINELAND CROTON OR GRANNYBUSH

Croton linearis Jacq.
Spurge family (Euphorbiaceae)

Description: Woody shrub, rarely reaching 6' tall, with narrowly linear, aromatic, alternate leaves on densely pubescent twigs. The leaves average 1"–1½" long and ¼"–⅜" wide. Male and female flowers are produced on separate plants and average ³⁄₁₆" wide. Fruits are 3-parted capsules.

Bloom Season: All year

Habitat/Range: Pinelands from St. Lucie County south to the Florida Keys and West Indies

Comments: The name *linearis* is descriptive of the linear leaves. The common name grannybush originates from the plant's long history in Jamaica and the Bahamas as an herbal leaf tea to treat rheumatism in elderly women. It was also used medicinally by early settlers in Florida to treat colds, fever, and "women's problems." It is a larval host plant of the rare Florida leafwing and Bartram's scrub-hairstreak butterflies in southern Florida and is sometimes grown as a landscape plant by native-plant enthusiasts.

GRACEFUL SANDMAT
Euphorbia hypericifolia L.
(Also *Chamaesyce hypericifolia* [L.] Millsp.)
Spurge family (Euphorbiaceae)

Description: Herbaceous annual with erect stems and opposite, oblong-lanceolate, glabrous leaves with finely toothed margins and an asymmetric base. Leaves average ¾"–1" long and ⅜"–½" wide. Tiny white to pinkish flowers are in round clusters. All parts exude milky sap when broken.

Bloom Season: All year

Habitat/Range: Open disturbed areas of the southern United States through the neotropics

Comments: *Euphorbia* honors Trojan War hero Euphorbus, physician to King Juba II of the ancient kingdom of Numidia in northwest Africa. The name *hypericifolia* relates to the similarity of the leaves to a *Hypericum* (Clusiaceae). This species is common in residential landscapes and disturbed natural areas. It is regarded as native in the *Atlas of Florida Plants* but the *Flora of North America* alludes to it being native to the new-world tropics and adventive in the United States.

COASTAL BEACH SANDMAT
Euphorbia mesembrianthemifolia Jacq.
Spurge family (Euphorbiaceae)

Description: Shrubby perennial to about 36" tall but usually half that height, with glabrous, opposite, ovate to elliptic leaves reaching about ½" long and ¼" wide. Small flowers appear in the upper leaf axils.

Bloom Season: All year

Habitat/Range: Beach dunes and saline flats from Levy and Flagler Counties south along both Florida coasts to the Florida Keys, West Indies, Bermuda, Mexico, and coastal Central America

Comments: The cumbersome name *mesembri-anthemifolia* (originally published with a spelling error) alludes to its leaves resembling those of a *Mesembryanthemum* (Aizoaceae). The species was first described in 1760 by Austrian physician and botanist Nikolaus Joseph von Jacquin (1727–1817), who collected specimens near Cartagena, Colombia. This is an attractive plant of frontline dunes and other coastal habitats but is practically unknown in cultivation except for beach dune restoration projects. It is called coast spurge in the Bahamas.

SOUTHERN FLORIDA SANDMAT
Euphorbia pergamena Small
Spurge family (Euphorbiaceae)

Description: Herbaceous perennial with prostrate or ascending stems lined with opposite, oblong to ovate leaves ¼"–⅜" long and half as wide. The leaves are glabrous on the lower surface, slightly hairy above, with an asymmetrical base. The red-centered white flowers are axillary and measure about ¹⁄₁₆" wide.

Bloom Season: All year

Habitat/Range: Pinelands of Miami-Dade County, Collier County, and Big Pine Key in Monroe County, Cuba, and Hispaniola

Comments: The name *pergamena* is Latin for "parchment" and is how, in 1898, botanist John Kunkel Small (1869–1938) described the leaf texture. This is a state-listed threatened species due to its limited range and habitat in southern Florida. Although the flowers are tiny, the bright white color makes them quite noticeable. The plant is also called rockland spurge. Look for it in cleared firebreaks and trail margins on Big Pine Key.

BROWNE'S INDIAN ROSEWOOD
Dalbergia brownei (Jacq.) Schinz
Pea family (Fabaceae)

Description: Sprawling or climbing shrub with long, ropelike branches and single, ovate to elliptic leaflets measuring 2"–4" long and 1"–1¾" wide. The flowers are produced in short, axillary racemes, producing 1½" oblong to linear-oblong seedpods.

Bloom Season: April to June

Habitat/Range: Coastal hammocks and mangrove-buttonwood associations in Miami-Dade County and the Monroe County Keys into tropical America

Comments: *Dalbergia* was created in 1882 by the son of famed Swedish botanist Carolus Linnaeus (1707–1778), honoring Swedish botanist Nils Dalberg (1730–1820). The name *brownei* honors Irish naturalist and physician Patrick Browne (1720–1790), who explored Jamaica. The flower buds accompany the new growth, developing quickly and then bursting open all at once. A flowering plant is striking, but the flowers are very short-lived. Bees visit the flowers. Some species produce valuable timber that is sold as cocobolo and rosewood.

COINVINE
Dalbergia ecastaphyllum (L.) Taub.
Pea family (Fabaceae)

Description: Climbing or trailing shrub with very long branches and single, ovate to elliptic, dull green leaflets measuring 2"–4" long and 1½"–2½" wide. The flowers are about ⅜" long; the suborbicular fruits reach about 1" across.

Bloom Season: March to September

Habitat/Range: Dunes, shell mounds, and margins of coastal forests from Hillsborough and Seminole Counties south along both coasts to the Florida Keys, West Indies, tropical America, and western tropical Africa

Comments: The name *ecastaphyllum* is Greek and relates to bearing one leaflet, a distinctive characteristic for this and other members of the genus. The common name is for the flat, round, coin-like fruits. It is used as a fish poison and medicinally to increase urine flow, to cleanse the gastrointestinal tract, and to instigate menstruation. It is a larval host plant of the statira sulphur.

WHITE LEADTREE
Leucaena leucocephala (Lam.) de Wit
Pea family (Fabaceae)

Description: Tree to 15' tall with alternate, bipinnate leaves bearing 4–9 pairs of lanceolate, pointed, inequilateral leaflets ⁵⁄₁₆"–½" long and about ⅛" wide. Globose flower heads are about 1" across followed by flat, linear, clustered pods to 5" long and ½" wide.

Bloom Season: All year

Habitat/Range: Invasive along forest margins and disturbed sites discontinuously from the Florida Panhandle to the Florida Keys. Native to the West Indies.

Comments: *Leucaena* is a Greek word referring to white flowers. The name *leucocephala* means "white head," for the white heads of flowers of this species. This is a very weedy Category II invasive species, often forming dense stands along roads that bisect natural habitats. It is a larval host plant of the gray ministreak butterfly and is cultivated in developing countries as a fast-growing source of firewood.

WILD TAMARIND
Lysiloma latisiliquum (L.) Benth.
Pea family (Fabaceae)

Description: Deciduous tree averaging 30'–50' tall but can reach more than 100' in height. Alternate, bipinnate leaves bear 10–33 pairs of sessile, linear-oblong leaflets measuring ⁵⁄₁₆"–½" long and ⅛"–³⁄₁₆" wide. Flowers are in globose heads to about 1" across. The pods are linear-oblong, 3"–4" long and 1"–1¼" wide, often wavy.

Bloom Season: April to November

Habitat/Range: Hammocks and pinelands in Indian River, Lee, Collier, Miami-Dade, the Monroe County mainland and Keys, West Indies, Mexico, and Central America

Comments: *Lysiloma* refers to the separation of the pod valves from the margins. The name *latisiliquum* alludes to the broad pods. This is an excellent tree to attract warblers, vireos, gnatcatchers, and flycatchers that feast on small moth caterpillars, butterfly larvae, young thorn bugs, and other insects. It is a larval host plant of the large orange sulphur, mimosa yellow, and Cassius blue butterflies. The 111'-tall national champion wild tamarind was in Castellow Hammock (Miami-Dade County) but was felled by Hurricane Andrew in 1992.

JAMAICAN DOGWOOD OR FISHPOISON TREE
Piscidia piscipula (L.) Sarg.
Pea family (Fabaceae)

Description: Deciduous tree to 40' tall or more with alternate, gray-green, odd-pinnate compound leaves with 5–9 elliptic-oblong to obovate-oval leaflets 3"–3½" long and 2"–2½" wide. Flowers are congested along the branches, typically when the tree is leafless. Papery pods cover the branches.

Bloom Season: April to June

Habitat/Range: Coastal hammocks and mangrove fringes from Pinellas and Hillsborough Counties south along the west coast to Miami-Dade County and the Monroe County Keys, West Indies, and tropical America

Comments: *Piscidia piscipula* combine to mean "to kill little fish." The leaves, twigs, and bark contain toxins that kill small fish and are used in the Caribbean as a fish poison. The common name Jamaican dogwood relates to Jamaican shipbuilders using an L-shaped piece of heartwood from the tree to strengthen the union where the deck and bow meet; this piece of wood is called a "dog." The heartwood is used medicinally to treat a variety of ailments, including to "divert evil eye" in adults; the bark is used to treat herpes in people and mange in dogs. It is a larval host plant of the hammock skipper and fulvous hairstreak.

CATCLAW BLACKBEAD
Pithecellobium unguis-cati (L.) Benth.
Pea family (Fabaceae)

Description: Spiny shrub or small tree to about 18' tall. Evenly bipinnate, alternate leaves bear 2 obovate to oblong inequilateral leaflets per pinna, each about 1"–1½" long and ¾"–⅞" wide. Globose heads of flowers are in terminal racemes, each measuring ¾"–1" wide. Pods are twisted or contorted.

Bloom Season: April to October

Habitat/Range: Hammocks in Brevard County and from Hillsborough County south along the west coast to Miami-Dade County and the Monroe County Keys; the West Indies to northern South America

Comments: *Pithecellobium* refers to the contorted seedpods of the type species. The name *unguis-cati* means "cat's claw," for the sharp spines on the branches. The species can be confused with white-flowered forms of *Pithecellobium keyense* (see "Pink Flowers" section), but the base of the individual flowers in the heads of that species are pink, and *P. unguis-cati* are green.

PARASITIC GHOSTPLANT
Voyria parasitica (Schltdl. & Cham.) Ruyters & Maas
(Also *Leiphaimos parasitica* Schltdl. & Cham.)
Gentian family (Gentianaceae)

Description: Herbaceous annual with thin, frail stems reaching 3"–6" tall, branching near the top, somewhat resembling a candelabra. The plant lacks chlorophyll. Erect flowers range from beige to off-white and measure about ⅜" long.

Bloom Season: March to October

Habitat/Range: Hammocks of Miami-Dade County and the Monroe County Keys, West Indies, Mexico, and Central America

Comments: *Voyria* is a name from French Guiana. The name *parasitica* relates to the plant deriving nutrients by parasitizing fungi in decomposing leaves, a trait called myco-heterotrophy. This state-listed endangered species forms small colonies but can be overlooked because it blends in perfectly with the leaf litter, where it is loosely rooted. In the Florida Keys it is known from Elliott Key (Miami-Dade County) and on Key Largo and Middle Torch Key in Monroe County.

INKBERRY

Scaevola plumieri (L.) Vahl
Goodenia family (Goodeniaceae)

Description: Succulent shrub forming dense mounds to 6' tall or less with dark green, fleshy, obovate to oblanceolate leaves averaging 3" long and 1½" wide. Flowers are fanlike, to about ⅝" wide, with 5 lobes. Black, globose fruits are ½" wide.

Bloom Season: All year

Habitat/Range: Beaches and coastal flats from Hillsborough and Brevard Counties south along both coasts to the Monroe County Keys, West Indies, and tropical America

Comments: *Scaevola* means "left-handed" and is symbolic of the left hand of legendary sixth-century war hero Gaius Mucius Scaevola, who burned off his right hand in an altar fire to prove his courage to Etruscan king Lars Porsena after an assassination attempt, convincing Porsena to make peace with Rome. The name *plumieri* honors French botanist and Franciscan monk Charles Plumier (1646–1704). This state-listed threatened species is also called beachberry, black soap, and mad moll.

BEACH NAUPAKA

Scaevola taccada (Gaertn.) Roxb.
Goodenia family (Goodeniaceae)

Description: Succulent, mounding shrub to 8' tall or more with light green, spatulate leaves from 4"–6" long and 2"–2½" wide (either pubescent or glabrous). The fan-shaped flowers are about ⅝" wide. Globose, ½" fruits ripen white.

Bloom Season: All year

Habitat/Range: Invasive along beaches and other coastal habitats from Hillsborough and Brevard Counties south along both coasts to the Florida Keys. Native from Hawaii to Malaya.

Comments: The name *taccada* is a vernacular name in Sri Lanka. This is a Category I invasive species made popular for coastal landscaping by the Florida nursery trade. Another common name is gullfeed because gulls feast on the fruits. In Hawaiian lore, two lovers got into an argument. The man gave her a naupaka flower back when they were full flowers, but she tore it in half; from then on, the shrub only produced half flowers.

LOVEVINE
Cassytha filiformis L.
Laurel family (Lauraceae)

Description: Parasitic vine with orange to green-ish, leafless stems that may entirely engulf the host. The stems reach about ⅛" thick with globose flowers to ⅛" wide and globose white fruits to about ¼" wide.

Bloom Season: All year

Habitat/Range: Parasitic on herbaceous and woody plants in a wide array of habitats in Taylor County and from Hillsborough and Brevard Counties south through the Florida Keys, Texas, and warm temperate and tropical regions worldwide

Comments: *Cassytha* is Greek for a parasitic plant. The name *filiformis* relates to the threadlike stems. It is very noticeable while driving through the Florida Keys, as it forms tangles of orange stems over its roadside hosts. The stems are fragrant when crushed, which is a reminder that it is closely related to fragrant-leaved plants such as redbay, laurel, and avocado. It is called lovevine for its alleged aphrodisiac properties.

LANCEWOOD
Damburneya coriacea (Sw.) Trofimov & Rohwer
(Also *Nectandra coriacea* [Sw.] Griseb.; Ocotea
coriacea [Sw.] Britton)
Laurel family (Lauraceae)

Description: Tree to 25' tall or more with smooth, light gray bark and leathery, lanceolate leaves 4"–5" long and 1½"–2" wide, fragrant when crushed. Fragrant, 6-lobed flowers are about ½" wide followed by oval or subglobose fruits to about ⅜" wide, ripening dark blue to black, atop a red or yellow calyx base.

Bloom Season: Mostly May to August

Habitat/Range: Hammocks from Volusia, High-lands, and Collier Counties south to the Florida Keys, West Indies, and Central America

Comments: *Damburneya* was created in 1838 by Constantine Samuel Rafinesque (1783–1840) to honor French merchant Louis Auguste Damburney (1722–1795), who wrote about making dyes from native plants. The name *coriacea* means "leath-ery," alluding to the leaves. Butterflies visit the flowers, and birds feast on the fruits.

MARLBERRY

Ardisia escallonioides Schltdl. & Cham.
Myrsine family (Myrsinaceae)

Description: Shrub or small tree typically 8'–14' tall with alternate, dark green, oblanceolate to elliptic leaves averaging 2"–4" long and 1"–2" wide. Fragrant flowers are in terminal clusters, each measuring about ¼" across. Fruits ripen dark purple and measure about ¼" wide.

Bloom Season: All year

Habitat/Range: Hammocks and pinelands from Citrus and Flagler Counties south through the Florida Keys, the Bahamas, Cuba, Hispaniola, Mexico, Guatemala, and British Honduras

Comments: *Ardisia* is Greek for "pointed," alluding to the pointed anthers. The name *escallonioides* alludes to its resemblance to an *Escallonia* (Escalloniaceae). The common name marlberry is a corruption of an earlier name, marbleberry. It is also called dogberry in parts of its range. The Miccosukee called it the "black tobacco seasoning tree" and added dried leaves to their tobacco. The fruits are edible and slightly tart. Small, iridescent-green halictid bees are pollinators.

MYRSINE OR COLICWOOD

Myrsine cubana A. DC.
(Also *Myrsine floridana* A. DC.; Rapanea punctata [Lam.] Lundell)
Myrsine family (Myrsinaceae)

Description: Small tree to 16' tall with alternate, glossy, oblong-obovate leaves averaging 2"–3½" long and 1"–1½" wide, mostly bunched toward the branch tips. Flowers are in small clusters that line the branches. Fruits are about ³⁄₁₆" in diameter, ripening black.

Bloom Season: November to February

Habitat/Range: Hammocks and pinelands from north-central Florida south through the Florida Keys, West Indies, and the tropical Americas

Comments: *Myrsine* is Greek for "myrtle"; the name *cubana* relates to Cuba, where the species was collected in 1829 and described in 1841 by Swiss botanist Augustin Pyramus de Candolle (1778–1841). Birds eat the small fruits of this common hammock tree. The Seminole and Miccosukee dried the leaves and added them to their tobacco to make it last longer. The common name colicwood suggests its use as a treatment for colic.

WHITE STOPPER
Eugenia axillaris (Sw.) Willd.
Myrtle family (Myrtaceae)

Description: Small tree 10'–18' tall with opposite, ovate to elliptic leaves measuring 1"–2" long and ½"–¾" wide. Flowers are in axillary clusters and are followed by round, ⅜" fruits that ripen black.

Bloom Season: May to August

Habitat/Range: Hammocks and pinelands from St. Johns and Levy Counties south through the Florida Keys and West Indies

Comments: *Eugenia* honors French-born Austrian military officer and patron of the arts François Eugene de Savoy-Carignan (1663–1736), who became Prince Eugene of Savoy. The name *axillaris* is for the axillary flowers. This species emits a faint skunky odor that is especially noticeable in hammocks on calm mornings. Early settlers ate the fruits to cure diarrhea, hence the common name stopper. The root is boiled and used as a sexual enhancer for "building up men's energy and body" and as a bath for women after childbirth.

REDBERRY STOPPER
Eugenia confusa DC.
Myrtle family (Myrtaceae)

Description: Small to medium-size tree that averages 18'–30' tall with opposite, stiff, glossy, elliptic-lanceolate leaves with an elongated apex. The leaves average 1½"–2¼" long and ¾"–1" wide, with revolute margins. Flowers are on ½" peduncles, are clustered or solitary along the stems, and produce subglobose, scarlet fruits to about ¼" wide.

Bloom Season: Mostly March to July

Habitat/Range: Coastal hammocks from Martin, Miami-Dade, and the Monroe County Keys to the West Indies

Comments: The name *confusa* relates to Swiss botanist Augustin Pyramus de Candolle (1778–1841) becoming confused when trying to describe this species because of its similarity to other members of the genus. This state-listed endangered species is found on Elliott Key, Totten Key, and Key Largo but is most common in the coastal hammocks along Biscayne Bay in Coconut Grove. The 57'-tall national champion is at Vizcaya in Coconut Grove.

SPANISH STOPPER

Eugenia foetida Pers.
Myrtle family (Myrtaceae)

Description: Slender, multi-trunk tree to 18' tall with opposite, oblong leaves averaging 1"–1½" long and ½"–¾" wide, with blunt tips. Flowers are produced along the stems and are followed by oval, ³/₁₆" fruits that ripen black.

Bloom Season: Mostly June to August

Habitat/Range: Hammocks from Manatee and Brevard Counties south into the Florida Keys and the West Indies

Comments: The name *foetida* means "stinking" or "fetid," alluding to the slightly unpleasant odor of the flowers. It is cultivated by native-plant enthusiasts and lends itself well as a tall privacy screen because of its tendency to produce multiple trunks and root suckers. The small fruits are eaten by birds. In Cuba and the Bahamas, the roots of Spanish stopper and white stopper are boiled as a tea and taken to increase sexual potency, or for "building up men's energy and body."

RED STOPPER

Eugenia rhombea (O. Berg) Krug & Urb.
Myrtle family (Myrtaceae)

Description: Tree to 18' tall or more with smooth, peeling bark and opposite, ovate to rhombic leaves measuring 1"–2" long and ½"–¾" wide and always widest above the middle. Axillary flowers are solitary or in clusters of 2–8 followed by oval fruits that ripen dark red to nearly black.

Bloom Season: April to August

Habitat/Range: Coastal hammocks of the Florida Keys (Miami-Dade and Monroe Counties), West Indies, and from Mexico south into South America

Comments: The name *rhombea* alludes to the rhombic (somewhat diamond-shaped) leaves. This handsome tree is a state-listed endangered species due to its rarity and its limited natural range in Florida, being found only in the Florida Keys. The hard, chestnut-colored wood is prized for cabinetry in the Greater Antilles; the flexible stems are used in Cuba to hang tobacco leaves to dry.

LONG-STALKED STOPPER

Mosiera longipes (O. Berg) Small
(Also *Psidium longipes* [Berg.] McVaugh)
Myrtle family (Myrtaceae)

Description: Shrub or small tree to 15' tall with opposite, glossy, elliptic-lanceolate leaves averaging about 1" long and ½" wide. Solitary flowers are on long stalks, followed by ⅜" oval fruits that ripen red.

Bloom Season: Mostly April to August

Habitat/Range: Pinelands and hammocks of Miami-Dade County and the Monroe County Keys to the Bahamas

Comments: *Mosiera* honors Charles A. Mosier (1871–1936), the first superintendent of Royal Palm State Park, which was incorporated into Everglades National Park in 1947. This state-listed threatened species is typically found as a shrub in pine rockland habitat, so look for it in the National Key Deer Refuge on Big Pine Key. It is called mangroveberry, Bahama stopper, and wild guava in the Bahamas. The fruits are eaten by birds, raccoons, opossums, Key deer, and invasive green iguanas.

SPICEWOOD OR PALE LIDFLOWER

Myrcia neopallens A. R. Lourenço & E. Lucas
(Also *Calyptranthes pallens* Griseb.)
Myrtle family (Myrtaceae)

Description: Shrub or small tree to 18' tall or more with opposite, elliptical to somewhat lanceolate leaves reaching 2½" long and 1¼" wide. The midrib is not raised above the surface of the leaf blade, and the new growth is pinkish brown in color. Fragrant ⅜" flowers are in axillary clusters and can be so numerous to cover the entire canopy. Small, oval fruits ripen dark red.

Bloom Season: March to September

Habitat/Range: Hammocks, rarely pinelands, of Miami-Dade County and the Monroe County Keys, the Bahamas, and Greater Antilles

Comments: *Myrcia* is one of the ancient Greek names for Myrtle. The name *neopallens* combines "new" and "pale," alluding to the pale undersides of the leaves and the new species name change from *Calyptranthes pallens*.

MYRTLE-OF-THE-RIVER
Myrcia zuzygium (L.) A. R. Lourenço & E. Lucas
(Also *Calyptranthes zuzygium* [L.] Sw.)
Myrtle family (Myrtaceae)

Description: Shrub or small tree to 16' tall or more with opposite, elliptic to ovate leaves reaching 2½" long and 1¼" wide with a raised midrib (not present on the previous species). Fragrant flowers are about ⅜" across in axillary clusters. Small oval fruits ripen bluish black.

Bloom Season: April to June

Habitat/Range: Hammocks of southern Miami-Dade County and the Monroe County Keys into the West Indies

Comments: The name *zuzygium* is said to be native vernacular from tribes in the West Indies. This is a state-listed endangered species, with local populations in southern Miami-Dade County on the mainland and on Elliott Key within Biscayne National Park; also in Dagny Johnson Key Largo Hammocks Botanical State Park on North Key Largo (Monroe County). Birds feed on the fruits and are the likely vectors to have brought seeds of this and many other tropical trees to South Florida during spring migration from the Greater Antilles or the Bahamas

BRACTED COLICROOT
Aletris bracteata Northr.
Asphodel family (Nartheciaceae)

Description: Herbaceous perennial forming a rosette of pale green, linear-lanceolate leaves averaging 2"–3½" long and about ⅜"–½" wide, but may be longer. Mealy, tubular, white (rarely yellow) flowers range ¼"–⅜" long, appearing along the top third of an erect scape to 12" tall or more.

Bloom Season: Mostly February to July

Habitat/Range: Pine rocklands of southern Miami-Dade and Monroe (mainland and Keys) Counties to the Bahamas

Comments: Aletris was a legendary Greek slave woman who ground grain, so the genus *Aletris* relates to the mealy texture of the flowers. The name *bracteata* alludes to the bracts that subtend the flowers. This state-listed endangered species was first described by American botany professor Alice Rich Northrop (1864–1922), best known for advocating access to nature for schoolchildren. The roots have been used to treat colic in children. It is the only member of the genus that occurs in the Florida Keys.

SMOOTH HOGWEED OR ERECT SPIDERLING
Boerhavia erecta L.
Four O'clock family (Nyctaginaceae)

Description: Diffusely branched, herbaceous annual 12"–36" tall with opposite, broadly triangular-ovate to ovate-lanceolate leaves 1"–2" long and ½"–⅝" wide. Flowers measure about ³⁄₁₆" across and are in lax, few-flowered clusters on wiry stems.

Bloom Season: May to December

Habitat/Range: Beaches, roadsides, and disturbed hammock margins across the southern United States, Bermuda, West Indies, and tropical America

Comments: *Boerhavia* honors Dutch physician and botanist Herman Boerhaave (1668–1738), who was the first medical professor to teach students at patients' bedsides. The name *erecta* means "upright." The plant is used in traditional medicines throughout its range in the American tropics, where it is also eaten as a vegetable. It produces organs at the base of the plant that store nutrients so it can survive drought and fire. The native *Boerhavia diffusa* and the non-native *Boerhavia coccinea* also occur in the Florida Keys.

GOLD COAST JASMINE
Jasminum dichotomum Vahl.
Olive family (Oleaceae)

Description: Woody, twining, high-climbing vine with mostly opposite, glossy leaves that average 1½"–3" long and ¾"–1½" wide. Very fragrant flowers are in clusters, each flower measuring about ¾" wide, producing subglobose black fruits to ¼" in diameter

Bloom Season: All year

Habitat/Range: Invasive in hammocks and urban landscapes. Native to tropical central and western Africa.

Comments: *Jasminum* is latinized from the ancient Arabic word *yasemin*, for sweetly fragrant plants. The name *dichotomum* is for the dichotomous branching habit. This is a very aggressive Category I invasive species in Florida. Jasmines are popular landscape plants, principally for their intense floral perfume. Brazilian jasmine (*Jasminum fluminense*) is another Category I invasive species in the Florida Keys with similar flowers but with leaves divided into 3 leaflets. Both species can be found invading hammocks and are difficult to control. Birds disperse the fruits.

CARTER'S ORCHID
Basiphyllaea corallicola (Small) Ames
Orchid family (Orchidaceae)

Description: Terrestrial orchid with a single leaf that measures about 2" long and ⅛" wide. The flowering stem stands 3½"–6" tall and is topped with several flower buds that rarely fully open due to cleistogamy (self-pollinated in bud).

Bloom Season: October to November

Habitat/Range: Pine rocklands and hammock margins of southern Miami-Dade County and on Big Pine Key in the Lower Florida Keys into the Bahamas

Comments: *Basiphyllaea* refers to the basal leaf. The name *corallicola* means "growing on coral," alluding to the limestone rock substrate, but actually not coral. It is a state-listed endangered species first discovered in Florida in 1903 by botanist Joel Jackson Carter (1843–1912). Due to its small stature, rarity, and short flowering season, it is exceptionally difficult to find, and discovering a plant with a fully open flower is exceptionally rare due to cleistogamy.

MICHAUX'S ORCHID
Habenaria quinqueseta (Michx.) Eaton
Orchid family (Orchidaceae)

Description: Terrestrial orchid with succulent, lanceolate basal leaves measuring up to 6" long and 1" wide, becoming smaller up the flowering stem. The flowers are spindly, with a lip divided into 3 threadlike divisions.

Bloom Season: August to January

Habitat/Range: Marshes, prairies, and wet flatwoods from South Carolina to Texas south through all of Florida

Comments: *Habenaria* means "rein," alluding to the rein-like spurs on the lip. The name *quinqueseta* means "five bristles," for the narrow portions of the calyx and corolla. The common name honors French botanist and explorer André Michaux (1746–1802), who first discovered this species in South Carolina. Michaux is mostly known for his studies of the North American flora. In the Florida Keys this orchid is found within the National Key Deer Refuge on Big Pine Key but is locally common in the proper habitat across the Florida mainland.

SOUTHERN LADIES' TRESSES
Spiranthes torta (Thunb.) Garay & H. R. Sweet
Orchid family (Orchidaceae)

Description: Terrestrial orchid 8"–18" tall with 2 or 3 narrowly linear leaves reaching 3"–8" long that are absent when flowering. Small, nodding flowers with downward-pointing lateral sepals line a terminal spike, sometimes loosely spiraling.

Bloom Season: April to July

Habitat/Range: Rocky pinelands of Palm Beach, Broward, Collier, Miami-Dade, and the Monroe County mainland and Keys, West Indies, and Central America

Comments: *Spiranthes* means "coil" and "flowers," alluding to the spiraling flower arrangement on many species. The name *torta* means "twisted," also relating to the spiraling flowers. In the Florida Keys, this critically imperiled, state-listed endangered species is found only within the National Key Deer Refuge on Big Pine Key. Of the fifteen native members of this genus in Florida, this is surprisingly the only species found in the Florida Keys.

189

KEYS PASSIONFLOWER
Passiflora multiflora L.
Passionflower family (Passifloraceae)

Description: Woody, high-climbing vine that attaches to twigs and branches with tendrils. Softly pubescent, oblong leaves averaging 2"–3" long and ¾"–1½" wide. Flowers are about ½" wide and produced in axillary clusters. The ⅜" globose fruits are dark blue.

Bloom Season: July to November

Habitat/Range: Hammocks of Elliott Key (Miami-Dade County) and the Monroe County Keys, the Bahamas, Cuba, and Hispaniola

Comments: *Passiflora* means "passion flower" or "crucifixion flower" and relates to the crucifixion of Jesus, or the Passion. The name *multiflora* alludes to the numerous flowers. In Florida, this state-listed endangered species is restricted to the Florida Keys but is sometimes cultivated by butterfly gardeners on the southern mainland to attract zebra longwing, gulf fritillary, and Julia heliconian butterflies. It is on plant lists for Dagny Johnson, John Pennekamp, and Lignumvitae Key State Parks, Crocodile Lake National Wildlife Refuge, and Elliott Key in Biscayne National Park. Mature vines can produce hundreds of blossoms, but the species has limited availability in nurseries that specialize in native plants.

ROUGEPLANT OR BLOODBERRY
Rivina humilis L.
Petiveria family (Petiveriaceae)

Description: Perennial subshrub to 6' tall with lanceolate to elliptic, glabrous or finely pubescent leaves to about 3" long and 1¼" wide. Flowers are about ³⁄₁₆" wide in terminal or axillary spikes. Fruits are about ⅛" across.

Bloom Season: All year

Habitat/Range: Hammock margins and disturbed sites throughout Florida, west to Arizona, and through the West Indies and tropical America

Comments: *Rivina* honors German professor and botanist August Quirinus Rivinus (1652–1723). The name *humilis* translates to "low growing." This species is weedy in garden settings but is culti-vated by native-plant enthusiasts. The sap from the fruit is red and stains the skin, hence the name rougeplant. If eaten, the fruits may cause numb-ness of the mouth followed by coughing, thirst, vomiting, and bloody diarrhea. The leaves and roots are even more toxic. It was formerly placed in the Phytolaccaceae, or Pokeweed family.

PENINSULA AXILFLOWER
Mecardonia acuminata (Walter) Small subsp.
peninsularis (Pennell) Rossow
Plantain family (Plantaginaceae)

Description: Herbaceous perennial with angled stems that branch near the base, with toothed leaves reaching ½"–⅝" long and about ¼" wide. The 5-lobed, tubular flowers are on long stalks, with the posterior lobes of the flower united about two-thirds of the length.

Bloom Season: April to November

Habitat/Range: Pinelands and flatwoods of central and southern Florida

Comments: *Mecardonia* honors Spanish botanist Antonio de Meca y Cardona, an eighteenth-century Spanish patron of the Barcelona Botanical Garden and Marquis of Ciutadilla. The name *acuminata* means "tapering to a long narrow point," alluding to the leaf shape. The name *peninsularis* means "growing on a peninsula," in this case, Florida. This subspecies is endemic to central and southern Florida and, in the Florida Keys, is known only from the National Key Deer Refuge on Big Pine Key.

DOCTORBUSH
Plumbago zeylanica L.
Leadwort family (Plumbaginaceae)

Description: Shrubby perennial with vine-like stems bearing alternate, elliptic-lanceolate leaves 1½"–4" long and up to 2" wide. Flower spikes are lined with tubular, 5-lobed flowers averaging ½" wide. Linear fruits are prism-shaped and cling to hair and clothing.

Bloom Season: All year

Habitat/Range: Coastal strand and open disturbed sites across the southern United States through the neotropics, Hawaii, and Southeast Asia

Comments: *Plumbago* was used by Dioscorides (AD 40–80) for a metal and a plant, which led to the common name leadwort for this plant. The name *zeylanica* means "of Ceylon," referring to modern-day Sri Lanka. Leaves or roots rubbed on the skin can cause reddening and blistering, giving rise to the Spanish names *malacara* (bad face) and *erva de diablo* (devil's herb). It is a larval host plant of the cassius blue butterfly but is seldom cultivated.

PIGEON PLUM
Coccoloba diversifolia Jacq.
Buckwheat family (Polygonaceae)

Description: Tree to 20' tall with ovate to elliptic, alternate leaves with bark that peels off in short flakes. Juvenile leaves reach 24"; mature leaves are much smaller. A distinguishing characteristic is the ocrea, which makes the petiole appear to wrap around the stem. Flowers are on slender racemes. Fruits on female trees are suborbicular, to about ⅜" wide.

Bloom Season: April to July

Habitat/Range: Hammocks of Brevard, Lee, and Hendry Counties south through the Florida Keys, West Indies, Mexico, Belize, and Guatemala

Comments: *Coccoloba* describes the fleshy hypanthium surrounding the fruits. The name *diversifolia* is for the diverse size of the leaves. Female trees can often be identified by the scratch marks on the trunk created by raccoons climbing the trees to access the fruits. The common name alludes to pigeons eating the fruits; in Cuba it is called *fruta de paloma*, or dove fruit.

SEA GRAPE

Coccoloba uvifera (L.) L.
Buckwheat family (Polygonaceae)

Description: Tree to 24' tall or more with widely spreading branches and round, red-veined leaves averaging 4"–6" long and wide. Flowers are on spikes to 6" long; females bear round, purple fruits about ½" wide.

Bloom Season: All year

Habitat/Range: Sandy coastlines from Flagler and Pasco Counties south along both coasts to the Florida Keys, West Indies, and tropical America

Comments: The name *uvifera* means "grapelike," alluding to the fruits. This is a popular landscape tree in coastal regions of Florida and is often used as a tall hedge. The fruits are used to make sea grape jelly, which tastes much like apple jelly. The wood is prized by woodworkers to make cabinets, butcher blocks, bowls, shoe lasts, and lumber for building material. Bees visit the flowers, and beekeepers place hives near thickets of trees for sea grape honey sold in marketplaces.

SEA PLUM

Coccoloba x *hybrida* Castañeda-Noa
Buckwheat family (Polygonaceae)

Description: Hybrid tree to 20' tall or more with alternate, obovate to elliptic leaves averaging 4"–8" long and 2"–4" wide. Flowers are on slender, axillary racemes. Suborbicular fruits are about ⅜" wide.

Bloom Season: April to July

Habitat/Range: Coastal hammocks of Palm Beach County and the Monroe County Keys (possibly elsewhere within the range of the parent trees)

Comments: The name *hybrida* relates to the species being a hybrid. The parents of this rare hybrid are the pigeon plum (*Coccoloba diversifolia*) and the sea grape (*Coccoloba uvifera*), but it much more resembles the pigeon plum in appearance. Hybrids may occur wherever the parent trees grow close enough together for bees to transfer pollen. It is propagated vegetatively for the South Florida nursery trade. In the Florida Keys it is known from Sugarloaf Key, perhaps elsewhere.

SEVENYEAR APPLE
Casasia clusiifolia (Jacq.) Urb.
Madder family (Rubiaceae)

Description: Dioecious shrub or small tree to 10' tall with opposite, dark green, glossy, obovate leaves 3½"–5" long and 2"–3" wide, rounded at the tip. Male flowers are in axillary clusters with flowers on females usually solitary. Ovoid to obovoid fruits reach 3" long and 1¾" wide, ripening from green to black. The pulp is black.

Bloom Season: All year

Habitat/Range: Coastal hammocks of Broward, Lee, Collier, Miami-Dade, and the Monroe County Keys, Bermuda, the Bahamas, and Cuba

Comments: *Casasia* commemorates the Spanish governor of Cuba, Luis de las Casas y Arragorri (1745–1800). The name *clusiifolia* relates to the resemblance of the leaves to a *Clusia*. The black pulp in ripe fruits resembles licorice in flavor, although Dr. Dan Austin (1943–2015), author of *Florida Ethnobotany*, considered the flavor to be "disgusting." Hummingbirds, sphinx moths, butterflies, and bees visit the fragrant flowers. The unripe fruits contain genipin, which turns black when exposed to the skin and has been widely used for tattoos and to dye clothing. It is a larval host plant of the tantalus sphinx moth.

DUNE LILYTHORN
Catesbaea parviflora Sw.
Madder family (Rubiaceae)

Description: Woody shrub 2'–6' tall with many erect branches arising from the base that are crowded with orbicular, dark green leaves that often hide the stiff, sharp thorns. The leaves average ⅜" long. Small flowers appear from the leaf axils, each with 4 pointed lobes. White, round fruits are about ⅛" wide.

Bloom Season: All year

Habitat/Range: Pine rocklands, coastal salt flats, and dunes of the Florida Keys and West Indies

Comments: *Catesbaea* honors English naturalist Mark Catesby (1679–1749). The name *parviflora* means "few flowers." This state-listed endangered species occurs from Bahia Honda State Park west to the National Key Deer Refuge on Big Pine Key. There are seventeen members of the genus found in the Bahamas, Hispaniola, and Cuba, but this is the only species native to Florida; it is known from Bahia Honda State Park and the National Key Deer Refuge on Big Pine Key.

BLACKTORCH
Erithalis fruticosa L.
Madder family (Rubiaceae)

Description: Perennial shrub or rarely a small tree to 8' tall or more with opposite, dark green, broadly obovate or elliptic-oblanceolate leaves averaging 1½"–2½" long and ¾"–1¼" wide. Flowers are about ⅜" wide and are followed by round, black, ¼" fruits.

Bloom Season: All year

Habitat/Range: Hammock margins and edges of mangroves from Martin County south along the Atlantic coast to Miami-Dade and the Monroe County Keys, West Indies, Mexico, and Central America

Comments: *Erithalis* has been interpreted as meaning "growing luxuriantly" or "very green," obviously for its growth habit and leaf color. The name *fruticosa* means "shrubby." This state-listed threatened species can be locally common, especially along trails and roads that bisect its habitat. Because the hard wood is very flammable, another common name is candlewood. Birds eat the fruits; small bees visit the flowers.

CARIBBEAN PRINCEWOOD
Exostema caribaeum (Jacq.) Roem. & Schult.
Madder family (Rubiaceae)

Description: Small tree, rarely to 16' tall, with opposite, elliptic to lanceolate leaves that average 2"–3" long and ¾"–1" wide, often wavy. The flowers have linear, recurved lobes and appear in the leaf axils, emitting a vanilla-like fragrance at night. Lustrous brown capsules are 2-valved.

Bloom Season: Periodically all year

Habitat/Range: Hammocks of Miami-Dade County (Elliott Key) and the Monroe County Keys into the West Indies, Mexico, and Central America

Comments: *Exostema* relates to the exserted stamens. The name *caribaeum* is for the Carib Indians, an indigenous people from the Lesser Antilles. This state-listed endangered species is on plant lists for Elliott Key, Key Largo, Windley Key, and Big Pine Key. It is used medicinally and is effective in combating malaria. The highly flammable wood is used for torches. Sphinx moths visit the vanilla-scented flowers after dark.

EVERGLADES VELVETSEED
Guettarda elliptica Sw.
Madder family (Rubiaceae)

Description: Shrub or rarely a small tree to 15' or more with opposite, suborbicular to oval leaves, mostly 1"–2" long and ½"–1½" wide. Fragrant flowers are white to creamy-white with 4 or 5 lobes, to about ¼" wide, followed by round, velvety, 5⁄16" fruits that ripen purplish.

Bloom Season: Mostly May to August

Habitat/Range: Hammocks and pine rocklands of Lee, Broward, Miami-Dade, and the Monroe County mainland and Keys, West Indies, and tropical America

Comments: *Guettarda* honors French physician, naturalist, mineralogist, and botanist Jean-Étienne Guettard (1715–1786), who studied the relationship between plants and soil types. The name *elliptica* references the elliptic leaves. The species is also called hammock velvetseed, but it is more commonly found in pine rockland habitat. This is a locally common shrub of pine rocklands on Long Pine Key in Everglades National Park and Big Pine Key in the Lower Florida Keys.

ROUGH VELVETSEED OR VELVETBERRY
Guettarda scabra (L.) Vent.
Madder family (Rubiaceae)

Description: Upright shrub or small tree to 20' tall or more with rough-textured, elliptic to obovate, rather stiff leaves 2"–4" long and 1"–2" wide. Fragrant, white to pinkish-white flowers measure about ¾" long. Pubescent, ovoid fruits ripen red, to about ⅜" across.

Bloom Season: Mostly May to August

Habitat/Range: Hammocks and pinelands of Lee, Palm Beach, Miami-Dade, and the Monroe County Keys, West Indies, and tropical America

Comments: The name *scabra* references the scabrous, or rough, leaf surface. Rough velvetseed is typically an erect shrub 4'–5' tall in pine rocklands, with larger leaves than the previous species. The flowers emit a sweet perfume at night to attract sphinx moths as pollinators, but butterflies and hummingbirds also visit the flowers by day. West Indian girls place flowers in their hair as perfume.

FLORIDA DIAMONDFLOWERS
Houstonia nigricans (Lam.) Fernald var. *floridana* (Standl.) Terrell
(Also *Hedyotis nigricans* [Lam.] var. *floridana* [Standl.] Wunderlin)
Madder family (Rubiaceae)

Description: Herbaceous perennial with thin, erect, ascending, or sprawling stems and opposite, sessile, filiform leaves averaging ½"–1" long and ¹⁄₁₆"–⅛" wide. Flowers are in leafy cymes, white or sometimes pink, with 4 spreading lobes to about ¼" across.

Bloom Season: All year, but mostly August to April

Habitat/Range: Pine rocklands of Miami-Dade County and the Monroe County Keys to the Bahamas

Comments: *Houstonia* honors Scottish botanist William Houstoun (1695–1733), who collected plants in the American tropics but died unexpectedly of heatstroke in Jamaica. His name is sometimes spelled Houston. The name *nigricans* means "blackish," alluding to the color of dried plants. The name *floridana* means "of Florida." In the Florida Keys it is only known from the National Key Deer Refuge on Big Pine Key.

REDGAL OR CHEESE SHRUB

Morinda royoc L.
Madder family (Rubiaceae)

Description: Shrubby perennial with long, vine-like branches and opposite, linear-lanceolate to oblanceolate leaves averaging 1½"–2½" long and ¾"–1" wide. The 5-lobed flowers are about ⅜" wide, produced in axillary heads. Fruits are globose, about ¾" wide or more, ripening yellow.

Bloom Season: All year

Habitat/Range: Hammock margins, pinelands, and disturbed sites from Hillsborough and Brevard Counties south through the Florida Keys, West Indies, and tropical America

Comments: *Morinda* is Latin for "Indian mulberry," alluding to the fruits, but may also commemorate French physician Louis Morin (1636–1715). The name *royoc* is probably based on *hoyoc*, the Mayan name for *Morinda yucatanensis*. Fully ripe fruits smell strongly of Limburger cheese. Butterflies visit the flowers, and it is a larval host plant of the pluto sphinx moth. This and other species have a wide range of medicinal uses.

BAHAMA WILD COFFEE

Psychotria ligustrifolia (Northr.) Millsp.
Madder family (Rubiaceae)

Description: Woody shrub to 6' tall with opposite, obovate or lanceolate leaves, typically 1½"–2½" long and 1"–1½" wide. The ¼" flowers are in terminal panicles followed by red, ellipsoid fruits measuring about ³⁄₁₆" long.

Bloom Season: March to June

Habitat/Range: Hammocks of Miami-Dade County, Monroe County Keys, Bermuda, the Bahamas, and the Greater Antilles

Comments: *Psychotria* means "to give life," for the plant's medicinal uses. The name *ligustrifolia* alludes to the resemblance of the leaves to a Ligustrum (Oleaceae). This state-listed endangered species is mostly found in the Monroe County Keys but has been documented in mainland Miami-Dade County. It is the most uncommon of the three species native to Florida. Butterflies and sphinx moths visit the flowers, and birds are attracted to the red fruits. Members of this genus are larval host plants of the tersa sphinx moth.

WILD COFFEE
Psychotria nervosa Sw.
Madder family (Rubiaceae)

Description: Woody shrub to 8' tall with opposite, shiny, dark green obovate or lanceolate leaves averaging 2½"–4" long and 1"–2" wide, with elevated lateral nerves. The ¼" flowers are in terminal panicles and produce red, ellipsoid fruits to about ⁵⁄₁₆" long.

Bloom Season: March to June

Habitat/Range: Hammocks, pinelands, and occasionally coastal habitats of peninsular Florida, the Florida Keys, West Indies, and tropical America

Comments: The name *nervosa* alludes to the prominent lateral nerves on the leaves. The flowers are frequented by butterflies, especially ruddy daggerwings, and the red fruits are savored by many birds, making it a choice landscape plant for semi-shady areas. Tersa sphinx moth larvae feed on the leaves. The common name wild coffee comes from it being related to coffee (*Coffea arabica*), but the seeds have no caffeine. In Mexico the seeds are ground and carried in a shirt pocket as a love charm. Crushed leaves are used medicinally to stop bleeding and are combined with other plants to treat respiratory problems, swollen feet, boils, and other maladies. The tropical American *Psychotria viridis* is an ingredient in a powerful psychoactive brew called *ayahuasca*, used by indigenous tribes in the Amazon basin.

WHITE INDIGOBERRY

Randia aculeata L.
Madder family (Rubiaceae)

Description: Woody shrub or small tree to about 10' tall, sometimes with paired axillary spines. Obovate, oblanceolate, to orbicular leaves tend to be clustered toward the branch tips and average ¾"–1" long and about ½" wide. Axillary flowers are solitary or in small clusters. Fruits ripen white and measure about ⅜" wide.

Bloom Season: All year

Habitat/Range: Pinelands and hammocks from Brevard, Pinellas, and Hillsborough Counties south along both coasts to the Florida Keys, West Indies, and tropical America

Comments: *Randia* was named to honor English botanist and apothecary Isaac Rand (1674–1743), who was the director of the Chelsea Physic Garden from 1724 to 1740. The name *aculeata* alludes to the axillary spines. Although the fruits are white, the seeds are embedded in purplish pulp, hence the common name. It is a larval host plant of the tantalus sphinx moth.

FLORIDA FALSE BUTTONWEED

Spermacoce keyensis Small
(Also *Spermacoce floridana* Urb.)
Madder family (Rubiaceae)

Description: Herbaceous annual or short-lived perennial with prostrate, angled, scabrous (rough) stems that are typically red with elliptic to elliptic-lanceolate, opposite leaves averaging ⅝"–¾" long and ⅜"–½" wide, and often purple in color or with purple margins. Flowers are ³⁄₁₆" wide, clustered in the leaf axils.

Bloom Season: All year

Habitat/Range: Open sandy or wet marl habitats of Miami-Dade and the Monroe County Keys, Texas, and the Bahamas

Comments: *Spermacoce* alludes to the calyx teeth on the fruits. The name *keyensis* means "of the Florida Keys." Botanist John Kunkel Small (1869–1938) first described this species in 1933. Other names applied to this species are *Spermacoce floridana* and *S. tenuior* var. *floridana*. It is on the plant list for Long Key State Park but probably occurs elsewhere in the Florida Keys, because it can easily be overlooked or mistaken for the related *Spermacoce prostrata*.

WOODLAND FALSE BUTTONWEED
Spermacoce remota Lam.
Madder family (Rubiaceae)

Description: Herbaceous annual or perennial with 4-angled glabrous or slightly pubescent stems and lanceolate leaves ¾"–2" long and ¼"–⅝" wide. White to pink-tipped, 4-lobed flowers are few to many in terminal and axillary heads.

Bloom Season: All year

Habitat/Range: Wet soils of flatwoods, marshes, floodplain forests, and disturbed sites from Georgia, Alabama, and Florida through the West Indies and tropical America

Comments: The name *remota* relates to the widely separated flower clusters along the stem. Leaves of many species of *Spermacoce* are used medicinally to treat conjunctivitis, gallstones, and to relieve headaches. Small bees and butterflies visit the flowers. It was described in 1792 by French naturalist Jean-Baptiste Lamarck (1744–1829), who was one of the first proponents of biological evolution. This species is somewhat weedy and is found in almost all of the parks and preserves throughout the Florida Keys.

PINELAND BUTTONWEED
Spermacoce tetraquetra A. Rich
Madder family (Rubiaceae)

Description: Herbaceous perennial, usually erect, and covered with bristly hairs. The stems are 4-angled with opposite, ovate to lanceolate hairy leaves averaging 1"–2" long and ½"–1" wide. The 4-lobed flowers are in few-flowered, terminal clusters.

Bloom Season: All year

Habitat/Range: Pinelands, rock barrens, and disturbed sites across much of Florida to the West Indies, Mexico, and Central America

Comments: The name *tetraquetra* means "with four sharp angles," relating to the stems. The coarse, bristly hairs that cover the stems and leaves of this species make it easy to identify. It is on the plant list for the National Key Deer Refuge on Big Pine Key but does not appear on plant lists for any of the state parks in the Florida Keys, although it could easily be overlooked. Bees and small butterflies visit the flowers.

SHRUBBY FALSE BUTTONWEED
Spermacoce verticillata L.
Madder family (Rubiaceae)

Description: Herbaceous perennial with erect or ascending stems that are slightly 4-angled and typically less than 10" tall. Leaves are linear to linear-lanceolate ranging ¾"–2" long and ¼"–⅜" wide. Flowers are in terminal and axillary clusters along the stem.

Bloom Season: All year

Habitat/Range: Invasive in disturbed sites, including trail margins, roadsides, and residential landscapes throughout Florida. Native to tropical America.

Comments: The name *verticillata* relates to the whorls of leaves. An infusion from the flowers is used in Brazil to relieve pain, and in Africa the roots and leaves are prepared with *Cuscuta* and *Zebrina* to treat bacterial skin infections and leprosy. It is a Category II invasive species. *Spermacoce neoterminalis*, with larger flower clusters only in the top 2 leaf axils, is known from Big Pine Key, but some botanists lump it under synonymy with this non-native species.

SEA TORCHWOOD
Amyris elemifera L.
Citrus family (Rutaceae)

Description: Tree to 16' tall with opposite to subopposite compound leaves bearing 3 (rarely 5) broadly ovate to rhombic-ovate leaflets that are fragrant when crushed. Flowers are in glabrous, terminal or axillary panicles and produce black, globose ⅜" fruits.

Bloom Season: All year

Habitat/Range: Hammocks and coastal habitats from Flagler County south along the eastern coastal counties of Florida through the Florida Keys, West Indies, and Central America

Comments: *Amyris* is Greek for "much balsam," alluding to the aromatic resin. The name *elemifera* is Greek for "bearing a fragrant gum." The common name torchwood relates to the highly flammable, resinous wood. This is a larval host plant of the giant swallowtail, Bahamian swallowtail, and the critically imperiled Schaus swallowtail. Another species, *Amyris balsamifera*, was collected once in 1925 on North Key Largo and again from "Miami" without label data. It is presumed extirpated.

BALLOON VINE OR FAUX PERSIL
Cardiospermum corindum L.
Soapberry family (Sapindaceae)

Description: Herbaceous perennial vine with ribbed stems that climbs by tendrils and bears compound leaves divided into 3 ovate, coarsely toothed leaflets. The flowers produce balloon-like, angled pods to about 1" wide. Round, hard, black seeds have a white, semicircular hilum.

Bloom Season: All year

Habitat/Range: Hammock margins of Miami-Dade and Monroe Counties (mainland and Keys). Pantropical.

Comments: *Cardiospermum* means "heart seed," alluding to the white, heart-shaped hilum on the seeds of some species. The name *corindum* is said to mean "heart of India." The common name faux persil is French for "false parsley," relating to the shape of the leaflets. Amazonian men believe bracelets made from the seeds prevent snakebite. The native *Cardiospermum microcarpum* and the non-native *C. halicacabum* also occur in the Florida Keys. They are larval host plants of the silver-banded hairstreak, Miami blue, and gray hairstreak butterflies; also the silvered prominent moth.

INKWOOD
Exothea paniculata (Juss.) Radlk.
Soapberry family (Sapindaceae)

Description: Tree to 40' tall or more with alternate, evenly pinnate compound leaves bearing 4–6 oblong to oblong-lanceolate leaflets averaging 2"–4" long and ¾"–1" wide. Flowers are in terminal and axillary panicles and produce ⅜" subglobose fruits that ripen red to dark purple.

Bloom Season: January to August

Habitat/Range: Hammocks of Volusia and Collier Counties south along the coasts through the Monroe County Keys, West Indies, and Central America

Comments: *Exothea* means "to expel" and relates to the species' separation from the genus *Melicoccus*. The name *paniculata* alludes to the panicles of flowers. The plant is also called butterbough in parts of its range. Ink was once made from the fruits, and the hard wood has been used for boat-building, marine pilings, tool handles, and railroad ties. It is a very attractive tree and deserves more use as a landscape tree in South Florida.

203

WHITE IRONWOOD

Hypelate trifoliata Sw.
Soapberry family (Sapindaceae)

Description: Tree to 18' tall or more with alternate leaves divided into 3 obovate leaflets, averaging ¾"–1¼" long and ⅝"–¾" wide. The flowers are in open panicles, each about ¼" across. Small, round fruits ripen black.

Bloom Season: May to November

Habitat/Range: Coastal hammocks of the Florida Keys and pine rocklands of Long Pine Key in Everglades National Park into the West Indies

Comments: *Hypelate* is the Greek name for butcher's broom but later used for this tree. The name *trifoliata* relates to the 3 leaflets. The genus is represented by this single state-listed endangered species, one of Florida's rarest trees. In the Florida Keys, it is on plant lists for Key Largo, Windley Key, Lignumvitae Key, and Long Key. Bees, wasps, and small butterflies visit the flowers. It is quite attractive and deserves horticultural attention as a landscape tree in South Florida.

SAFFRON PLUM

Sideroxylon celastrinum (Kunth) T. D. Penn.
(Also *Bumelia celastrina* Kunth)
Sapodilla family (Sapotaceae)

Description: Thorny shrub or small tree to about 18' tall with oblanceolate to obovate leaves clustered along the stems and thorns, reaching 1"–1½" long and ¾"–⅝" wide. Fragrant flowers are in clusters and produce small, obovoid, blue-black fruits.

Bloom Season: December to April

Habitat/Range: Coastal hammocks of Central Florida south through the Florida Keys, Texas, West Indies, and Mexico south to South America

Comments: *Sideroxylon* is Greek for "iron wood," alluding to the hard wood of members of the genus. The name *celastrinum* is Latin for "an evergreen tree." A survey conducted in 2006 revealed that a fruiting saffron plum had one of the highest visitation rates of fruit-eating birds, and many species of warblers were observed eating the flowers. The fruits are edible and sweet tasting; deer are very fond of eating the leaves.

WILLOW BUSTIC
Sideroxylon salicifolium (L.) Lam.
(Also *Bumelia salicifolia* [L.] Sw.)
Sapodilla family (Sapotaceae)

Description: Tree to 24' or more with the young growth covered with golden pubescence. The alternate leaves are oblanceolate to broadly elliptic, 2"–4" long and 1"–1¼" wide. Fragrant flowers are numerous along the branches or sometimes in leaf axils. Subglobose ¼" fruits ripen black.

Bloom Season: May to November

Habitat/Range: Hammocks from Martin, Hendry, and Collier Counties south through the Florida Keys, West Indies, and Central America

Comments: The name *salicifolium* alludes to the resemblance of the leaves to a species of *Salix* (Salicaceae), or willow. This fast-growing hammock tree sometimes invades pinelands, where it is kept shrubby, or killed, by fire. Warblers, vireos, and flycatchers have been observed consuming the flowers; thrushes, blue jays, and mockingbirds eat the ripe fruits. The leaves serve as larval food for the ello sphinx, a common hummingbird-like moth in South Florida.

GOATWEED
Capraria biflora L.
Figwort family (Scrophulariaceae)

Description: Herbaceous subshrub to 6' tall or less, usually much branched, with alternate, oblanceolate, toothed leaves averaging 1"–2" long and ½"–¾" wide. Axillary flowers are on long stems, often paired, and measure about ½" wide.

Bloom Season: All year

Habitat/Range: Open coastal habitats, especially along trails, from Martin and Lee Counties south through the Florida Keys, West Indies, and tropical America

Comments: *Capraria* is a Latin word pertaining to goats, because goats will eat the plant when other barnyard animals avoid it. The name *biflora* alludes to the paired flowers. Although the leaves contain toxins, they are widely used as a tea substitute in the neotropics and as a medicinal tonic to treat a wide assortment of ailments, including colds, coughs, diabetes, fevers, venereal diseases, kidney problems, measles, and to expedite labor. Although butterflies visit the flowers, the species is seldom purposely cultivated.

BIRD PEPPER

Capsicum annuum L. var. *glabriusculum* (Dunal)
Heiser & Pickersgill
Nightshade family (Solanaceae)

Description: Woody shrub to 6' tall with alternate, ovate-lanceolate leaves averaging ½"–1½" long and ⅜"–¾" wide. White, 5-lobed flowers measure about ⅜" across, producing globose to ellipsoid fruits to about ⅜" long, ripening red.

Bloom Season: All year

Habitat/Range: Coastal hammocks of northern peninsular Florida south into the Florida Keys and the neotropics

Comments: *Capsicum* is taken from a Latin word for "a box," alluding to the fruit shape of some species. The name *annuum* means "annual" and *glabriusculum* means "without hairs." The fruits are ranked 90,000 on the Scoville unit heat scale, making them ten times hotter than the jalapeño pepper. Mockingbirds gulp the small fruits whole, and Bahamians eat the fruits to "excite the appetite." The "heat" in peppers is caused by capsaicin, used in shark repellents and pepper sprays for personal protection.

MULLEIN NIGHTSHADE

Solanum donianum Walp.
Nightshade family (Solanaceae)

Description: Shrub to 6' tall or less with the young branches, petioles, and flower stems covered with dense pubescence. The alternate leaves are elliptic-oblong, averaging 4"–8" long and 1½"–3" wide. Fruits ripen red, measuring ¼"–⅜" wide.

Bloom Season: All year

Habitat/Range: Mangroves and open marshy habitats of southern Florida, Mexico, the Bahamas, and Belize

Comments: The meaning of *Solanum* is obscure but may come from the Latin *solamen*, meaning "a comfort," or "soothing," relating to the pharmacological uses of psychoactive species. The name *donianum* honors British botanist George Don (1798–1856), who collected plants in Brazil, West Indies, and Africa for the Royal Horticultural Society. The common name mullein relates to plants used for medicinal purposes to treat respiratory problems. It is a state-listed threatened species and a larval host plant of the Carolina sphinx and five-spotted hawk moths.

POTATOTREE

Solanum erianthum D. Don

Description: Large shrub or small tree to 10' tall with copious pubescence covering the stems and leaves. The ovate to elliptic leaves are alternate and reach 10" long and 4" wide. Terminal flower clusters are followed by round yellow fruits measuring about ½" across.

Bloom Season: All year

Habitat/Range: Hammock margins, canopy gaps, and disturbed sites across much of peninsular Florida into the Florida Keys; widespread in tropical and warm temperate regions worldwide

Comments: The name *erianthum* means "woolly-flowered." The leaves smell strongly of tar when rubbed—a good identifying characteristic. Many birds, including red-bellied woodpeckers, are fond of eating the fruits. It is quick to colonize canopy gaps in hammocks created by tropical storms and hurricanes. Although it is regarded as native to Florida, some botanists suggest it may be native to tropical Asia and now widespread in the Americas.

RUSTWEED

Polypremum procumbens L.
Tetrachondra family (Tetrachondraceae)

Description: Much-branched herbaceous annual or short-lived perennial with opposite, sessile, linear to narrowly lanceolate leaves that may become rust-colored. The stems spread flat on the ground, with terminal and axillary flowers to about ⅛" wide.

Bloom Season: All year

Habitat/Range: Pinelands, dunes, and disturbed sites from Maryland to Illinois and Texas south through all of Florida, West Indies, and tropical America

Comments: *Polypremum* alludes to the species' numerous stems; *procumbens* relates to its procumbent growth habit. Botanists have had a difficult time deciding where to place this monotypic genus, and has been included in the Buddlejaceae, Lamiaceae, and Loganiaceae. The name rustweed refers to the leaves becoming rust-colored. It is also called juniper leaf and is used medicinally in El Salvador as a remedy for uterus inflammation.

JOEWOOD
Jacquinia keyensis Mez
Theophrasta family (Theophrastaceae)

Description: Small tree, often shrubby, with smooth light gray bark. The alternate, oblong to obovate, stiff leaves usually have revolute margins and average ¾"–1" long and ⅜"–½" wide. Very fragrant white flowers are about ½" wide. Small, round fruits ripen orange-red.

Bloom Season: All year

Habitat/Range: Coastal hammocks and rock barrens of Lee, Miami-Dade, and Monroe Counties (mainland and Keys), the Bahamas, and the Greater Antilles

Comments: *Jacquinia* honors Austrian physician and botanist Nikolaus Joseph von Jacquin (1727–1817), who collected plants in Central America and the West Indies. The name *keyensis* means "of the Florida Keys." Another common name is cudjoewood, with *cudjoe* originating from the Akan people of Ghana, who frequently named their children for the day of the week they were born. Cudjoe is a name given to boys born on a Monday, and it is believed there was an enslaved man from Ghana who lived on the island now named Cudjoe Key in the Lower Florida Keys. The tree's name was later shortened to joewood. Bracelet wood (*Jacquinia arborea*) is a related non-native species sparingly naturalized in the Florida Keys and bearing much larger leaves and similar, but larger flowers.

FLORIDA FIDDLEWOOD

Citharexylum spinosum L.
(Also *Citharexylum fruticosum* L.)
Verbena family (Verbenaceae)

Description: Dioecious tree to 18' tall or more with glossy, opposite, oblanceolate leaves averaging 3"–4" long and 1½"–2" wide with orange petioles. Very fragrant ⅜" flowers are on pendent spikes. Fruits are globose, to about ⅜" wide, ripening from orange to purplish black.

Bloom Season: All year

Habitat/Range: Hammocks and pinelands of central and southern Florida through the West Indies to South America

Comments: *Citharexylum* is Greek for "fiddle wood," for the use of the wood to make musical instruments. The name *spinosum* alludes to the spines on the margins of seedling leaves. A leaf tea is used in the Caribbean to treat allergies, asthma, and chest pain. Trees may be defoliated each year by fiddlewood leafroller moth caterpillars, which cover the canopy with silky tents. Butterflies visit the flowers, and the fruits are eaten by birds.

WILD SAGE OR BUTTONSAGE

Lantana involucrata L.
Verbena family (Verbenaceae)

Description: Widely branched woody shrub to 6' tall with opposite, oblong-ovate to broadly ovate leaves, rounded at the tip, and averaging about 1" long and ¾" wide. The yellow-centered white flowers are sometimes blushed with pink or lavender, and are in dense clusters to about ¾" across. Fruits are purple, to ⅛" wide.

Bloom Season: All year

Habitat/Range: Pinelands, beach dunes, and hammock margins in coastal counties of central and southern Florida, West Indies, Bermuda, and Mexico south to South America

Comments: The genus *Lantana* was named because of the resemblance of the type species to *Viburnum lantana*. The name *involucrata* means "having an involucre," relating to the leafy bracts below the flowers. The leaves are fragrant when crushed. In the Bahamas, a leaf tea is used to sponge sores caused by measles and chicken pox. Butterflies commonly visit the flowers.

CAPEWEED OR FOGFRUIT
Phyla nodiflora (L.) Greene
Verbena family (Verbenaceae)

Description: Mat-forming herbaceous perennial with opposite, toothed leaves that measure 1" long and ½" wide or less. Axillary flower stalks are 1½"–2½" tall, topped by a flower head that is round and flattened when young, becoming cylindrical with age. The white to pinkish flowers are about ⅛" wide, forming a ring.

Bloom Season: All year

Habitat/Range: Wet habitats, beaches, roadsides, and lawns of tropical and subtropical regions worldwide

Comments: *Phyla* is Greek for "tribe," alluding to the tight head of flowers. The name *nodiflora* refers to the flower stalks appearing from the leaf nodes. Other common names are creeping charlie, matchsticks, and turkey tangle fogfruit. The common name fogfruit is often corrupted as "frogfruit." The flowers attract bees and butterflies; the leaves are larval food for the phaon crescent and white peacock butterflies, so it should be encouraged in lawns or purposely planted as a ground cover.

VELVETBURR
Priva lappulacea (L.) Pers.
Verbena family (Verbenaceae)

Description: Herbaceous annual or short-lived perennial to about 30" tall with hairy, quadrangular stems. Ovate to triangular leaves are opposite with hairy petioles and blades measuring ¾"–6" long and ⅜"–3" wide. Flowers are loosely arranged on a rachis and are followed by round, green fruits covered with short bristly hairs. The flowers can be white, blue, or pinkish.

Bloom Season: All year

Habitat/Range: Disturbed sites, including residential landscapes, of Collier, Miami-Dade, the Monroe County mainland and Keys, Texas, West Indies, and tropical America

Comments: *Priva* is Latin for "alone," or "single," without explanation. The name *lappulacea* means "bur-like," alluding to the fruits that stick to clothing, hair, and feathers. Although native to Florida, this species can be weedy in garden settings, where people and pets serve as vectors to transport the bristly fruits to new locations. Another common name is cat's tongue, for the raspy hairs on the fruits.

VIRGINIA CREEPER
Parthenocissus quinquefolia (L.) Planch.
Grape family (Vitaceae)

Description: Woody vine climbing by adhesive disks along the stem. Leaves are alternate, averaging 2"–3" long and wide, typically divided into 5 toothed leaflets. Flowers are in dense clusters bearing round fruits to about ¼" wide, with 1–3 seeds.

Bloom Season: January to August

Habitat/Range: Woodlands of Canada, the United States, the Bahamas, Bermuda, and Cuba

Comments: *Parthenocissus* is Greek for "virgin" and "ivy," which influenced the name Virginia creeper. The name *quinquefolia* alludes to the 5 leaflets. This can be an aggressive vine, both in natural habitats and home landscapes. The leaves can be a skin irritant on sensitive people and have been used medicinally to treat lockjaw, venereal disease, and dropsy. The species is a larval host of the pandorus, Abbott's, lettered, nessus, and hog sphinx moths; also the grape leaf skeletonizer, lesser grapevine looper, eight-spotted forester, beautiful wood nymph, and copper underwing moths.

TALLOW WOOD OR HOG PLUM
Ximenia americana L.
Ximenia family (Ximeniaceae)

Description: Thorny hemiparasitic tree typically reaching about 12' tall, but may be taller. Leaves range from elliptic, lanceolate, ovate, or obovate and average 1"–1¾" long and ½"–1" wide. Very fragrant white to pale yellow, hairy flowers are clustered in the leaf axils. The oblong fruits ripen yellow and measure about 1¼" long and ¾" wide.

Bloom Season: April to December

Habitat/Range: Wooded swamps, pinelands, hammock margins, and coastal scrub throughout peninsular Florida and the Florida Keys through the neotropics to Africa, Asia, and Australia

Comments: *Ximenia* honors Francisco Ximénez (1570–1620), a Franciscan monk dedicated to botany. The name *americana* means "of America." The ripe fruits are tasty and are a favorite of black bears and raccoons in Florida. The fruits are used to brew beer in South America; the seeds are eaten as a purgative in religious cleansing rituals.

GLOSSARY

achene: A small, dry, one-seeded fruit

acute: Sharp-pointed

annual: Completing its life cycle in one year

anther: The pollen-bearing part of the stamen

areole: A spine-bearing area on a cactus

aril: An extra covering around a seed

axillary: Arising from the angle between a leaf petiole and the stem

biennial: Completing its life cycle in its second year

bract: A leaflike structure below a flower or inflorescence

calyx: The outermost whorl of parts that form a flower, or, collectively, the sepals

ciliate: Fringed with hairs on the margin

cladode: A flattened leaflike stem that functions like a leaf

cordate: Heart-shaped with the notch at the base

cyme: A broad, flattened inflorescence with the central flower maturing first

dentate: With sharp teeth along the margin

dioecious: Producing male and female flowers on separate plants

drupe: A one-seeded fruit

elliptic: Broadest at the middle and tapering to both ends

endemic: Restricted to a specific geographical range

glabrous: Smooth or without hairs

gland: A depression or appendage on the surface of an organ that secretes a sticky fluid

glaucous/glaucescent: Appearing bluish gray in color or becoming so

globose: A sphere, like a globe

hemiparasite: A parasitic plant that also photosynthesizes

hemispheric: Shaped like half a sphere

hilum: The scar at the point of attachment on a seed (like the black portion of a black-eyed pea)

hirsute: Rough, with coarse or shaggy hairs

hypanthium: A cuplike or tubular enlargement of the receptacle of a flower

inflorescence: The arrangement of flowers on an axis

involucre: The bracts that surround a flower or a cluster of flowers

lanceolate: Lance-shaped

lenticel: Raised pores on woody stems that allow for atmospheric gas exchange with the internal tissues

linear: Long and narrow with parallel sides

neotropics: The region encompassing Mexico, Central America, South America, and the West Indies (including the Bahamas)

oblanceolate: Broadest at the tip and tapering gradually toward the base

obovate: Broadest above the middle and rounded at both ends

orbicular: Circular in outline

ovate: Broadest below the middle and rounded at both ends

pedicel: The stalk of a single flower

peduncle: The stalk of an individual flower or a head of flowers

perennial: Living three or more years

perianth: Collectively, the floral envelopes; usually used when the calyx and corolla are not clearly defined

petiole: The stem of a leaf

pistillate: Producing female flowers

plicate: Folded like a fan

procumbent: Trailing across the ground

prostrate: Lying flat on the ground

pseudobulb: The thickened bulblike basal stem of certain epiphytic and terrestrial orchid species

pubescent: Covered with short, soft hairs

raceme: A simple, elongated, indeterminate inflorescence

revolute: Curled under

rhizome/rhizomatous: An underground stem, or possessing underground stems

rhombic/rhomboid: Diamond-shaped

rosette: A circular cluster of leaves at the base of a plant

scabrous: Rough to the touch

scape: A leafless flower stalk

scorpioid: Curled at the tip and uncurling as the flowers open

sessile: Lacking a petiole

spadix: A spike on a succulent axis enveloped in a spathe

spathe: A broad, sheathing bract surrounding a spadix

staminate: Producing male flowers

suborbicular: Somewhat circular in outline

type: The species used to describe a family or genus

NATIVE PLANT RESOURCES

National Parks and Refuges

Biscayne National Park
9700 SW 328 St.
Homestead, FL 33033
Phone: (305) 230-1144

Everglades National Park
40001 SR 9336
Homestead, FL 33034
Phone: (305) 242-7700

Crocodile Lake National Wildlife Refuge
Mile Marker 106.3
10750 CR 905
Key Largo, FL 33037
Phone: (305) 451-4223

National Key Deer Refuge
Mile Marker 30.5 (Visitor Center)
30587 Overseas Hwy.
Big Pine Key, FL 33043
Phone: (305) 872-0774

Florida State Parks

Bahia Honda State Park
Mile Marker 37.0
36850 Overseas Hwy.
Big Pine Key, FL 33043
Phone: (305) 872-2353

Fort Zachary Taylor Historic State Park
601 Howard England Way
Key West, FL 33040

Curry Hammock State Park
Mile Marker 56.2
56200 Overseas Hwy.
Marathon, FL 33050
Phone: (305) 289-2690

Indian Key Historic State Park
Mile Marker 78.5 (offshore oceanside)
Islamorada, FL 33036
Phone: (305) 664-2540

Dagny Johnson Key Largo Hammock
Botanical State Park
CR 905
Key Largo, FL 33037

John Pennekamp Coral Reef State Park
Mile Marker 102.5
102601 Overseas Hwy.
Key Largo, FL 33037
Phone: (305) 451-6300

Lignumvitae Key Botanical State Park
Mile Marker 78.5 (offshore bayside;
    ferry service)
77720 Overseas Hwy. (offshore)
Islamorada, FL 33036
Phone: (305) 664-2540

Long Key State Park
Mile Marker 67.5
67400 Overseas Hwy.
Layton, FL 33001
Phone: (305) 664-4815

Windley Key Fossil Reef Geological
    State Park
Mile Marker 85.5
84900 Overseas Hwy.
Islamorada, FL 33036
Phone: (305) 664-2540

SELECTED REFERENCES

Austin, Daniel F. 2004. *Florida Ethnobotany*. Boca Raton, FL: CRC Press.

Correll, Donovan S., and Helen B. Correll. 1982. *Flora of the Bahama Archipelago*. Vaduz, Liechtenstein: A. R. G. Gantner Verlag K.-G.

Hammer, Roger L. 2004. *Florida Keys Wildflowers*. Guilford, CT: Globe Pequot.

Hammer, Roger L. 2014. *Everglades Wildflowers*, second edition. Guilford, CT: Globe Pequot.

Hammer, Roger L. 2018. *Complete Guide to Florida Wildflowers*. Guilford, CT: Globe Pequot.

Institute for Regional Conservation: www.regionalconservation.org.

Luer, Carlyle. 1972. *The Native Orchids of Florida*. New York: New York Botanical Garden.

Majure, Lucas, et al. 2017. *Taxonomic Revision of the* Opuntia *humifusa complex (Opuntieae: Cactaceae) of the Eastern United States*. Phytotaxa 290 (1) 001–065. Auckland: Magnolia Press.

Minno, Marc C., Jerry F. Butler, and Donald W. Hall. 2005. *Florida Butterfly Caterpillars and Their Host Plants*. Gainesville: University Press of Florida.

Weakley, Alan S., Derick B. Poindexter, Hannah C. Medford, Bruce A. Sorrie, Carol Ann McCormick, Edwin L. Bridges, Steve L. Orzell, Keith A. Bradley, Harvey E. Ballard, Jr., Remington N. Burwell, Samuel L. Lockhart, and Alan R. Franck. 2020. "Studies in the Vascular Flora of the Southeastern United States. VI". *Journal of the Botanical Research Institute of Texas* 14 (2), 199-239.

Wunderlin, Richard P., and Bruce F. Hansen. 2011. *Guide to the Vascular Plants of Florida*, third edition. Gainesville: University Press of Florida.

INDEX

INDEX

ABOUT THE AUTHOR

Roger L. Hammer is a professional naturalist and survivalist instructor for the Discovery Channel's reality TV show *Naked and Afraid*. He grew up in Cocoa Beach and served in the US Army from 1965 to 1968 as a tank gunner, ship winch operator, education specialist, and Army recruiter. He was the manager of the 120-acre Castellow Hammock Nature Center for the Miami-Dade County Parks Department from 1977 to 2010. He received the first Marjory Stoneman Douglas Award presented by the Dade Chapter of the Florida Native Plant Society in 1982, Tropical Audubon Society honored him with the prestigious Charles Brookfield Medal in 1996, and in 2003 he received the Green Palmetto Award in Education from the Florida Native Plant Society. He has given keynote speeches at Florida Native Plant Society state conferences, the 2008 World Orchid Conference, and the 2016 Florida Wildflower Foundation symposium. He was also the opening speaker at the American Orchid Society's one-hundred-year anniversary celebration held at Miami's historic Biltmore Hotel in 2022. In 2012 he received an honorary Doctor of Science degree from Florida International University. He is the author of *Everglades Wildflowers, Central Florida Wildflowers, Complete Guide to Florida Wildflowers, Attracting Hummingbirds and Butterflies in Tropical Florida, Exploring Everglades National Park and the Surrounding Area, Paddling Everglades and Biscayne National Parks, Florida Icons: 50 Classic Views of the Sunshine State*, and *Attracting Hummingbirds and Butterflies in Tropical Florida*. He lives in Homestead with his wife, Michelle.